HOOVER INSTITUTION PUBLICATIONS

NATIONALISM AND REVOLUTION IN EGYPT

The Role of the Muslim Brotherhood

NATIONALISM AND REVOLUTION IN EGYPT

The Role of the Muslim Brotherhood

by

CHRISTINA PHELPS HARRIS

Published for

THE HOOVER INSTITUTION ON WAR,
REVOLUTION, AND PEACE

Stanford, California

by

MOUTON & CO. · THE HAGUE / LONDON / PARIS

1964

The Hoover Institution on War, Revolution, and Peace, founded at Stanford University in 1919 by Herbert Hoover, is a center for advanced study and research on public and international affairs in the twentieth century. The views expressed in its publications are entirely those of the authors and do not necessarily reflect the views of the Hoover Institution.

For my husband, DAVID HARRIS

PREFACE

Studies such as the present one rarely see the light of day without the help of many generous-spirited scholars and friends. Especially is this the case in writing of a politico-religious movement that has received so little publicity abroad, except in the nature of adverse criticism.

My grateful thanks are due Professor Nabih Amin Faris of the American University of Beirut, Professor David Harris of Stanford University, Professor Albert H. Hourani of St. Antony's College, Oxford, Professor Enver Ziya Karal of the University of Ankara, Professor George Lenczowski of the University of California at Berkeley, President C. Easton Rothwell of Mills College, formerly director of the Hoover Institution, Visiting Associate Professor Fayez A. Sayegh of Stanford University, Professor Emeritus Graham H. Stuart of Stanford University, Mr. Edwin M. Wright of the Foreign Service Institute of the U.S. Department of State, and Professor Costi K. Zurayk of the American University of Beirut, for their great kindness in reading the whole of this study and making many helpful comments and suggestions.

I am also greatly indebted to Dr. Kenneth Cragg, formerly editor of *The Muslim World*, Sir Hamilton Gibb, who is Director of the Center for Middle Eastern Studies at Harvard University, and Dr. Harold W. Glidden of the U.S. Department of State and the Library of Congress, for their kindness in reading all the chapters on Islam and the Muslim Brotherhood, namely chapters III to VIII inclusive, and for giving me most useful suggestions.

Dr. Harold H. Fisher, Emeritus Professor of History, Stanford University, was so very kind as to read and comment upon chapters i and ii.

To an Egyptian friend, Professor Mohamed Kafafi of the University of Cairo, I am deeply indebted for the opportunity of discussing many problems relevant to Islam in modern Egypt and to the background and early history of the Muslim Brotherhood. Dr. Kafafi read and commenced upon chapters III and IV of the manuscript.

I should like to express particular appreciation for the opportunity of consulting certain unpublished materials of the United States government on the Muslim Brotherhood.

Mr. Nasuh Adib, now serving as a Middle East specialist in the United Nations, was helpful to me in many different ways, both here and in Egypt. I am specifically indebted to Mr. Adib for translating all the cited quotations from Arabic texts, and also for reading chapters iii through viii.

For the onerous task of proofreading and checking English sources, I am grateful for the help of Mr. Howard Koch, Jr. I also desire to acknowledge my indebtedness to Mrs. Daja Adib and to Dr. Abdur Rahman al-Hassun, both of whom were most helpful in the checking of Arabic books and references. For typing the final revisions, I am much indebted to Mr. William J. Bradford. I also greatly appreciate all the assistance given me by Mr. Jesse Phillips and Miss Liselotte Hofmann, and by numerous members of the staff of the Hoover Institution. The author is especially grateful to Dr. W. Glenn Campbell, Director of the Hoover Institution, who has made the publication of this book possible.

The major portion of the research for this study was done in the library of the Hoover Institution. The Arabic- and Western-language materials of its Middle East collections provided me with indispensable, in some cases unique, sources, including publications of the Muslim Brotherhood.

For all the conclusions reached in this study, as well as for any errors, I take full responsibility.

June, 1963   CHRISTINA PHELPS HARRIS,
                                              Department of Political Science
                                              Stanford University

CONTENTS

NOTE ON TRANSLITERATION OF ARABIC

The system of Arabic transliteration used throughout this book follows in general the system established in the Hoover Library for the cataloguing of Arabic materials. A few concessions, however, have been made with a view to the problems of printing – e.g., the dots under letters normally under-dotted have been omitted, as have all long-vowel marks.

In the case of many proper names and the better-known Arabic words and place names currently used in the press and by writers about the Middle East, the generally accepted Anglicized form of the name or word is used: for example, Muhammad Ali Pasha, the Khedive Ismail, King Fuad and King Farouk, Arabi Pasha, General Naguib, Colonel Gamal Abdel Nasser, Ali Maher Pasha, Caliph and Caliphate, the Koran, the Ulama, and place names such as Mecca, Saudi Arabia, Nejd, Ismailia, and Tel el-Kebir.

INTRODUCTION

Our world today is an unquiet place. From west to east, across the globe, mounting revolutionary struggle has followed hard upon two world wars. Western eyes have watched fearfully the relentless expansion of communism; Western minds have seemingly been hypnotized by the character and the dimensions of the international Communist movement. And yet, this movement is only one among many contemporary struggles for power. The continent of Africa and subcontinents of Asia have bred a variety of revolutions, some of which have been taken over wholly or in part by Communist revolutionaries. But not all. A great number of the new Asian and African states have no direct concern with communism at all. They are intent upon their own battles for freedom. These are their valiant years: they seek liberation from real or imagined oppressions. Some have already thrown off the shackles of colonialism, and they strive to preserve their new-won freedom from political domination, or to secure immunity from economic subjection. Others, more politically mature, seek strength to pursue their own policies without fear or favor, and reach for power in order to remain independent between the contending forces of East and West.

Notable among these last is the government of Egypt, which became – in its brief union with Syria – the United Arab Republic. Its president, Gamal Abdel Nasser, is a leader of Arab nationalists who grope toward Arab unity; and he is the principal and most articulate Arab spokesman for the doctrine of "positive neutrality" and "nonalignment."

In 1953, a year after the establishment of the Revolutionary Government of Egypt, Colonel Gamal Abdel Nasser – as he then was –

published *The Philosophy of the Revolution*. In this booklet he invited the reader to look closely at a map of the world and then to consider the three spheres of Egyptian destiny. These spheres, which he called circles, he identified as follows: first and foremost, the "Arab circle," the life and history of whose peoples are "intermingled with ours" in Egypt; second, the "circle of the continent of Africa," wherein fate has placed Egypt, and from whose heart the Nile – "the artery of life of our country" – draws its waters; and third, the Islamic circle, a monotheistic religion, a civilization, and a heritage which bind Egyptian Muslims to all the Muslims of the world.[1]

More than 400 million Muslims inhabit the third of these circles, roughly one seventh of the total world population.[2] Their religious community has its being within the framework of a relatively rigid Sacred Law; it is a society founded upon an all-embracing legal system bequeathed to its Believers between the 7th and 10th centuries and held by all orthodox Muslims to embody a directive from God. Consequently, Islamic developments within this sphere, which stretches from the Atlantic Ocean to the Pacific – from the western shores of Africa to the Philippines – will have vital repercussions among all the inhabitants of these continents and islands. The ultimate fate of its Muslims and their regeneration in our time will be directly affected by movements for Islamic reform and progress. On the other hand, fundamentalist and reactionary religious movements which arise within the community of Islam may affect, adversely, the relations between Muslims and non-Muslims and could prejudice the effective role of Muslim peoples in international affairs.

The following study is primarily concerned with a specific religious association, the Muslim Brotherhood. This militant, fundamentalist organization, which originated in Egypt in the interwar years, became a powerful and implacable enemy of the Government of the Revolution.

In late October of the year 1954, early in the third year of the Revo-

---

[1] Gamal Abdel Nasser, *The Philosophy of the Revolution* (Buffalo, N.Y., 1959), pp. 59-78.
[2] Estimate based upon figures in *Atlas of Islamic History,* comp. Harry W. Hazard (Princeton, N. J., Princeton University Press, 1951; 3d ed., rev., 1954), p. 5.

lution, amid nationwide mass meetings to celebrate the final achievement of Egypt's unqualified independence, the outside world was
startled by a near tragedy in the country. Gamal Abdel Nasser, a
young lieutenant colonel who was then premier of Egypt, had recently become *de facto* head of the military dictatorship launched by
General Naguib two years earlier. On October 26, Colonel Nasser was
touring the Nile Delta to explain to his countrymen the advantages of
the new Anglo-Egyptian agreement on the evacuation of the Suez
Canal Base. While he was addressing a mass meeting in Alexandria,
and the assembled crowd was hanging on his words, an Egyptian
workingman fired eight shots at him at close range. Happily for the
Government of the Revolution, the premier was not harmed. But the
would-be assassin gave the military junta its chance to take action
against a powerful subversive organization in Egypt. The man who
fired the shots, a tinsmith, was identified as a member of the Muslim
Brotherhood. The subsequent arrest of more than a thousand members of this organization and the trials of its leaders, on charges of
treason and conspiracy to overthrow the regime by force, uncovered
a vast plot against the Revolutionary Government. The head of the
Brotherhood's underground terrorist organization in Cairo confessed
that plans had been elaborated to carry out wholesale assassinations
of the leaders of the Revolution, preparatory to the establishment of
a new government supported by the Muslim Brotherhood. And in the
course of the trials various leaders of the Brotherhood, including its
head or "Supreme Guide," admitted that the activities of the terrorist
wing of the organization, if unchecked, would have led to civil war
and widespread terrorism in the country.

The attempted assassination of Colonel Gamal Abdel Nasser was
the dramatic climax of a two-year struggle for supremacy between
the military leaders of the Revolution and the powerful Muslim
Brotherhood, an organization that had been active in Egypt for more
than a quarter of a century.

This Brotherhood of orthodox Muslims, which was in origin and
essence a religious revivalist association, burgeoned into a politico-
religious movement in the late 1930's. And simultaneously it developed as a storm center in the life of independent Egypt, a country
that stands at the intellectual, geographical, and strategic crossroads
of East and West.

This study has a twofold objective. In the first place, it is necessary to create an intelligible setting for a discussion of the Brotherhood movement and to identify adequately the various political, social, and spiritual tensions that gave it birth. In the second place, the Brotherhood itself must be described with sufficient clarity to illumine the critical nature of the struggle that took place between the Muslim Brethren and their fellow countrymen – a struggle that produced a situation fraught with grave danger to the body politic.

To accomplish this dual purpose, the material here presented has been divided into two parts. The first three chapters are designed to give as succinct a review as possible of the founding of modern Egypt: the rise and development of nationalism, the birth of modern constitutionalism and the rise of political parties, the British occupation of the country and the reasons for it, the political crises generated by the First World War, the economic and social legacy of the war years, and the early modern movements for Islamic reform and regeneration. The subsequent chapters describe the founding of the Muslim Brotherhood, its history, and the relations between this organization and the Government of the Revolution.

The establishment of the Muslim Brotherhood in 1928 was the natural, one might almost say the inevitable, result of Egyptian history during the 19th and early 20th centuries. And its development coincided with the growth of a new feeling of solidarity between Muslims throughout the Arab world. The Brotherhood was an Islamic nationalist organization and movement that derived its special strength from the acute tensions built up in Egyptian society during the modern era. In its Islamic manifestation, it was an outgrowth of ultraconservative Muslim reaction against the Western Christian penetration of Egypt from the middle of the 19th century. In its nationalism, it was a product of the Egyptian nationalist movement from 1879 to 1936. The gradual westernization and modernization of Muslim society, joined with the wholly unpalatable fact of foreign domination, shaped the ideology of the movement, as did the increasingly depressed economic and social conditions of life among the Muslim masses of Egypt. And the attendant intellectual conflict in 20th-century Egypt between the forces of conservatism and modernism contributed its own special influence.

The early development and expansion of the Brotherhood organization took place in a country where two political struggles were joined: the one for national independence, and the other for the achievement of political maturity. The tensions generated by these struggles were ominously complicated by the nature of the society in which they took place. For more than a century Egyptians had been in the process of emerging from medieval social and economic conditions. They had been trying to get rid of alien political controls at a time when they were also forced to cope with the multitudinous problems attendant upon the modernization of their society. They had entered the 20th century hopefully, only to find that inherited social and economic conditions painfully hampered their march toward modern living. Concomitant with their political struggle was a conflict between the intellectual and the religious forces of conservatism and modernism. In this complex struggle for advancement, the Muslim Brotherhood was recognized as a bastion of religious conservatism in modern Egypt.

In spite of being a politico-religious movement born in the 20th century, the Muslim Brotherhood in its motivation and religious objectives was an ideological throwback to the 18th and 19th centuries – to militant Arabian Wahhabism and to the later Pan-Islamic ideal of Jamal al-Din al-Afghani. Yet the Brotherhood cannot be considered a purely reactionary organization. It sponsored an up-to-date program for social and economic reform, albeit within a rigid and inhibiting religious framework. The Muslim Brethren rejected intellectual and educational progress along Western rationalist lines, but they planned meticulously for social welfare, especially among the impoverished masses. Thus the Brotherhood represented religious reaction against contemporary secular influences in Egyptian life, and at the same time this militant movement transformed faith into positive social action.[3]

The influence of the Muslim Brethren and the implications of their struggle reach far beyond Egypt, because this movement has most of the characteristics of the "nativistic" type of "revitalization" movement – to borrow a definition current among anthropologists. For this reason many observers consider the Muslim Brotherhood to be

[3] Werner Caskel, "Western Impact and Islamic Civilization," in *Unity and Variety in Muslim Civilization*, ed. Gustave E. von Grunebaum (Chicago, 1955), p. 348.

the most significant contemporary movement in the world of Islam. Almost a quarter of a century after the founding of the Brotherhood a distinguished Egyptian Muslim, Ahmad Hasan al-Zayyat, wrote of the movement as follows:

The Muslim Brethren alone represent the real faith of Islam and the true mentality of the Muslim in this misshapen society; they do not conceive of religion as being an isolated hermitage and the world as a far away market place but they understand the Mosque and the market place to be one; the former is, as it were, the minaret and the latter is the main structure . . . . The Muslim Brethren have a tongue for guidance, a hand for economics, an arm for Holy War and an opinion for politics. They have followers in every one of the Arab countries. They have partisans in all the Islamic countries. The awakening of general consciousness in Egypt, the Sudan, Iraq, Syria, Yemen, Hijaz, Algeria, and Morocco was but the radiation of this spirit which will in the future have a great role to play.[4]

---

[4] Published in the magazines al-Risalah, No. 966 (January 7, 1952), and al-Daʿwah, No. 48 (January 15, 1952). Cited in Ishak Musa Husaini, The Moslem Brethren: The Greatest of Modern Islamic Movements (Beirut, 1956), p. 98. Husaini makes the following comment about the author of this quotation (p. 168, n. 281): "[Ahmad Hasan al-Zayyat] is a member of the Academy of the Arabic Language and the former editor-in-chief of al-Azhar magazine. His magazine is famous and popular. It has begun lately [1952] to support the Brethren and to praise their movement."

I

EGYPT ENTERS THE MODERN WORLD

For twenty-four centuries and well into modern times Egypt was incorporated in a succession of foreign empires or was ruled over by non-Egyptians who established alien dynasties in this rich and strategically desirable country. The cumulative shadow of centuries of foreign rule was darkly mirrored in the renaissance of modern Egypt. And the determination of Egyptians to free themselves completely from alien rule became a recurrent factor in the rise and development of their nationalist movement after the middle of the 19th century. In order to interpret the modern scene, one must therefore take account of certain historical developments.

The first Asiatic conquest of Egypt was undertaken by the Assyrians. But the final subjugation of the Egyptian Pharaohs was not accomplished until the Persians extended their imperial rule over the country in 525 B.C. The Persian occupation paved the way for the conquest by Alexander the Great in the 4th century. Subsequently the ancient civilization which had flourished in the Nile Valley for some three thousand years was gradually metamorphosed, first under Hellenistic Greek, later under Roman, and eventually under Byzantine domination.

In A.D. 641-642 Egypt, with its composite civilization – a blend of Pharaonic, Persian, Hellenistic, Roman, and Byzantine elements – was conquered by the inspired armies of Arab Islam and was largely Arabicized and Islamicized. Egypt thereafter shared fully in the cultural glories of the golden age of Islam, but its political fortunes rose and fell unevenly. Periods of greatness and decline alternated as Arab and Turkish dynasties dramatically succeeded each other in the land of the Nile. When the Abbasid Caliphate of Baghdad was destroyed by the Mongols (Tatars) in the 13th century and the Asiatic Arab world gradually sank to impotence under the weight of political anarchy, Egypt inherited the intellectual and religious leadership of the whole Sunni, or orthodox, Islamic world.

Previous to the 13th century the Arab dominions of the eastern Mediterranean had been invaded and partly occupied by Crusader armies from western Europe. But Egypt suffered less from these onslaughts than the Arabs of Palestine and Syria, thanks in part to the military capacities of its great Kurdish-Arab ruler, known to the Crusaders as Saladin. And it was the powerful Turkish Mamluk rulers of Egypt, a military slave dynasty, who finally forced the Crusaders to withdraw from Palestine in 1291. The era of the Crusades signalized, unhappily, the first overt hostility of the West against the Muslim world. Early in the 16th century a Western power, Portugal, closed the eastern trade routes to Egyptians by denying their ships and traders access to the Arabian Sea and the Indian Ocean. Wherefore Egypt – richest of all the Arab countries – entered into a period of economic stagnation that was not in any way relieved by the Ottoman Turkish conquest of the country in 1517.

From the 16th to the 19th century, Egypt remained a stagnant province of the Muslim Ottoman Empire. It became a pashalik, governed by a Pasha under the overlordship of the Turkish Sultan-Caliph who ruled the empire from Constantinople. But in the 19th century there were significant developments in the country and important changes in Turko-Egyptian relations. General Bonaparte's invasion of Egypt in 1798 set in motion a series of chain reactions within the Ottoman Empire as well as externally, among the Great Powers of Europe. The "Eastern Question," with all its complexities and confusions, was given a new shape and substance, and one of the startling developments was the emergence of Egypt as a powerful state.

Muhammad Ali, the founder of modern Egypt, was a Turkish military adventurer of great ability and ambition, with exceptional gifts of energy and imagination.[1] He rose to the surface of Egyptian political life after the brief but pregnant period of French occupation. In 1805 the Ottoman Sultan, yielding to the demand of the

---

[1] According to modern Turkish historians, Muhammad Ali was a Turk, the commander of an Albanian regiment. (Information received from Professor Enver Ziya Karal of the University of Ankara.)

Ulama (Muslim religious leaders) and the notables of Cairo, appointed him governor of Egypt with the title of Pasha. Thereafter, until his death in the middle of the century, Muhammad Ali Pasha devoted himself to securing the *de facto* independence of his adopted country under his own authoritarian rule. To achieve this end, he began the modernization of Egypt. With the help of French advisers and technicians he centralized the administration, imposed a monopolistic economy, built up a strong army and navy, opened the door to a great number of European merchants, and, primarily to supply his formidable military establishment, introduced new industries. He also devoted meticulous attention to the development of agriculture.

Historically, the wealth of Egypt has been based on the land, and the great river artery of the Nile, with its branches in the Delta of Lower Egypt, has supplied the lifeblood of its agriculture. Before the French occupation it is believed that less than two per cent of the land was cultivated – more than 98 per cent of Egypt was desert.[2] But, thanks to the Nile and its annual flood, the cultivated area was extraordinarily fertile. Muhammad Ali excavated new canals, cleaned or repaired old canals, built and restored dikes, and initiated the construction of the first great barrage across the Nile at the head of the Delta. One of his major enterprises was the fifty-mile-long Mahmudiyyah Canal, built both for irrigation and for the transport of goods between Cairo and his new port at Alexandria. Unfortunately there were many technical imperfections in the construction of this great canal, which cost the lives of thousands of peasants conscripted for the work. Furthermore, the cropping area of the whole of Lower Egypt was expanded by extending summer irrigation, made possible by heavy exactions of forced labor from the peasantry. The normal crop production of Egypt was greatly increased in this way and also new crops, notably long-staple cotton, were introduced. Cotton cultivation resulted in the founding of the Egyptian cotton-textile industry in the 1820's. Short-staple cotton had been grown in the Delta and in Upper Egypt long before the 19th century, but it was the new long-staple cotton that became the vital cash crop for export to Europe.

Early in his reign (1813), Muhammad Ali Pasha ordered a cadastral survey of the cultivable area of Egypt, for the purpose of in-

[2]   The area of Egypt is roughly 386,000 square miles.

troducing a systematic collection of land taxes and thus increasing his revenues. Then he gradually took over the direct administration of almost all the cultivable land in the country. In some cases, land was confiscated outright; in others, compensation (in the form of life pensions) was given to the holders of large estates or to the tax farmers of certain districts. In the case of waqf land – i.e., the landed property of religious endowments which were held in mortmain – the Pasha took over its administration personally without violating the terms of the trusts. By 1844 the total cultivable land was estimated to be close to four million acres (3,890,423 faddans), about 2.5 per cent of Egypt; at that time the population was probably not more than 2,500,000 persons.[3]

After completing the expropriation of the land at the end of 1815, Muhammad Ali administered Egypt, through his government hierarchy, as though it were a state farm. All revenues from the land were taken in directly by the state treasury, but these were used by the Pasha for both state and private purposes. Thereafter he experimented with various land policies and so-called landholding reforms, with a view to increasing the revenues so urgently needed for his planned development of Egypt. By 1846, the date of his final land law, more than one and a half million acres of land were held by large landholders and tax farmers – members of the ruling family, Turkish officers and high government officials, and some favored foreigners (notably Greek settlers), whereas more than two million acres had been reallocated to the peasantry. The peasants were granted possession of the land, often on a hereditary basis, but they were not given title to it; they only had rights of usufruct. They were, however, safeguarded against permanent alienation from the land. Muhammad Ali extended the cutivable area through reclamation of recently abandoned land and promoted the cultivation of trees (especially acacias) and walled gardens. Some experienced farmers

---

[3]   Helen Anne B. Rivlin, *The Agricultural Policy of Muhammad ʿAlī in Egypt* (Cambridge, Mass., 1961), pp. 269-270, 279. Reliable statistics were then unobtainable, and also Muhammad Ali Pasha preferred to act upon the basis of exaggerated and optimistic population estimates — because "The successful achievement of [his] goals ... required a supply of manpower far in excess of the one available to him" (p. 278). For information on the "landholding reforms" see, *ibid.*, pp. 60-64, 72-73, 270; on irrigation, pp. 214, 219-223, 238-240, 270; on cotton cultivation, pp. 73, 137-144.

were assisted with loans to buy animals, agricultural implements, and seeds. But the peasants continued to be heavily oppressed by excessive taxation, onerous government controls, and conscription for forced labor (the corvée) and for the army. In the Delta, the newly irrigated land best suited to cotton cultivation was transferred to the large landholders, leaving the peasants with the relatively poor land.

In his many plans to modernize the economy and develop the military strength of Egypt, Muhammad Ali consciously imitated the West and looked to Europeans, notably Frenchmen, for expert guidance. He gave Egypt its first secular state schools and its first hospitals. And in his desire to import Western knowledge and techniques he sent 339 Egyptians to European schools and universities.[4] He put priority upon the study of military science, engineering, industry, and medicine. In the field of public administration, on the other hand, this first ruler of modern Egypt discouraged education for responsible public office. He was unashamedly a despot and never saw the slightest reason to allow his subjects to participate in the government of their country.

New light has recently been shed upon the contribution of Muhammad Ali to the intellectual revolution that took place in 19th-century Egypt. By sending so many young men to study in Europe, and by adopting Bonaparte's printing press, he fostered the creation of a new educated class in Egypt. This first small group laid the earliest foundation for modern Egyptian nationalism and for the subsequent reforms brought about in Egyptian society. And the cultural renaissance of Egypt may be dated from the establishment of the still famous Arabic printing-press at Bulaq, on the outskirts of Cairo, in 1822. "Of all his activities those connected with education were the only unmixed advantages his rule bestowed on Egypt, and were definitely his most important contribution to the creation of an Egyptian nation."[5] In addition to the specialist military and medical schools opened by Muhammad Ali, a School of Languages was found-

[4] In Muhammad Ali's period 230 Egyptians studied in France, 95 in England, and 14 in other countries. Of these students, 310 studied engineering and industry, 15 medicine, and 2 agriculture. Only 12 of the total number were students of the humanities. M. M. Mosharrafa, *Cultural Survey of Modern Egypt* (London, 1948), II, 54.

[5] Jamal Mohammed Ahmed, *The Intellectual Origins of Egyptian Nationalism* (London, 1960), pp. 9-10.

ed in 1835. Its director, who had led the first educational mission to France, was Rifa'ah Rafi al-Tahtawi. He and his pupils, with the active encouragement of Muhammad Ali, translated 2,000 European books and pamphlets, many of which were published by the new official printing press. According to a distinguished Egyptian scholar, the School of Languages "played a central part in forming the political mind of Egypt." [6] Al-Tahtawi himself wrote some seventeen books, "made a conscious effort" to modernize the Arabic language, and sought to popularize European sciences in Egypt. His earliest work gave the Arab world of his day its first book on Europe and on European thought. One of his last and most famous books analyzed the needs and duties of Egyptians, emphasized almost every aspect of needed social reforms, and laid the foundation of a distinctive Egyptian nationalism associated with basic reform movements. In short, al-Tahtawi was the first intellectual reformer of modern Egypt, and he did much to "recreate the mind and society" of his country. [7]

Despite multitudinous activities on the home front, Muhammad Ali Pasha never lost sight of his need to build up his political power vis-à-vis the Sublime Porte (as the Ottoman government was then known to Europeans). He had taken the first step in this direction by contriving the defeat of part of a British expeditionary force that invaded the Delta in 1807. When the British withdrew from Egypt, they negotiated a peace directly with Muhammad Ali, though he was only a vassal of the Sultan. He took a second step to consolidate his power in Egypt when he accomplished the destruction of the Mamluk Beys (1811), many of whom had intrigued against him with the British. The Mamluks were a Turko-Circassian military caste that had long oppressed Egypt and intimidated the Pashas appointed by the Sultan to rule over the country. Muhammad Ali then responded to the various and urgent demands of his suzerain, the Sultan, for military assistance, but always at a stiff price. He sent his armies to northern Arabia to suppress the Wahhabi rebellion against the Turks; he sent troops and a fleet of sixty ships to help the Turkish army crush the Greek war of independence. And Egyptian troops

---

[6] *Ibid.*, p. 10

[7] For information on al-Tahtawi see, *ibid.*, pp. 11-15. Muhammad Ali had al-Tahtawi's first book, *al-Taklis*, read aloud to him and "instructed school-masters to read it with their students" (p. 13).

were overwhelmingly successful in both Arabia and Greece – though the Greeks were rescued from irreparable disaster by European intervention at Navarino in 1827. In between these prolonged campaigns Muhammad Ali dispatched Egyptian forces southward to conquer the Sudan; Khartum was founded by Egyptians in this first Sudanese campaign. Finally, the great Pasha turned openly against the Sultan, and his troops fought the Ottoman army to a standstill in order to establish Egyptian rule over Syria and Palestine. There are grounds for believing that he and his son Ibrahim nourished grandiose plans to create an Arab empire under Egyptian hegemony. So strong did Muhammad Ali become that the European Powers eventually intervened to save the Ottoman Empire from destruction at his hands.

Before his death in 1849, though deprived by a coalition of the Great Powers of the fruit of all his victorious campaigns in western Asia and Arabia, Muhammad Ali Pasha succeeded in establishing his Turkish dynasty in Egypt upon a hereditary basis. But it remained for Ismail Pasha, his third successor, to complete the political work of the founder of the dynasty. Under him, Egypt achieved its *de facto* independence. Ismail's turbulent period, however, can be better understood if one pauses first to consider certain internal aspects of the life of the country.

Of the Egyptian population of about two and a half million persons in the mid-19th century, about eighty per cent were fallahin, or peasants, illiterate and living on a uniform level of bare subsistence. The remaining twenty per cent of the population, chiefly artisans, merchants, officials, and religious dignitaries, lived in Cairo or Alexandria and in the towns and villages of the Delta. The Beduin, or nomads, formed a negligible part of the population. The overwhelming majority of the people were Sunni, or orthodox Muslims, but a varied assortment of religious-minority communities formed some eight per cent of the total population.

Coptic Egyptians, then as now, constituted the largest resident minority group. The Copts, descendants of the original, pre-Islamic inhabitants of Egypt who had resisted conversion to Islam, were peasants of Upper Egypt as well as city dwellers in the Delta. Arabic-speaking Christians, they traced their affiliation to the Monophysite Christians of the 4th century.

A large community of Lebanese and Syrian Arabs established itself in Egypt during the second half of the 19th century. This Syro-Lebanese community was partly Sunni Muslim and partly Christian – Orthodox and other Eastern Christian sects. There were also small minority groups of Armenians and Jews, long-time residents of Egypt, and both of these groups were relatively wealthy and influential. Because most of the resident minorities were urban peoples, they earned their livelihood primarily in commerce and the professions, and some of them were artisans. The Copts and the Armenians supplied many officials, and a few members of both communities attained high office; the Syro-Lebanese Arabs provided Egypt with some of its most distinguished journalists and literati; the Copts and Jews monopolized financial activities.[8]

Muhammad Ali Pasha's spectacular program of rehabilitation unquestionably laid the foundations of modern Egypt. But many of the reforms he instituted had failed, even during his lifetime, to achieve the results anticipated by him. Certain inadequacies could be laid to the totalitarian character of his program and to the lack of adequate and trained manpower, and certain failures were chargeable to a general weakness in management techniques. But one or two special factors deserve mention because they serve to explain recurrent problems in the development of modern Egypt.

The outstanding disappointment of Muhammad Ali's reign was the failure, admitted by Egyptian historians, of his program for industrialization. There were many reasons for this, including administrative inexperience and excessive production costs. But extraneous events were primary causes of the failure of this first attempt to transform Egypt into an industrial country. In the first place, the Pasha was obliged for political reasons, after 1841, to reduce his Egyptian army to 18,000 men. After this cutback of almost ninety per cent became effective, the domestic market for products of the new state factories fell off sharply. And shortly thereafter, when the Anglo-Turkish commercial treaty of 1838 became operative in Egypt, Muhammad Ali was no longer able to protect his infant industries against European competition.

[8] For a brief, illuminating survey of the minority communities see Albert F. Hourani, *Minorities in the Arab World* (London, 1947), chaps. i-iv and, especially, chap. v. See also Charles Issawi, *Egypt at Mid-Century* (London, 1954), chaps. i-iii, and Sesostris Sidarouss, *Des Patriarcats dans l'Empire Ottoman* (Paris, 1907).

The agricultural program of Muhammad Ali, on the other hand, was relatively successful. But even here the germs of future problems began to develop. The peasant, on whom hinged the ultimate success of all plans for economic development, received a sharp reminder that his perennial miseries were by no means at an end. Conscription, whether for the army or for industry, terrorized the peasant families and emphasized their general insecurity under the authoritarian regime. The grave problems that were later to be posed by the almost incredible increase of population in the 20th century were absent in the 19th century; but the hardships attendant upon heavy taxation and forced labor were endured by the whole peasantry. Furthermore, the primary role of Egypt as an agricultural nation in the world economy was firmly established some decades before the British Occupation in 1882. And the growing dependence of Egypt upon a one-crop economy was foreshadowed early in the regime of Ismail Pasha. During the American Civil War the English demand for Egyptian long-staple cotton caused agricultural interests in Egypt to place almost exclusive reliance upon a single cash crop. In other words, British Advisers after 1882 promoted, but did not initiate, the growing of cotton for export to the mills of Lancashire. Moreover, Egyptian administrators, when confronted by the flourishing state of commerce and agriculture under Ismail Pasha, were naturally reluctant to try to revive the industries which had failed so dismally in the period of Muhammad Ali.

The forward momentum of Muhammad Ali Pasha's domestic policies came to a standstill under his two immediate successors. Many constructive reforms and innovations, including his educational program, languished for lack of state support. It is true, however, that the obscurantist Abbas I (1848-1854) laid the first railway in Egypt, with the help of the British, and that Said Pasha (1854-1863) gave a concession to a Frenchman, Ferdinand de Lesseps, for the construction of the Suez Canal. In 1856, the Compagnie Universelle du Canal Maritime de Suez, with its headquarters in Paris, was given a definitive concession for ninety-nine years from the date of completion of the canal. But the terms of the concession were excessively onerous for the Egyptians; and with the development of communications in the country the threat of European intervention or occupation loomed ominously on the Egyptian horizon.

The one domestic reform worthy of mention in this interim period
was the establishment of the principle of private ownership of land.
Said Pasha recognized, by decree in 1858, the right of the Egyptian
peasant to own land and to sell, bequeath, or mortgage it. All the
peasants who had been allocated land with usufruct rights by Muhammad Ali, became overnight the legal owners of the plots of land
they inhabited and tilled. But even this reform had its obverse side,
because peasant ownership of land opened the door to all the cumulative evils of peasant indebtedness. Whenever thereafter the peasants
needed to raise money, most often to meet the costs of excessive
taxation, their possession of land made them the prey of unscrupulous moneylenders.

Ismail Pasha (1863-1879), who inaugurated a new era of political
and cultural development, boasted that the Egypt of his day had become in reality a part of Europe. In words that have since become
famous, he said: "Mon pays n'est plus en Afrique; nous faisons partie
de l'Europe actuellement."

Between 1867 and 1873 Ismail succeeded in achieving administrative and financial independence from the Ottoman Sultan – the
Sublime Porte – though Egypt remained juridically a part of the
Ottoman Empire until the First World War. He did not challenge
the Sultan on the battlefield because he realized, after witnessing the
defeat of his grandfather, Muhammad Ali Pasha, by a European
coalition (1840-1841), that any military victory over Turkish armies
would undoubtedly bring about further intervention by the Great
Powers. He had recourse instead to the weapons of bribery and diplomacy. He bought for himself and his descendants a new title, that
of Khedive; he further stabilized the dynasty by securing the right of
governing Egypt in accordance with the principle of primogeniture
– thereby eliminating controversies over the succession. As Khedive
he was given full powers to enact all domestic legislation for Egypt,
to conclude commercial and financial agreements with foreign governments, to negotiate modifications of the existing capitulations, and
finally – what proved to be disastrous for his personal rule – "full
power to contract, without leave, in the name of the Egyptian Government, any foreign loan, whenever he may think it necessary." He
was also given authority to provide for the defence of Egypt and to
"increase or diminish" the number of Egyptian troops. In recognition

of his new status, the Khedive almost doubled the annual tribute of Egypt, binding his successors to pay LT 750,000 (about 3.2 million dollars) a year into the Ottoman treasury.[9]

The most significant event of Ismail's reign was the opening of the Suez Canal to international maritime traffic on November 16, 1869. With the completion of this link between the Mediterranean and Red seas, Egypt became the guardian of the shortest highway between Europe and Asia. This meant, *ipso facto*, that Egypt became simultaneously guardian of the imperial and commercial communications of the Great Powers. From that time forth it became a matter of practical politics for the European powers to take whatever steps might seem necessary to ensure freedom of passage for their ships through the canal. Stated another way, it meant that thenceforth Egypt could not dissociate itself from international power politics. Ironically enough, the very Khedive who obtained complete administrative and financial autonomy for Egypt from the Ottoman Empire was also the one to celebrate with Oriental splendor the opening of this international waterway through his country. And it was this very waterway that created the one insuperable obstacle to the achievement by Egypt of its unqualified independence. The Khedives of Egypt, in dealing with the European powers, were on their own after 1873, without the benefit of legal protection from the Sultan of the Ottoman Empire. They were therefore more vulnerable to the conflicting pressures of the Great Powers.

Many aspects of Egyptian life received the diligent attention of "Ismail the Magnificent." Under him, the unveiled face of Egypt became more recognizably modern and westernized. Even a brief list of the public works he completed is staggering in its implications: 910 miles of railway, including a line to Upper Egypt, 8,400 miles of canals, more than 5,000 miles of telegraph, some 500 bridges, and several thousand miles of roads were built during the sixteen years of Ismail's reign. Port Said was founded, and a fine deep-water harbor was constructed at Alexandria – making this city the second port in the Mediterranean. A merchant fleet was established – the Khedivial

[9] The *firman* (decree of the Sultan of the Ottoman Empire) of June 8, 1873, consolidating the special privileges conferred on the Khedive of Egypt. Text in J. C. Hurewitz, *Diplomacy in the Near and Middle East: A Documentary Record: 1535-1914* (Princeton, N. J., 1956), I, 175-177.

Mail Line, with more than a dozen ships for service in the Mediterranean and Red seas – and fifteen coastal lighthouses were erected. The post office service became a department of government, with more than 200 post offices. But this was not all. The Egyptian historian, Professor Rifaat, quotes the Khedive Ismail as saying "Everyone has a mania for something – mine is for stone and mortar." [10] He built sumptuous palaces and villas and other impressive buildings, and the face of Cairo was lifted for the edification of foreign crowned heads who visited Egypt at the time of the opening of the Suez Canal. The opera house, numerous public gardens, and the famous Kasr al-Nil Bridge, connecting Cairo with the island of Ghezireh, were constructed, as well as a new road from Giza to the Pyramids. The great cities of Cairo and Alexandria were given gas, pure water, and drainage. And Helwan, then known as Helouan-les-Bains, became an aristocratic suburb of Cairo.

Ismail also gave great attention to agriculture and cultivated the land intensively. Despite Said Pasha's acknowledgment of the principle of freehold tenure, Ismail looked upon the whole of Egypt as his personal estate, subject to his exploitation, and he acquired for himself – through purchase, "gifts," or expropriation – nearly one fifth of all the cultivable area. By modernizing agricultural methods and exploiting the peasantry, he increased the productivity of his estates; and by cultivating cotton on a large scale during the American Civil War, he initiated an agrarian revolution. Pashas and beys soon followed his example, and even the peasants gave up their traditional rotation of wheat and clover to share in the profits of cotton. The Khedive next turned to the development of sugar plantations in Upper Egypt. A sugar boom succeeded the cotton boom, and Egypt began to export sugar to European markets. A fateful by-product of large-scale sugar cultivation was the beginning of a change in the age-old system of irrigation, necessitated by the dependence of the sugar-cane crop on ample water supplies during the greater part of the year. A system of perennial irrigation was inaugurated in Middle and Upper Egypt. The resultant rural prosperity of the early years of Ismail's reign was, however, later offset by various other factors,

[10] M. Rifaat Bey, *The Awakening of Modern Egypt* (London, 1947), p. 106. For the statistics given during the reign of Khedive Ismail see, *ibid.*, pp. 107-109, 122-124, and George Young, *Egypt* (London, 1927). p. 82.

such as the decline in the price of Egyptian cotton after the end of the American Civil War, inefficiency and waste in administering new experiments (notably in the large-scale development of sugar plantations), the intolerably heavy taxation of the Egyptian peasantry, and the concomitant growth of peasant indebtedness. Under Ismail, taxation of the land was increased by about fifty per cent.[11]

From the domestic point of view, the intellectual developments of the period were of paramount importance. Until Muhammad Ali's day, the education of Muslim Egyptians had been entirely in the hands of religious teachers and theologians. Elementary mosque schools served the villages; the University of al-Azhar and its affiliated institutes, the advanced mosque schools, served Cairo and the larger towns. The Christian and Jewish minority groups by tradition had their own community schools. Muhammad Ali did not touch the systematized religious education of Egypt for either the majority or the minority groups. He established state schools, parallel to the religious centers of instruction, for the purpose of educating Egyptians for the army and for assistance to him in the administration of the country. His new schools were primarily utilitarian; they were run on military lines and controlled (until 1837) by the Defense Department. Ismail perpetuated this dual system of religious and secular education. But his principal purpose was to spread enlightenment throughout Egypt – to stimulate education for its own sake and to educate as many Egyptians as possible. After promulgating an organic law of public instruction in 1868, Ismail established primary, secondary, and higher schools, divorced from the Defense Department. These were given new curricula, they were subject to medical inspection, and almost all of their pupils were educated and supported at the expense of the state. Additional special schools for law, languages, medicine, music, and other subjects were also founded. A teachers' training institute, the Dar al-ʿUlum, was opened in 1872, the first normal school of Egypt. The year following, one of the Khedive's wives established the first school for girls. Even the European mission schools were aided with donations of land and money. Altogether some 100,000 students attended more than 4,800 schools in the 1870's.[12]

[11] Alfred Milner, *England in Egypt* (London, 1894), p. 216.
[12] Rifaat, *op. cit.*, pp. 122-124. Further confirmation is given in the "Cave

Education, however, constituted only one facet of the intellectual renaissance of Ismail's era. The first national library and the first national museum were founded by the Khedive; Egyptological studies were promoted; and 172 Egyptian students were sent to Europe by the government, for specialization in different fields. The Egyptian press began its flourishing existence and played an important role in the general literary renaissance of the time.

Intimately connected with the spread of education and the growth of intellectual activity was an embryonic constitutional movement. Muhammad Ali had established a consultative council, presumably in imitation of the various councils appointed during the Napoleonic occupation of Egypt, but this council had failed to survive its founder. A state council instituted later by Said amounted to no more than a private cabinet for the convenience of the Pasha. Ismail, early in his reign, decided to create an assembly of notables. On November 10, 1866, he opened the first session of the newly elected "Consultative Assembly of Deputies" (*Majlis shura'l-nuwwab*) with an address in Arabic. Ismail's speech on this occasion, significantly making no reference to the Sultan, included a judicious quotation from the Koran which enabled him to make the point that a Muslim ruler ought to govern with the advice of his people.[13] The seventy-five deputies of the Assembly were elected for a three-year term by electors who, in the first instance, had been chosen by popular vote. Sixty-nine of the seventy-five were chosen in rural areas. Many of the regulations governing the powers and procedure of the Assembly were drawn up in obvious imitation of the French Assemblée Nationale.

Report" of the British mission to Egypt in 1876 (see p. 39, footnote 20).

[13] ". . . and I (Isma'il) thought often about establishing a Chamber of Deputies because its advantages are recognized and cannot be denied. Its characteristics are that matters are decided through consultation between the ruler and the people, as is the case in most countries. Suffice it to say that God encouraged it by saying 'Consult them in the matter' and also 'Solution of their affairs depends on consultation.' " See 'Abd al-Rahman al-Rafi'i, *'Asr Isma'il* [The era of Ismail] Cairo, 1932), II, 100. – See also Jacob M. Landau, *Parliaments and Parties in Egypt* (New York, 1954). Chap. i of Landau's monograph is devoted to the First Assembly of 1866-67, chap. ii to the Assemblies from 1868 through 1878, chap. iii to the Assembly of 1879 (which produced the first *draft* of a constitution).

Various motives have been attributed to Ismail for the calling of the first assembly elected in Egypt. Most European writers assumed that this Pasha, who shortly thereafter became the first Khedive, merely wished to pose as a constitutional ruler – in the interests of promoting better, or more lucrative, relations with the governments of Europe. Some thought that he was prompted primarily by a desire to raise new funds, of which he stood in perennial need. Others have suggested that the creation of a political body over which he presided was a device to gain more effective control of the village notables, since it was they who contributed almost all of the deputies. Only a few observers seem to have credited him with any desire to initiate representative government.

Whatever his motives, the first Assemblies exercised a purely advisory function between 1868 and 1878. They were empowered to deliberate on the domestic affairs of the country and to render opinions on various government projects. The Khedive could adjourn, prorogue, or dissolve them at will, ignore their recommendations or veto their decisions. But, undeniably, the convocation of the Assembly in 1866 marked the first step taken by Egypt toward parliamentary institutions. Many proposals initiated by the first Assemblies were approved and acted upon by the Khedive. And the deliberations of the deputies, though confined for the most part to matters pertaining to agriculture, irrigation, village administration, property, and the judiciary, gave invaluable training to later leaders of the constitutional movement. The Assembly of 1866-1867 took a great interest in education and the creation of new schools; and the Assembly of 1876 enquired into the financial proceedings of the government. The Khedive himself hinted, in his address to the Assembly of 1877, that the deputies might be given some share in the financial administration of the country. And from that time forth the deputies gained in self-assurance and independence. In 1879 they demanded a written constitution for their Assembly – which was, significantly, no longer called the "Consultative Assembly of Deputies." The Majlis shura'l-nuwwab had become the Majlis al-nuwwab, simply the "Assembly of Deputies."

The efforts of the constitutionalists were all the more significant because, by 1879, they had come to form part of a three-pronged movement for the reform of Egyptian society. An articulate campaign for Islamic regeneration was initiated in the 1870's, inspired by a foreign Muslim, Sayyid Jamal al-Din al-Afghani, and led eventually by the greatest of his Egyptian disciples, Shaykh Muhammad 'Abduh. This movement for the total reformation of Muslim society gathered strength and momentum throughout the lifetime of Muhammad 'Abduh, until the very day of his death in 1905.[14]

The most militant phase of the national reform movement was embodied in the army, which had been built up and reorganized by the Khedive for his expeditions into equatorial Africa. A number of secret societies were founded in Egypt during Ismail's reign. Among them was a secret association of Egyptian officers, representative of the fallah or peasant elements in the army. In 1879 this military group established the first "national party" (al-hizb al-watani), for the primary purpose of combating foreign influence in Egypt. The nationalist character of the army movement did not emerge until the end of the Khedive's reign, and it did not develop into a full-fledged revolt until after Tawfiq had succeeded Ismail as Khedive. But the discontents and grievances of the Egyptian elements in the army had their origin, at least in great part, in Ismail's African adventures and must be understood in this context.

According to one account, no less a person than Edward, Prince of Wales, while on a visit to Egypt in 1868, had suggested to the Khedive the prestige value of civilizing the "Dark Continent." Ismail responded with lavish enthusiasm and raised the twin banners of geographical exploration and suppression of the slave trade to inaugurate a series of costly campaigns in tropical Africa. For this purpose he took into his service a great number of foreigners, to lead his army and train his soldiers. Under the leadership first of Sir Samuel Baker and later of General Charles Gordon ("Chinese Gordon"), Egyptian troops brought the northern Sudan once more under effective Egyptian control and conquered the southern Sudan, temporarily blocked the normal slave-trade routes, and penetrated to the headwaters of the White Nile. A number of distinguished European and American officers participated in these campaigns, under the command of General Gordon. And some forty Americans, all of whom had had practical military experience in the Civil War, took

[14] Because of its importance, the problem of Islamic reform in Egypt is dealt with separately, in the third chapter of this study.

service with the Khedive as staff officers.[15] They helped him to re-organize his army and transform it into an efficient fighting force. But initial successes in Africa were ultimately checked, first by the Abyssinians, who defended themselves savagely against Egyptian en-circlement, and then by a political and financial crisis in Egypt that forced Ismail to withdraw and retrench his forces. The morale of the army accordingly declined rapidly after 1875. Egyptian troops had suffered heavy losses in the field; they had also been victimized by the fatal bickering and lack of co-operation among non-Egyptian officers in the top commands; and they suffered finally from reduc-tions in pay – necessitated by the financial crisis that overtook the Egyptian government. And worst of all, from their point of view, the Egyptian officers of the Khedive's army were discriminated against, in matters of promotion and pay, in favor of the Turko-Circassian officer group.

One receives the impression, in viewing the various facets of Is-mail's period, that Egypt was inundated by foreigners. One reason was that the Khedive himself took the lead in promoting a great influx of Europeans. He needed them and their skills for every mod-ernizing enterprise which he set on foot. At the technical level they were indispensable, and for the new education they were greatly to be desired. Eventually, also, as his need for larger revenues grew urgent, Ismail wanted Europeans to help him exploit the wealth of his country. He sought to attract European capital to Egypt by all manner of enticements, including very generous interest rates. And European speculators, in that age of "bubbles" and overseas expan-sion, were quick to respond. The inpouring of foreign merchants and businessmen had actually begun in the early 1840's, directly after the Anglo-Turkish and Franco-Turkish commercial agreements of 1838 became operative in Egypt. These agreements had resulted in the destruction of Muhammad Ali's commercial monopolies, and Euro-peans were given free access to Egypt and allowed to do business there unhampered by any restrictions. But this foreign penetration was accentuated by the financial policies of the Khedive Ismail, with

---

[15]   For a lively account of their varied activities in Egypt see William B. Hes-seltine and Hazel C. Wolf, *The Blue and the Gray on the Nile* (Chicago, 1961). An appendix gives full identification of the forty Americans and their posts in Egypt, pp. 253-260.

the result that during the 1870's Egyptian economic and social life became more accessible to Western commercial and cultural influences and at the same time more vulnerable to Western political pressures. Thus the country was subjected to the competitive commercial activities of multitudes of Europeans – many of whom were frankly rapacious and viewed Egypt as a God-given land ripe for their exploitation. Between 1836 and 1878 the foreign population of Egypt increased from about 3,000 to more than 68,000. One reliable author estimates that there were as many as 80,000 foreigners living in Egypt in 1875.[16] Small wonder that Egyptians became foreigner-conscious and increasingly preoccupied with the presence and activities of Europeans in their midst.

Moreover, the special position of Europeans in Egypt, who enjoyed financial and judicial protection under the Capitulations, made them suspect and eventually resented by Egyptians. During the 19th century fourteen foreign communities enjoyed privileged positions in Egypt, based on extraterritorial rights granted in capitulatory treaties. The Capitulations guaranteed far-reaching but varying judicial, police, and fiscal immunities to the nationals of governments that had entered into this type of treaty relationship, first with the Ottoman and later with the Egyptian governments.[17] After the firman of autonomy of 1873, the Khedive further extended the rights and im-

---

[16]   Issawi, *op. cit.*, p. 25. The total of 80,000 foreigners – "a solid little army sheltered behind the bulwark of the Capitulations" – is given by Jasper Yeates Brinton (Justice of the Court of Appeals, Mixed Courts of Egypt), in *The Mixed Courts of Egypt* (New Haven, Conn., 1930), pp. 28-29. Of the 80,000 foreigners, according to Justice Brinton, about 35,000 were Greeks, 17,500 French, 14,000 Italians, 6,000 British, 6,000 Austrians, 1,000 Germans, 500 Persians, 200 Dutch, 150 Spaniards, 100 each of Russians and Belgians, and finally a miscellaneous group of Swedes, Danes, Portuguese, Swiss, Americans, and others numbering about 40 in all. A. E. Crouchley in *The Economic Development of Modern Egypt* (London, 1938), p. 125. tends to support Brinton's figures: he gives 79,696 as the foreign population of Egypt in 1871, and he states further that their number had increased to 90,886 by 1882. He also notes that the total population of Egypt had risen from 5,250,000 (in 1873) to 6,804,021 (in 1882).

[17]   The Capitulations, officially terminated by the Montreux Conference of 1937, were not completely liquidated until the abolition of the Mixed Courts in 1949. There is an interesting section on this subject in the *Annual Survey* of the Royal Institute of International Affairs for 1937, I, 581-607. *L'Egypte Indépendante*, by Le Groupe d'Etudes de l'Islam (Paris, 1938). Part II, chap. i, pp. 111-116, contains a fairly detailed analysis of the Capitulations in Egypt

munities of certain foreign nationals in return for financial aid or loans to his government. And as the century progressed, the increasingly privileged position of foreigners led to unfair discrimination against Egyptian nationals. The judicial immunities of the various foreign residents, together with the asylum afforded them by their consulates in time of need, made it virtually impossible for the Egyptian government either to hold them to account for their actions or to maintain law and order on an equitable basis wherever foreigners and Egyptians lived cheek by jowl in mixed communities. Judicial chaos was the result. So long as Europeans formed a negligible group in the country, the problems occasioned by the extraterritorial provisions of the Capitulations resulted in but little ill-feeling. But once their numbers drew attention to the obvious injustices occasioned by their special status, the abuses of extraterritoriality caused Egyptians to suffer from an intense feeling of discrimination.

This situation precipitated one of the most notable reforms of Ismail's period – the one for which posterity has given him the greatest credit. His able Armenian minister, Nubar Pasha, after eight years of unremitting effort and numberless visits to all the great capitals of Europe, introduced a unified system of mixed courts for the foreign nationals. These new Egyptian, strictly national courts replaced in large part the individual consular courts. All civil and commercial cases between foreigners and Egyptians, as well as between foreigners of different nationalities, were brought under their jurisdiction. The new courts were "mixed" in the sense that foreign and Egyptian justices and judges sat together to try the cases brought before them, but the foreign judges – perhaps inevitably, since this reform was dependent upon the agreement of the powers concerned – were in a fixed majority. The foreign judicial appointees were selected from among the nationals of all the European powers and the United States without discrimination – even those of the non-Capitulatory powers were eligible for appointment. In practice, they were nominated by their own governments, but they were appointed and paid by the Khedive of Egypt. So far as possible, diplomatic and

---

and their importance in Egyptian social, legal, and administrative life. And in his book *Egyptian Service, 1902-1946* (London, 1949), Sir Thomas Russell Pasha gives many illuminating examples of the conflicts and problems created by the Capitulations.

prestige issues were circumvented in their selection. The Courts of the Reform, as they were popularly known, were four in number. There were three District Courts of the First Instance, at Cairo, Alexandria, and Mansourah, and one Court of Appeals in Alexandria. Of their first forty justices and judges, twenty-four were foreign; but as time went on the ratio of foreigners to Egyptians increased until, by 1930, only twenty-three out of a total of sixty-nine were Egyptian.[18]

The Mixed Courts administered their own law. Egyptian civil, commercial, and maritime codes, founded upon the French codes and totaling in all 2,500 articles, were drawn up by a French lawyer in the service of the Egyptian government. So also was a code of civil and commercial procedure. All of these new Egyptian codes were supplemented by a slowly growing body of statute law, promulgated by the government of Egypt and made applicable to foreigners with the consent of the powers. And finally all of these written law codes were supplemented and in some matters of procedure actually modified by usage (*La Coutume*), which has always been a source of law in Egypt. In cases where the written law was silent, insufficient, or obscure, the justices and judges of the Mixed Courts were authorized by their charter to follow the principles of natural law and equity.

The Mixed Courts constituted a noteworthy experiment in reform. They stabilized and elevated the judicial relationship between Egyptians and foreigners. They gave a great impetus toward the study of European law in Egypt. They likewise resulted in 1883 in the establishment of still other national Egyptian courts based on a modified version of the *Code Napoléon* – modified in that they took cognizance of the Muslim law of the land. But the Mixed Courts in practice proved to be a very mixed blessing. In the first place, because they were largely foreign in composition, they conducted their business in foreign languages. The law itself, moreover, and the procedure were too European for the country – many hardships were consequently inflicted upon illiterate Egyptians, particularly through laws govern-

[18] For the above and subsequent material on these national courts I have drawn on Brinton, *op. cit.*, pp. 13, 15-17, 21, 74, 77, 79, 83, 84, 145-152, 154, 367-370. See also Rifaat, *op. cit.*, p. 119, and the Earl of Cromer, *Modern Egypt* (London, 1908), II, 316-320. Incidentally, though the Mixed Courts issued from the brain of Nubar Pasha, Riadh (Riaz) Pasha was actually prime minister when the Mixed Courts were first opened on New Year's Day, 1876.

ing indebtedness. Thirdly, their criminal jurisdiction was very narrowly circumscribed because the consular courts continued to exercise criminal jurisdiction over their own nationals in almost all cases. Worst of all, from the point of view of the constitutional development of Egypt, the Mixed Courts not only curtailed the power of the Khedive, but also encroached upon the legislative rights of the government.

The duration and difficulties of Nubar's struggle, before he could obtain European – and particularly French – agreement to his proposals for judicial reform, threw in its turn a sinister spotlight on the undue influence of Europeans in Egypt. And the commitment of the foreign powers to the support of privileged positions for their nationals injected a further element of unrest into the situation. The final catastrophe of Ismail's reign, resulting in the active intervention of two of the Great Powers in Egypt's internal affairs, produced consternation in the country. To the clear-sighted Egyptian, this was dramatic evidence that the dictation of foreign Christian states was to be substituted for the accustomed control of their Muslim Ottoman overlord – only a few years after the Sultan himself had agreed to renounce his right to interfere in the domestic affairs of the Khediviate. How this came about should now be explained.

An involved story lies behind the decline and fall of the Khedive Ismail. In a nutshell, Egypt's first Khedive took too many liberties with the natural wealth of Egypt, a wealth which, in view of his multifarious development schemes, must have seemed to him inexhaustible. Everything that Ismail planned and carried out for Egypt cost a great deal of money. The material and cultural benefits which he bestowed upon the country were too costly, and his own princely scale of living added to the burden. In the final accounting, it was shown that Ismail's personal expenditures, lavish though they were, would not alone have ruined Egypt. But instead of retrenching financially, he tried to maintain the fiction of solvency. He taxed his peasantry mercilessly, beyond endurance, but they could never contribute enough to save him. He then took to borrowing on a larger and larger scale from the willing private bankers of Europe, and these ruthless financiers charged him ruinous interest rates on their loans.

In order to convince his creditors that he was and that he would remain solvent, Ismail put on a public show of great wealth. He spent more and more on public works, on entertaining European crowned heads and envoys, and on developing the Khedivial establishment. Consequently he sank deeper into debt after every loan and promptly borrowed again in an effort to extricate himself. Next he pledged the revenues of the railways and the royal domains. In 1875 he sold his founders' shares (44 per cent of the total shares) in the Suez Canal Company to Great Britain for the relatively paltry sum of about four million pounds.[19] By the end of that year Egyptian treasury bills were discounted at 30 per cent. In 1876 payment on the foreign debt charges was, for the first time, postponed by Khedivial decree.

In March, 1876, Stephen Cave, who had led a special British mission to Egypt to inquire into the financial condition of the country, submitted his report to Parliament. This remarkably thorough report pointed out that "every available portion" of the revenue of Egypt had been pledged for the charges of existing loans. Upon his accession, the Khedive Ismail had inherited a national debt of £3,292,800 from his predecessor, Said Pasha. Between 1864 and 1873 Ismail contracted four more state loans with various international European banking houses. None of these cost the Egyptian government less than 12 per cent per annum (including sinking funds), and the 1866 loan raised for the construction of railways cost 26.9 per cent per annum. The ruinous loan of 1873 was contracted for the nominal amount of 32,000,000 pounds sterling, of which the Egyptian treasury actually received only 20,740,077 pounds. By the end of 1875 more than 29,500,000 pounds had been paid for the interest and sinking funds of the public loans. Unofficial and short-term loans, constantly prolonged on "ruinous" terms, cost the Khedive and his country even more dearly. Moreover, a large proportion of the money thus received was taken out of the country again as profit on foreign contracts. When all the debts of the state, including those of the Khedivial lands and the floating debt, were unified by decree on May 7, 1876, the total national debt of Egypt stood at approximately 91,000,000 pounds sterling.

Cave attributed the critical condition of Egyptian finances to "the combination of two opposite causes": the fact that the country was in a state of transition and suffered from the defects of the *ancien régime* on the one hand, and the defects of the new era of westerniza-

[19]   The market price of the shares at that time.

tion on the other. He added that "immense sums are expended on unproductive works . . . and on productive works carried out in the wrong way, or too soon." At the same time he maintained that Egypt's resources were "sufficient, if properly managed, to meet her liabilities." [20]

Ismail's insolvency led to European intervention. In May, 1876, the Khedive sanctioned the appointment of a foreign receivership, known as the Commission of the Debt (the *Caisse de la Dette*), on behalf of Egypt's foreign creditors. And the Anglo-French Dual Control was established. Under this arrangement an English controller-general took charge of the Revenue Office, and a French controller-general took charge of the Audit Office. Egypt's financial crisis, however, was not to be thus easily solved. During 1877/1878 there was a very low Nile, which made a serious crop problem for the peasantry, and Egyptian troops were forced to participate in the Russo-Turkish war at the bidding of the Sultan. The Mixed Courts gave judgments in favor of creditors against the Khedive, but these could not be enforced. And the separation of finance from administration resulted in a general deterioration of government. A European commission of inquiry brought in a severe indictment of Ismail's personal government; and its recommendation to limit the absolute power of the Khedive led to the appointment of two European ministers – one British and one French – to the national ministry. This development led quite naturally to general discontent and openly expressed anti-foreign feeling. Nationalist meetings took place, and anonymous protests emanated from secret societies.

Early in 1879 Egyptian army officers staged a potentially serious military demonstration in Cairo after arbitrary reductions had been made in their pay; the Khedive himself was called upon to disperse them. And soon thereafter Ismail, pushed too far by the representatives of the Powers, took the momentous decision of supporting the constitutional nationalists and their leader, Sharif Pasha. His next step was to defy the officials of the Dual Control. Once the Khedive

---

[20] "Report by Mr. Cave on the Financial Condition of Egypt," in Great Britain, Parliament, *Accounts and Papers: State Papers*, Vol. LXXXIII, Egypt, No. 7 (1876), pp. 1, 6-8, 12 (C. 1425). See also Alfred Milner, *England in Egypt*, 2d ed. (London, 1894), pp. 216, 218-219, and Young, *op. cit.*, pp. 72, 84, 87.

made common cause with the nationalists, and the European consuls and creditors began to feel insecure, Ismail's fate was sealed. All the Great Powers, at the instigation of Bismarck, put pressure on the Sultan to depose his vassal. On June 26, 1879, without any prior warning, a telegram was dispatched from Constantinople to "The Ex-Khedive Ismail," and immediately thereafter this once powerful and proud ruler received orders from the Powers to quit his country.

The reign of the Khedive Ismail has been dealt with at relatively great length because Egypt's future was conditioned in his era. Both the later political development of the nation and the role assigned to Egypt on the international political stage were inexorably predetermined during these sixteen fateful years.

Egyptians were profoundly shaken by the deposition of Ismail. They were humiliated as well as alarmed that the Great Powers could and did put pressure on the Sultan to depose their once powerful Khedive. The fallah officers, the religious leaders, and the educated elite all deeply resented this latest and most sinister evidence of European influence over their affairs. Inevitably, the Khediviate lost face in Egypt, as it lost prestige abroad. Tawfiq, the son of Ismail, became the new Khedive. But the firman of investiture limited the strength of the Egyptian Army to 18,000 men, though it left almost intact all the other powers granted to the Khediviate in the firman of 1873. Shortly thereafter, Khedive Tawfiq guaranteed the tenure of the Anglo-French financial controllers subject only to dismissal by their own governments. The stage was set for a fresh crisis, which was not long in coming.

Had the new Khedive been a strong man, or courageous, things might have worked out differently – at least, the inevitable crisis would have been postponed. Unhappily, Tawfiq, like Louis XVI of France at the beginning of the French Revolution, was incapable of coping with the situation that faced him. Like Louis he led an exemplary private life, but he was weak, vacillating, and wanting in intellectual vigor. The Khedive Tawfiq, moreover, was menaced on three fronts. He was under continual pressure from the Anglo-French controllers and from the nationalists in his own country, as well as under intermittent pressure from his suzerain, the Sultan in Constantinople. He kept always in mind the fate of his father, Ismail – a waking nightmare that undermined his moral strength.

Between 1879 and 1882 the National Party grew from a small secret association to a large popular movement. The omnipresence of the Dual Control, the shock of Ismail's fall from power, the anomalous position of the new Khedive, to say nothing of his vacillating character, were all factors that contributed to the strength of the national movement. The actual composition of this movement and the factionalism that it developed at the end of 1881 resulted in the military rebellion of 1882, better known as the revolt of Arabi Pasha.

Foremost in the National Party were the Constitutionalists, a group that had been gaining ground since 1876. In the eyes of many Europeans, particularly Englishmen in Egypt, the Constitutionalists' struggle against the absolute power of the Khedive was legitimate and entirely comprehensible. The Constitutionalists, however, posed a special problem for the Anglo-French controllers, particularly when they sought to gain control of the financial management of Egypt The Assembly of 1881-1882 drafted a constitution, demanded ministerial responsibility, and insisted upon its right to vote the budget. The last of these objectives was inevitably opposed by the Anglo-French officials of the Dual Control, since they had the responsibility for re-establishing the solvency of the Egyptian government.

The Muslim religious leaders in the National Party were in sympathy with the Constitutionalists and, to a lesser extent, with the Egyptian army officers. But they placed their emphasis primarily upon the attainment of fundamental reforms in Muslim Egyptian society. Furthermore, as members of an elite group, the Ulama of al-Azhar, they had little intercourse with Europeans.[21] Despite this fact, they recognized sooner than did other reformers in the National Party that active resistance to the Khedive or opposition to the Dual Control would lead to a dangerous situation in the country. Shaykh Muhammad 'Abduh was the leader of the intellectual movement for Muslim reform and was also an ally of the military reformers, but, as the military phase of the national movement progressed, he realized that incipient revolutionary activities were likely to render his desired reforms impossible of achievement, and he then became an opponent of the military movement. In the beginning, the military leaders had constantly sought his advice; when he opposed them, as

[21]   See chap. III, note 6 (p. 117).

he did with increasing vigor, and warned them of the danger of foreign intervention, they turned against him.[22]

The third group, the founders of the National Party, were the fallah officers. It was they who eventually, and disastrously for the national movement, became paramount in the councils of the party as well as numerically predominant. The army group had many grievances, all of them aggravated upon the accession of Tawfiq by the reduction of the army from 45,000 men to fewer than 18,000. Worst of all from their point of view was the appointment of a Circassian general, Osman Pasha Rifki, as Minister of War. He dismissed many Egyptian officers, put many more on half pay, and gave preferential promotion to Turks and Circassians. Three fallah colonels, sprung from peasant families, provided articulate leadership for the discontented Egyptian officers of the Khedive's army. It was Colonel Ahmad Arabi, known as "The Egyptian," who gave his name to the revolt. He was a sincere, eloquent, intensely religious man and was generally considered by his fellow Egyptians to be a talented young officer. His two friends and colleagues, Ali Fahmi and 'Abd al-'Al, were likewise able officers.

At first the three colonels merely protested against the Turko-Circassian policy of the Minister of War. When Rifki, however, attempted to arrest and court-martial them in February, 1881, these three Egyptian officers were forcibly rescued by their own troops. Khedive Tawfiq, frightened by this demonstration of fallah strength in the army, dismissed Osman Rifki and appointed – only temporarily, as it turned out – a new Minister of War acceptable to Colonel Arabi and his two associates. This evidence of the Khedive's weakness marked the beginning of the rise of the fallah colonels to popular power. When Tawfiq tried to regain control of the Ministry of War, as he did six months later, he precipitated a second and much

---

[22] See C. C. Adams, *Islam and Modernism in Egypt* (London, 1933), pp. 53-54 (including notes 5 and 6), quoting Rashid Rida in *al-Manar*, VIII, 413-467. See also Wilfrid Scawen Blunt, *Secret History of the English Occupation of Egypt* (New York, 1922), pp. 378-379. According to Shaykh Muhammad 'Abduh, quoted by Blunt from a written statement later given by the Shaykh to his English friend, on December 22, 1903, the Shaykh was in favor of a constitution and a free press in Egypt; he was not in favor of a revolution; he "urged Arabi to moderation" in September, 1881, and he foretold "a foreign occupation" at that time. Full text on pp. 378-379.

more serious demonstration on the part of three regiments, on September 9, 1881, in Abdin Palace Square in Cairo.

In December, 1881, the National Party, whose membership included some Egyptian Copts and Jews, as well as Muslims, drew up a moderate political program – their second party manifesto.[23]

In this document the National Party unwittingly prepared the ground for overt rebellion against the Khedive by confiding its interests to the army, "believing them to be the only power in the country able and willing to protect its growing liberties [and that] as soon as the people shall have established their rights securely the army will abandon its present political attitude." [24] This program also demanded that the army, "as the armed guardians of the unarmed people," should be efficiently maintained and its complement "made up to the full number [permitted by the Sultan's firman of 1879] of 18,000 men." At the same time, however, the party program explicitly recognized the Dual Control, "aware that all freedom and justice they have obtained in the past has been due to them" – i.e., the governments of England and France – and it accepted Egypt's foreign debt as a "matter of national honour" and "a necessity of their financial position, and the present continuance of it as the best guarantee of their prosperity." Finally, the National Party declared its loyalty to the Khedive in the following words:

They will continue to support Mohamed Tewfik's [Tawfiq's] authority as

[23] The first manifesto of this party was mentioned by the Official Gazette of the government of Egypt on April 13, 1879. The number of members of the National Party was never made public. But the manifesto of 1879 was signed by 327 Egyptians, of whom more than 28 per cent were army officers, 22 per cent officials (including retired employees), 18.3 per cent Deputies (a figure which represented 80 per cent of all the Deputies of the Assembly), 18.3 per cent religious representatives (including some Coptic and Jewish leaders, as well as members of the Ulama), and almost 13 per cent notables and merchants. By 1881, the National Party and its group of leaders would have grown considerably, but its leadership remained in the hands of the army officers. ʿAbd al-Rahman al-Rafiʿi, ʿAsr Ismaʿil (Cairo, 1932), II, 218. See also the interesting analysis made by Landau, op. cit., pp. 87-91.

[24] This and the following several quotations are from the English text prepared by Wilfrid Blunt and published in The Times, London, No. 30, 394, January 3, 1882, p. 4. Blunt was a staunch supporter of the National Party and a close friend of many of its leaders. He prepared this text in collaboration with Shaykh Muhammad ʿAbduh and several other Egyptian nationalists. He also sent a copy of this document to Prime Minister Gladstone – forwarded from Egypt on December 20, 1881.

long as he shall rule in accordance with justice and the law, and in fulfillment of his promises made to the people of Egypt in September 1881.
They declare, however, their intention to permit no renewal of that des-
potic reign of injustice which Egypt has so often witnessed, and to insist
upon the exact execution of his promise of Parliamentary government
and of giving the country freedom.

In the last paragraphs of the program, the National Party described
itself and its general aims thus:

The National party of Egypt is a political, not a religious party. It includes within its ranks men of various races and various creeds. It is
principally Mohamedan, because nine-tenths of the Egyptians are Mo-
hamedans; but it has the support of the Moors, of the Coptic Christians,
of the Jews, and others who cultivate the soil and speak the language of
Egypt. Between these it makes no distinction whatever, holding all men
to be brothers and to have equal rights, both political and before the law.
This principle is accepted by all the chief Sheikhs of the Azhar who support the party, holding the true law of Islam to forbid religious hatred
and religious disabilities .... The general end of the National party is
the intellectual and moral regeneration of the country by a better observance of the law, by increased education, and by political liberty,
which it holds to be the life of the people.

The following reassuring and significant statement was also included:

With Europeans resident in Egypt the National party has no quarrel,
either as Christians or as strangers, so long as these shall live conform-
ably with the laws and bear their share of the burdens of the State.

Unhappily for the Egyptian nationalists, they were soon constrained
to feel that they did have a "quarrel" with the Europeans. On
January 8, 1882, the governments of France and Great Britain sent
a gratuitous "Joint Note," often referred to as the Gambetta Note
because it was drafted at the Quai d'Orsay, to the Khedive Tawfiq to
assure him of their "support against the difficulties of various kinds
which might interfere with the course of public affairs in Egypt." In
this note they stated that "the English and French Governments consider the maintenance of His Highness on the throne, on the terms
laid down by the Sultan's *Firmans*, . . . as alone able to guarantee,
for the present and future, the good order and the development of
general prosperity in Egypt in which France and Great Britain are
equally interested." They further declared their belief that "the assurance publicly given of their formal intentions in this respect will

tend to avert the dangers [internal or external] to which the Government of the Khedive might be exposed, and which would certainly find England and France united to oppose them." [25] The precise nature of their "formal intentions," should France and Britain decide upon common action to support the Khedive vis-à-vis the Egyptian nationalists, was left unspecified.

Léon Gambetta, then Foreign Minister of France, seems to have feared that the Egyptians were about to become involved in a widespread Pan-Islamic movement. And as he was then faced with a Muslim revolt in Tunis and in Algeria which threatened the position of the French government in North Africa, he insisted upon taking a strong line with the Egyptians. The English, on the other hand, had no reason at that time to be alarmed by the situation in Egypt; they were not much moved by the predicament of the French in Algeria and Tunis; and they wished if possible to avoid any military action in Egypt. Yet the British Foreign Secretary, Lord Granville, allowed Gambetta to persuade him to agree to the Joint Note. This was all the more surprising in view of the fact that Granville had recently outlined a pacific policy for the guidance of the British Consul-General in Egypt. He had stated in a despatch to Sir Edward Malet on November 4, 1881, that "only . . . the occurrence in Egypt of a state of anarchy" could change his government's policy, which was to "maintain . . . the administrative independence of Egypt." [26]

The drafting of the Joint Note furnishes a classic example of the not infrequent lack of rapport between policy makers in London and

[25] *Accounts and Papers: State Papers*, Vol. LXXXII, Egypt, No. 2 (1882), "Despatch from His Majesty's Agent and Consul-General at Cairo, forwarding a copy of the Note presented to the Khedive by the English and French Agents," (C. 3106); France, Ministère des Affaires Étrangères, *Documents Diplomatiques Français (1871-1914)*, 1re Série (1871-1900), Tome IV (Paris, 1932), Documents Nos. 226, 227, pp. 217, 218.

[26] Great Britain, Foreign Office, *British and Foreign State Papers*, Hertslet ed. (London, 1890), LXXIII (1881-82), 1162, 1161. See also, *ibid.*, LXXIV, 369, Granville to Dufferin (in Constantinople), January 9, 1882, in which Granville summarizes his despatch to Malet of November 4, 1881, on the policy of Great Britain in regard to Egypt: "That policy aimed at the continuance of the *status quo*; the maintenance of the connection between Turkey and Egypt; the prosperity of the country; the maintenance of its liberties; and the absence of any preponderating influence on the part of any single Power. To this programme, and to the disclaimer of any ambitious designs on our part which the despatch contained, we fully adhered."

British representatives in the field – particularly before the development of aviation. British officials could not then make quick emergency trips to Cairo and back, or vice versa, and no one could be recalled from the field for immediate consultation. In this instance, the knowledge of experienced observers on the scene was entirely discounted. Gladstone, the great Liberal prime minister, and most of his government seem to have elected to believe that the national movement of Egypt was "wholly military," in disregard of all the evidence at hand.[27] They ignored the warnings of their representatives in Egypt, and they never opened their minds to the subject. Just before agreeing to the Gambetta Note, Granville had received an important memorandum from Sir Auckland Colvin, the British member of the Dual Financial Control. Writing on December 26, 1881, Colvin gave an account of the current Egyptian national movement, which he described as a "liberal" movement "directed to the good of the country." He advised strongly against "discouraging" or "thwarting" it. But he coupled this advice with a further recommendation:

But precisely because I wish it (the liberal movement now going on) to succeed, it seems to me essential that it should learn from the first within

---

[27]   The analysis and quotations in the text are from the Earl of Cromer (Evelyn Baring), *Modern Egypt* (London, 1908), Vol. I, especially p. 226. Evelyn Baring (1841-1917), later Lord Cromer, first served in Egypt under the Dual Control as a major in the British Army. He was the famous Proconsul during the first twenty-four years of the Occupation. In 1883, he was appointed British Agent and Consul-General, with plenipotentiary powers and diplomatic rank. He became Baron Cromer in 1892, viscount in 1899, and first Earl of Cromer in 1901. In his classic work on modern Egypt, Cromer gave it as his opinion that Granville had associated himself with Gambetta's note because he entirely misjudged the effect that such an official joint communication would produce in Egypt. Cromer also frankly criticized the British Government of the day in the following words: "One main point should surely have been borne in mind before the Joint Note was delivered. It was that a National Party existed in Egypt. On this subject, the British government appear to have been under a delusion from the first. They thought the movement was wholly military, and, therefore, undeserving of sympathy." He supported this criticism by quoting a speech delivered by Gladstone in the House of Commons on July 22, 1882, in justification of British intervention in Egypt during that month: "There have been periods," Gladstone declaimed, "at which it has been charitably believed, even in this country, that the military party was the popular party, and was struggling for the liberties of Egypt. There is not the smallest rag or shred of evidence to support that contention." For a full and authoritative analysis of events leading up to the Joint Note see also, *ibid.*, chap. xiii, pp. 214-253.

what limits it must confine itself . . . . In all that is doing or to be done, neither the Government nor the Chamber [the Assembly of Deputies] should be allowed to forget that the Powers have assumed a direct financial control over the country and intend to maintain it . . . . All that is designed to transfer the centre of financial authority from the [Dual] Control to the Chamber should be especially discountenanced and, if need be, negatived, as neutralising and nullifying the agency through which the Powers assure themselves of the efficient conduct of financial affairs, for which they have made themselves responsible in Egypt . . . . The line . . . that I advocate, is the open and firm recognition by the Powers, through their diplomatic agents, at this critical juncture when Egypt is remoulding her internal reorganisation, of the material interest they possess and intend to maintain in the administration, leaving full liberty to the Egyptians to frame what measures they please for their internal government, so far as they are not inconsistent with the status acquired by the Powers. In fact, the Egyptian administration is a partnership of three.[28]

Sir Edward Malet, in turn, warned his government against taking any step that might be construed as hostile to the national movement, and he urged Granville by telegram to give careful consideration to Colvin's memorandum before taking any action with respect to Egypt. He gave as his reasons that "It would be unadvisable that the Khedive should be encouraged to hope that we would support him in maintaining an attitude of reserve towards the Chamber . . . . To discountenance it would be to play into the hands of the Porte, increase the influence of the military, and diminish that which we are now obtaining as befriending moderate reform." [29]

But London ignored the constructive advice received and acted only upon Colvin's final recommendation, which he made in his official capacity as controller. In his memorandum, it is clear, he was thinking of protecting the Dual Control, rather than of obtaining unqualified support for the Khedive.

The Anglo-French note reached Cairo while the Assembly of Deputies was in process of drafting the first Egyptian constitution. The nationalists reacted instantaneously and with indignation. It was plain to them that a would-be autocratic Khedive was to be support-

[28] Quoted in Cromer, *op. cit.,* I, 221-222. Cromer states that Sir Auckland Colvin's memorandum reached the Foreign Office on January 2, 1882, i.e., six days before the presentation of the Joint Note of January 8, 1882.
[29] Quoted, *ibid.,* p. 218. Malet's prophecy was borne out, to the letter, in the events that took place after the delivery of the Anglo-French Joint Note.

ed against the national movement. All Egyptian nationalists forthwith united behind the army.

This much attention has been devoted to the British share in the
affair of the Gambetta Note for several reasons. First, because
France eventually abdicated its place in the Dual Control and Great
Britain became the sole occupying power in Egypt. Second, the joint
action of the two powers most vitally interested in that country has
also great historic interest because of some curious parallels, as well
as some interesting contrasts, with the Anglo-French position on the
Suez Canal crisis of 1956 – even though the latter incident lies outside the scope of this book. Finally, of course, the impact of the
Joint Note at the time was directly relevant to the subsequent story
of the Arabi Rebellion.

The day after the delivery of the note Malet thus informed the
Foreign Office:

The communication has, at all events temporarily, alienated from us all
confidence. Everything was progressing capitally, and England was looked on as the sincere wellwisher and protector of the country. Now, it is
considered that England has definitely thrown in her lot with France, and
that France, from motives in connection with her Tunisian campaign,
is determined ultimately to intervene here.[30]

On January 10 he followed up this despatch with another:

For the moment [the Joint Note] has had the effect to cause a more
complete union of the national party, the military, and the Chamber,
to unite these three in a common bond of opposition to England and
France, and to make them feel more forcibly than they did before that
the tie which unites Egypt to the Ottoman Empire is a guarantee to which
they must strongly adhere to save themselves from aggression.[31]

Lord Cromer, writing more than twenty years later, stated flatly that
"From the moment the Joint Note was issued, foreign intervention
became an almost unavoidable necessity." [32]

Outside Egypt the repercussions were almost equally unfortunate.
First the Sultan, and shortly thereafter various of the powers
– Russia, Italy, Austria-Hungary, and Germany – protested against

[30]   Quoted, *ibid.*, pp. 228-229.
[31]   Quoted, *ibid.*, p. 229. Malet's reference to the Ottoman Empire is an interesting foresight of Egyptian nationalist reaction after the British Occupation.
[32]   *Ibid.*, p. 235.

the Anglo-French note to the Khedive. Gladstone accordingly busied himself with an assortment of plans, all of them stillborn, to bring about the internationalization of the Egyptian question. On February 11, 1882, on the initiative of London, Britain and France backed down from the implications of their joint position with respect to Egypt. They stated unequivocally that, should intervention become necessary, they would desire "the united action and authority of Europe." [33]

The harm already done in Egypt by the Joint Note could not, however, be undone. The events of the next few months can be told fairly briefly. They form essentially a postscript to the delivery of the Anglo-French note to the Khedive.

In February, 1882, Colonel Arabi became Minister of War, and the constitution, Egypt's first, was completed. But difficulties developed straightway between the Assembly and the military. Colonel Arabi, who had become a pasha upon his appointment to the Ministry of War, grew more aggressive and highhanded. Both he and the Khedive renewed their earlier intrigues with the Sultan for his support; and the British and French consuls-general felt it necessary to meddle in both constitutional and military affairs. The situation steadily deteriorated. Finally, an Anglo-French squadron was sent to Alexandria, ostensibly to protect the foreign communities; and the consuls-general, heartened by its appearance, demanded that Arabi Pasha be exiled from Egypt and that his associates, Ali Fahmi and 'Abd al-'Al – who, like Arabi, had also been elevated to the rank of pasha – be retired to the provinces. These demands precipitated the final showdown between the Khedive and the nationalists.

Meanwhile, Tawfiq had formally requested the intervention of the Sultan on his behalf. But before a Turkish mission could reach Egypt, the Khedive began to fear for his personal safety. Accordingly he capitulated to the urgent nationalist demands to reinstate Arabi Pasha as Minister of War. The Turkish mission, when it arrived, found the impending revolt impossible to control. So the mission intrigued with both the Palace and the military, while Arabi and his

[33] "Foreign Office Circular Instructions to British Diplomatic Representatives in Berlin, Vienna, Rome and St. Petersburg, 11 February 1882", *Accounts and Papers: State Papers*, LXXXII (1882), 182, quoted in J.C. Hurewitz, *Diplomacy in the Near and Middle East* (Princeton, N. J., 1956), I, 194-196.

associates signed petitions for the deposition of the Khedive. Not until later, however, did the Sultan declare Arabi a rebel.

On June 11 riots broke out in Alexandria, in the course of which more than fifty persons were killed – most of whom were Europeans.[34] Arabi Pasha guaranteed order in the country and reassured the foreign consuls, but the Khedive, notwithstanding, left his capital to take refuge under the guns of the British squadron that remained anchored in Alexandria. Arabi restored order in the port city, but he then set his men to repair Alexandria's harbor fortifications, so the situation remained explosive. The British admiral ordered the Arabists to cease repair work on the harbor forts and batteries; when his ultimatum was ignored, the British ships bombarded the forts and silenced their guns. The British were forced to act without the French, whose ships had suddenly and inexplicably retired from the port. In this crisis the British Government invited France, no longer led by Gambetta, and Italy to join with them in putting down the Arabi Rebellion, but the governments of both France and Italy declined to take action. Although thousands of Europeans were leaving Egypt and many of the nationalists were becoming articulately xenophobic, the European Powers could not agree upon united action. The French Chamber, by a huge majority, voted against intervention, but the President of France gave his moral support to British unilateral intervention in Egypt.[35] In this knowledge, and with a promise

---

[34] Rifaat, *op. cit.*, p. 199, and *The Cambridge History of British Foreign Policy, 1783-1919* (Cambridge, 1923), III, 169; also Vice-Consul Calvert to Sir E. Malet and Earl Granville, June 12, 1882, *Accounts and Papers: State Papers*, Vol. LXXXIII, Egypt, No. 17 (1882), p. 28. For testimony of witnesses to the riots at Alexandria see, *ibid.*, Egypt, No. 16 (1882), "Correspondence Respecting the Riots at Alexandria on the 11th June, 1882" (C. 3390).

[35] On July 29, 1882, Georges Clemenceau attacked the government for its interventionist policy in Egypt, charging that European concerns and the threat of undue German influence were of paramount importance to France: "a fatal hand" – presumably Bismarck's — was "preparing a terrible explosion in Europe." De Freycinet's government fell, by an adverse vote of 416 to 75, and joint action with Britain in Egypt was thereafter out of the question. President Grévy, however, later gave the British expeditionary force his blessing and told the British chargé d'affaires at Paris that France wished England well and would rejoice at British success in Egypt. For a revealing discussion of French, British, Italian, German, and Turkish policies vis-à-vis Egypt, July to September, 1882, see Cromer, *op. cit.*, I, 302-320. See also William L. Langer, *European Alliances and Alignments* (New York, 1931), pp. 274-278. See also France, Ministère des Affaires Étrangères, *op. cit.*, Tome IV, Docu-

of military aid from the Sultan of the Ottoman Empire, the British Cabinet resolved to act alone.

Arabi Pasha was repudiated by the Khedive and proclaimed a rebel by the Sultan, but he gathered his forces to resist the now inevitable British intervention. The nationalist movement thereupon turned into an overt military rebellion. On September 13 at Tel el-Kebir – just west of the Suez Canal – a British expeditionary force under General Sir Garnet Wolseley summarily defeated Arabi's army. It was said in Egypt that 10,000 Egyptian troops were killed at Tel el-Kebir in a few hours. Arabi Pasha forthwith fled to Cairo and he and all the nationalists – with a single exception – surrendered themselves to the British.[36] Almost before it was begun, the revolt was ended.

In October and November of 1882, Arabi Pasha and his principal associates were tried in a special Khedivial court. At the insistence of the British, the trial was conducted in public and the prisoners were defended by British counsel. Arabi pleaded guilty to the charge of rebellion and was sentenced to death, but his sentence was commuted to perpetual exile. He and six of his associates were exiled to Ceylon. At the beginning of 1883 all the political prisoners who had escaped exile were released under a general amnesty.[37]

Many and various reasons have been given for the rout of Arabi and the fallah army. The soldiers were poorly equipped and inadequately trained. The military leaders themselves, including Arabi, were politically immature and ill prepared to shoulder responsibility. There was, moreover, considerable jealousy among the army officers, and there were instances of treachery to the three colonels. The Arabists were abandoned by their Khedive and outlawed by the Sultan. Many able Egyptian nationalists were discouraged by the hostility of Tawfiq and alarmed by the fact that the Sultan of the Ottoman Empire, after intriguing with both Arabi and Tawfiq, had decided to support the Khedive.

---

ment No. 525, September 14, 1882, pp. 499-500, congratulating the British on their victory at Tel el-Kebir.

[36] The single exception was ʿAbd Allah al-Nadim, as will be seen later.

[37] Eventually, in 1901, Arabi was pardoned and permitted to return to finish out his remaining years in Egypt. See Cromer, *op. cit.*, I, 334-337; A. M. Broadley, *How We Defended Arabi and His Friends* (London, 1884); and Blunt, *op. cit.*

Other factors, however, provide more fundamental reasons for the collapse of this revolt – leaving out the basic fact of British intervention. The three nationalist groups were seriously disunited. The Constitutionalists, in the person of Sharif Pasha, took umbrage as early as September, 1881, at the interference of the military in politics. Later, the influential fallah landlord Sultan Pasha was even charged with betraying the army. The Ulama (religious leaders) had not given wholehearted support to the fallah officers, particularly after the latter refused to be guided by Shaykh Muhammad 'Abduh. The military, for their part, were unprepared to fight European governments and armies, and they eventually sealed their own doom by invoking Pan-Islamic concepts and anti-European sentiments to bolster their cause. Brilliant but hotheaded journalists, notably 'Abd Allah al-Nadim, Salim al-Naqqash, and James Sanua (an Egyptian Jew), wielded their pens to incite the street Egyptian against foreign influences. A Syrian-Egyptian journalist coined the slogan "Egypt for the Egyptians."

Thus it was that a military movement which began as insubordination against the Turko-Circassian officer group in the highest army commands turned into a revolt against the authority of the Khedive. And when Tawfiq received support from two of the Great Powers, even though it had not been solicited by him, the militant nationalists inevitably turned against the Europeans. It was a constant source of irritation to the nationalists, moreover, that Europeans were guaranteed a privileged position in Egypt and were appointed to the most highly paid posts in the country. As early as September, 1881, the British consul-general had written to London:

During the late crisis (the army demonstration of September 9) there was a considerable panic in the large foreign population at Alexandria and Cairo, arising not so much from the expectation that the movement would turn against foreigners as from the sense of helplessness on their part if it did.[38]

---

[38] Malet to Granville, September 25, 1881, in *British and Foreign State Papers*, LXXIII, 1149. Five weeks later, however, and two months *before* the presentation of the Anglo-French Joint Note, Malet reassured Foreign Secretary Granville by telegram as to Arabi Pasha's position, in the following words: "Arabi Bey and two other Colonels came to see Mr. Colvin this morning. Arabi Bey's language produced the most favourable impression. He dis-

Whether or not Arabi could long have succeeded in restraining his supporters from attacking Europeans and confiscating foreign property in Egypt is, in a sense, beside the point, because a threat to the European communities was implicit in any nationalist military action. Street riots could be touched off by almost any provocation, as they were in Alexandria in June of 1882 – by the death of a donkey-boy who became embroiled in an altercation with a Maltese. Once a riot broke out, Europeans were bound to be hurt and their property damaged.

The feelings of the Europeans can readily be understood in this context. The foreign communities felt "helpless" and therefore unsafe, so they inevitably took fright. The European governments, their natural protectors in any crisis between Egyptians and foreigners, were called upon to protect them. There were foreign residents, as Lord Milner later pointed out, who were far from unsympathetic to the aims and aspirations of the nationalists. But most of the foreigners were doubtful that the nationalists would be able to achieve their desired reforms, and almost all were fearful lest Arabi's army should get out of hand. The foreign creditors of Egypt, intent upon getting their pounds of flesh, clamored for action by the governments of the Dual Control to protect their rights under the Commission of the Debt. Finally, a decisive consideration, the French and British governments deemed it necessary to maintain their joint position and their common interests in Egypt, and they were determined to safeguard the Suez Canal. When the French, preoccupied with their concerns in Europe, ultimately refused to participate in joint action with the British, the need for action was still felt in England. It was politically logical, therefore, that the British Government – after inviting the Powers and the Ottoman Sultan to intervene with them and after

---

claimed all hostility to foreigners, saying that what the Egyptians knew of liberty, and much that they had gained of it, was due to foreigners. He said that the object he, and those with him, had in view was by the progress of reform and the proper administration of justice to do away for ever with the arbitrary government of the Turkish Pashas, under which no man knew what the next day had in store for him. The programme which Arabi traced out is virtually in accordance with the policy which has always guided Her Majesty's Government in its action towards Egypt." Malet to Granville, November 1, 1881, *ibid.*, pp. 1159-1160.

receiving only varying degrees of moral support from the Powers – should determine upon unilateral action in Egypt.[39]

The next and inevitable step, after the defeat of Arabi's army, was for the British to occupy Egypt and set up a stable administration in the country. Officially, the British expeditionary force had been sent to put down the rebellion in order to restore the authority of the Khedive.[40] That, of course, could not be done in a day, or a month, or even a year. By the time it was done, no one could say with any certainty that the Khedive would be able to preserve his authority without the bulwark of an army of occupation – he had alienated too many Egyptian nationalists, and he had lost face in Muslim Egypt by putting himself under the protection of a foreign Christian power.

The re-establishment of stable government in Egypt, however, was not enough, nor was it an end in itself. Good government, as well as a strong and efficient administration, was needed to safeguard the European communities and their interests. Paramount among British interests was the securing of the Suez Canal and communications across Egypt, from Alexandria to the Isthmus. As early as 1879, Foreign Secretary Lord Salisbury had summarized the problem and laid down the general lines of future British policy in his instructions to Malet, upon the latter's taking up his post in Egypt. That policy did not change; it merely crystallized with the passing of the years. By 1882 four fifths of the total traffic through the Suez Canal was British; nationalist antagonism to every kind of foreign influence had

[39] When all is said, the scales were tipped against Arabi and the nationalists by foreign intervention. It is probable that Arabi's rebellion against the Khedive would have succeeded, had the forces opposing him been purely Egyptian. No less a person than Cromer stated categorically: "Had he [Arabi] been left alone, there cannot be a doubt that he would have been successful. His want of success was due to British interference." *Op. cit.*, I, 334.

[40] Malet to Granville, August 19, 1882, in *British and Foreign State Papers*, LXXIV, 575-576: "The following Proclamation has been issued by authority of the Khedive: *Proclamation to the Egyptians.* The General in command of the British forces wishes to make known that the object of Her Majesty's Government in sending troops to this country is to re-establish the authority of the Khedive. The army is therefore only fighting against those who are in arms against His Highness. All peaceable inhabitants will be treated with kindness, . . . Their religion, mosques, families, and property will be respected. Any supplies which will be required will be paid for, and the inhabitants are invited to bring them . . . G. J. Wolseley, General, Commander-in-chief of the British Army in Egypt, Alexandria, August 19, 1882."

reached the boiling point; and when the crisis came, the other Powers left it to Great Britain to act alone in defense of their collective interests.[41]

London foresaw three possible consequences of the immediate withdrawal of British troops. Either Egypt would slip into a state of anarchy, or the Sultan would seize the opportunity to reassert his effective control over Egypt, or one or more of the Great Powers would fill the vacuum left by the withdrawal of British forces. No one of these contingencies would have been tolerable from the point of view of London. It seems probable that a Turkish occupation of Egypt, per se, would not have been entirely unacceptable to the British Foreign Office. But it would have been intolerable to the French Foreign Office, and would therefore have eventually precipitated French intervention in Egypt, an act which would have been directly contrary to British policy. From 1879 on, Britain had held that no other power could be allowed to "be more powerful there than England."

At the same time, nothing seems clearer in retrospect than that the British neither desired nor intended to occupy Egypt indefinitely. Had they so intended, they would have simply annexed Egypt after the battle at Tel el-Kebir and the surrender of the Arabists, or else they would have established a protectorate over the country. As it was, they promised evacuation; but they stayed on "temporarily" to guarantee order and to initiate good government in Egypt. As Lord Cromer later pointed out, "the alternative policies of reform and evacuation were absolutely irreconcilable," because the actual presence of the British was essential to the requisite reforms. The trouble was that the Foreign Office "underrated the difficulties of getting out of the country," and so the temporary occupation drifted "insensibly into a condition of permanency." [42]

---

[41] See Hurewitz, *op. cit.*, I, 191-194, for text of the document, "British Policy on Egypt," October 16, 1879 (F.O. 78/2997). – The figure for British shipping through the Suez Canal is given in *British and Foreign State Papers*, LXXIII, 1164 – Barthélemy St. Hilaire to Sienkiewicz (French consul in Egypt), October 17, 1881.

[42] Cromer, *op. cit.*, II, 350-351.

II

THE BRITISH IN EGYPT

With the crushing of the Arabi Rebellion, on September 13, 1882, the British entered Egypt and remained for seventy-two years. In September, 1883, Lord Cromer, then Sir Evelyn Baring, was appointed British Agent and Consul-General. For the following twenty-four years he governed Egypt indirectly through an elite corps of British officials who acted as advisers and inspectors to the government ministries. By 1891 effective control over Egyptian affairs was exercised by an incredibly small group of thirty-nine officials (i.e., Advisers), without any display of undue authority. These Britishers formed the backbone of the Egyptian civil administration.[1] But they acted only in an advisory capacity. No machinery was ever set up to enforce the acceptance of their advice. Egypt continued to be ruled, *de jure*, by the Khedive and his ministers. *De facto*, however, Egyptian heads of departments customarily accepted the advice of the British officials. The ultimate sanction was, of course, the existence of a British garrison in the Citadel at Cairo. But the prestige of the Agency was so high, and its work on behalf of Egyptian reconstruction so notable, that no appeal had ever to be made to *force majeure*. An intricate system of administration was gradually worked out which depended for its success upon individual personal relationships – a system of "British heads and Egyptian hands." The forceful character of Lord Cromer, who came to be universally respected by

[1] Morroe Berger, *Bureaucracy and Society in Modern Egypt: A Study of the Higher Civil Service* (Princeton, N. J., 1957), pp. 26-30, citing Cromer's official report of 1891. There were of course many more than thirty-nine British officials in Egypt, but not in authoritative posts in the Khedivial administration.

Egyptians for the uprightness and justness of his dealings, made this anomalous system workable.[2]

The Khedivial machinery of government under the British occupation may be described briefly as follows. At the top, there were eight departments presided over by ministers: Foreign Affairs, Finance, Justice, War, Public Works, Education, Interior, and Waqfs (Muslim religious and charitable endowments). The last named was administered by a director-general who, in practice, took his orders directly from the Khedive. The Department of Finance included Customs, Lighthouses, and the Post Office. The Department of Interior included Sanitation and Prisons.

Before Cromer returned from a tour of duty in India to take up his new post in Egypt, the British ambassador at Constantinople, Lord Dufferin, was sent to Cairo to make recommendations with respect to the future administration of the country. After considerable study of current Egyptian problems, Dufferin wrote a comprehensive report advising the perpetuation of the Assembly of Deputies, together with the initiation of several other quasi-representative institutions. On May 1, 1883, an "Organic Law of Egypt" was promulgated by Khedivial decree, incorporating the recommendations made by Lord Dufferin. Simultaneously, a new Electoral Law was also published by decree. The Organic Law provided for the establishment of fourteen Provincial Councils, a Legislative Council, and a General Assembly (which included the Legislative Council). The Provincial Councils, with from three to eight members each, were set up to deal with purely local village matters – such as roads, canals, markets. The Legislative Council, with purely advisory functions, was composed of thirty members. Fourteen of the thirty, including the President of the Council, were named by the Khedivial government; the other sixteen were elected by the Provincial Councils and the urban areas (i.e., one to represent Cairo, and one to represent Alexandria and six towns of the Delta). The departmental ministers were also entitled to representation in the Council, and six of them normally attended. The Assembly consisted of eighty-two deputies:

---

[2] The Khedive Tawfiq was always amenable to British advice, for obvious reasons. But once, shortly after Tawfiq was succeeded by Abbas Hilmi, Cromer was forced to take a stern line with the young Khedive. He succeeded in convincing the Khedive that British "advice" had to be followed.

six ministers of the Khedive's government, the thirty members of the Legislative Council, and forty-six elected delegates. The Assembly's functions were also advisory, with an important exception: no new direct tax could be imposed without its approval. A high property qualification and minimum age and literacy qualifications were required for election to the Assembly.

Such was the extent of representative government during most of the period of the British Occupation. A Council of State was also provided for in the Organic Law, but it never took shape – owing to acrimonious disagreements concerning its role in the Khedivial government. According to Cromer, the purpose of the Organic Law was "to give the Egyptian people an opportunity of making their voices heard, but at the same time not to bind the executive Government by parliamentary fetters, which would have been out of place in a country whose political education was so little advanced as that of Egypt." [3]

Toward the end of the Occupation, Lord Kitchener – Cromer's second successor in the British Agency at Cairo, from 1911 to 1914 – moved to establish a more popular Assembly. A new Organic Law and a new Electoral Law led to the inauguration of the Legislative Assembly in November, 1913. Kitchener made this move partly in response to bitter nationalist criticisms of the unrepresentative character of existing quasi-parliamentary institutions. As its name implies, the new body was a merger of the Legislative Council and the General Assembly. It remained primarily consultative, but it was intended to work much more closely with the Khedive's Council of Ministers, it was more broadly representative, and it was held to constitute a "modest and cautious advance" toward a more democratic system of government.[4] Unfortunately, the Legislative Assembly had less than a year in which to function before the outbreak of the First World War.

In December, 1914, Egypt was declared a British protectorate and placed under martial law. And after the armistice of 1918 the con-

---

[3]   The Earl of Cromer, *Modern Egypt* (London, 1908), II, 274; the text of the Organic Law is in Great Britain, Foreign Office, *British and Foreign State Papers* (Hertslet ed.; London, 1890), LXXIV (1882-83), 1095-1103.
[4]   Jacob M. Landau, *Parliaments and Parties in Egypt* (New York, 1954), pp. 55-58.

stitutional situation in Egypt was radically altered, owing to the breakup of the Ottoman Empire and the Egyptian rebellion of 1919. Before turning to the new era of the 1920's, it might be well to summarize the problems and the achievements of the period between 1883 and 1914.

The unique character of the Occupation administration was, of course, related to the anomalous position of the British vis-à-vis the government of Egypt. The Khedive was the nominal ruler of the country, but at the same time he remained a vassal of the Sultan of the Ottoman Empire – a suzerain who continued to exact a yearly tribute, but who made no other demands upon the Khedive. Before 1914 the British had no wish to weaken the Ottoman Empire, for reasons of international politics, and no desire to change the juridical position of Egypt within that empire. Furthermore, the "permanent" nature of the British Occupation was not acknowledged by the European Powers until after the Anglo-French Entente of April, 1904. European jealousy of England's special position in Egypt was a complicating factor for the Foreign Office in London, and the French were particularly resentful of a situation that they had created by default. In fact, Anglo-French rivalry in Egypt was a principal characteristic of the period between 1882 and 1904 – when the French finally renounced their special interests in Egypt in return for a free hand in Morocco. Consequently, the British felt called upon to make repeated declarations of their intention to terminate the Occupation.

The problem of the Sudan proved to be a major obstacle to the British evacuation of Egypt. In 1883, a fervid Muslim leader known as the Mahdi made himself master of practically all the southern and eastern Sudan and was endeavoring to liberate the northern Sudan from Egyptian rule. There had been much Sudanese discontent with Egyptian administration after 1879. The disaffected elements, including countless frustrated former slave-traders, had joined the Mahdi's holy war. All the isolated Egyptian garrisons were surrounded by his Dervishes and were in danger of annihilation. The Mahdi-led rebellion had taken so many lives, and inflicted such severe losses on a number of Anglo-Egyptian expeditions, that the decision was finally taken in Cairo and in London to entrust General "Chinese" Gordon with the task of evacuating all Egyptians from the Sudan. Since evacuation of the northern Sudan alone would have meant the abandonment and consequent massacre of all Egyptian garrisons stationed south of Khartum, total evacuation was decided upon. But, as it turned out, total evacuation proved to be impossible of achievement. While General Gordon was attempting to discharge his mission, disaster overtook him and his troops at Khartum. After his death there, in January, 1885, the Nile frontier was established at Wadi Halfa, and surviving Egyptian forces were retired thither. For a decade thereafter, the Sudan was left derelict. The Mahdi died in the summer of 1885, but his successor, the Khalifa, renewed the holy war in the Sudan and threatened an invasion of Egypt. This made it more necessary than ever to keep Egypt strong and prepared to defend itself against Sudanese aggression – for the sake of the European communities as well as for the sake of the Egyptians. Consequently Lord Cromer superintended the building up of an efficient army. The new Egyptian Army was recruited from the fallahin and commanded by British officers, and it later proved its worth to Egypt.

Eventually, it became obvious to the British that the main branch of the Nile – known as the White Nile – had to be adequately safeguarded in the long-range interests of Egypt. For one thing, the Abyssinians (Ethiopians) were a perennial source of uneasiness. They were thought to have designs upon the White Nile, and they were strong enough to inflict a staggering defeat upon invading Italians at Adowa in March, 1896. Moreover, the Blue Nile rises in Abyssinia's Lake Tana. It was unthinkable that these or any other potentially hostile people should ever be allowed to gain control of both branches of the Nile. Therefore an Anglo-Egyptian expedition reconquered the whole of the Sudan between 1896 and 1898. And just as the Anglo-Egyptian troops under General Kitchener ("Kitchener of Khartoum") were consolidating their newly won position in the southern Sudan, a small contingent of French forces – the Marchand mission – succeeded in reaching the White Nile at Fashoda, from the west. Their unexpected appearance caused a grave diplomatic crisis in September, 1898, because the British had reason to fear that the French and the Abyssinians were planning to establish claims to the left and the right banks of the Nile, respectively.[5] Six weeks later, the

[5] At this same time, another French expedition was reported to be on its way inland from the Red Sea port of Jibuti – presumably to reinforce the

French evacuated Fashoda; but the result of all these alarums and excursions was the establishment of the Anglo-Egyptian Condominium, or joint rule, over the Sudan in January, 1899. The indirect result of these military activities in and about the Sudan was the British conviction that the time had not come for them to withdraw from Egypt.

Another factor which contributed to the prolongation of the Occupation was the success of British policies in Egypt, notably the financial rehabilitation of the country and the establishment of internal security. At the same time, the refusal of European Powers to contemplate any change in the regime of the Capitulations made Britain's self-imposed task harder vis-à-vis the Egyptians.

With the replacement of the Anglo-French Dual Control by the British Occupation, it became Britain's primary responsibility to put the finances of Egypt on as sound a footing as possible. In any case, financial reform was basic and therefore prerequisite to all other reforms, so this problem received the earliest attention of the occupying power. By 1896, financial recovery was complete; the Egyptian government had become solvent, and its credit abroad was restored. In that year, revenue reached the figure of LE 10,693,577 – roughly one million pounds Egyptian in excess of expenditure.[6] Ten years later, revenue had increased to approximately LE 14,500,000 and the reserve fund stood at LE 13,381,000. Reductions in taxation totaled more than two million pounds between 1883 and 1906. One distinguished official of the time held the view that the only gift which alien rule could bestow upon a foreign people, to justify its existence, was unprecedented "freedom from onerous fiscal burdens" and that "fiscal moderation, fiscal security, and fiscal equity, are his [the alien ruler's] credentials." [7] By this yardstick, the government of Britain was amply justified in its Egyptian administration.

Of almost equal importance for the reconstruction of Egypt was the need to increase the productivity of the country. Hence the Brit-

---

Marchand mission in the Sudan; and still a third French expedition was known to be on its way from Addis Ababa in Abyssinia for the same purpose.

[6] The value of the Egyptian pound (LE) was then always pegged to the pound sterling.

[7] Sir Auckland Colvin, *The Making of Modern Egypt* (London, 1906), pp. 210-211; see also pp. 219, 419-420, for the figures on the Egyptian budget (1896 and 1906).

ish also paid great attention to agricultural development, including irrigation works, and various reforms on behalf of the peasantry. The Aswan Dam on the Upper Nile was completed in December, 1902. Its great reservoir and distribution barrages doubled the available supply of Nile water and made possible the progressive conversion of the existing Pharaonic system of "basin" irrigation in Upper and Middle Egypt into the modern system of perennial irrigation.[8]

Substitution of perennial water storage for the ancient system of flooding increased the total yield of the land as well as that of the two principal export crops, cotton and sugar. Other public works included the construction of several thousand miles of new canals and drainage ditches, agricultural roads, and light railways. Life was at the same time made much easier for the peasants by a reassessment of the land tax – with a view to distributing the burden over the land in proportion to the fertility of the soil – and by the final abolition of the age-old tyranny of the corvée and the *kurbash*.[9]

The peasantry was also partly protected against moneylenders through the founding of an agricultural bank. Eventually, under Kitchener, the lot of the peasants was further eased by a law restricting land sales to protect them from the loss of their lands to moneylending usurers. The whole population of Egypt was also benefited by the establishment of a postal savings bank and by much needed prison reforms.

An enduring legacy of British administration – *monumentum aere perennius* – was the slow inculcation of a new concept, that of incorruptibility in office. A root-and-branch reorganization of all the ministries was accompanied by new working principles. Bribery, nepotism, and favoritism were officially discountenanced. And this elevation of moral standards was particularly noticeable in the Department of Justice and in the police service, where those of low social and economic status could most benefit.

The spectacular material improvements effected under British direction did not, however, reconcile all Egyptians to the British

---

[8]   Sir Eldon Gorst, "Egypt in 1904", Appendix III in Alfred Milner, *England in Egypt* (4th ed.; 1907).

[9]   The corvée was forced labor on government canals and lands. The *kurbash* — literally, a rhinoceros-hide whip – was traditionally used to punish the peasants, to extort taxes from them, and to exact corvée work. "Government by kurbash" was a symbol of medieval despotism.

Occupation, though the inarticulate peasants were early conciliated and reconciled to the new order. The upper ten per cent of the Egyptian population became critical of a foreign Christian regime, once financial and agricultural reforms had been instituted. Economic advantage in itself was powerless to overcome nationalist prejudice, though the benefits of the British Occupation were many and manifest.

There were two principal grievances. In the first place, Egyptians resented the fact that the British made no effort to train them in the art of administration. Unquestionably, Egyptians must have learned some modern administrative techniques when working with their British colleagues – if only by a process of osmosis. But no consistent effort was made to prepare them for the task of governing themselves. Sir Eldon Gorst, the first successor of Lord Cromer, from 1907 to 1911, was sent out to take up his post in Egypt with instructions to inaugurate a new policy, and he sought to give a greater measure of responsibility to Egyptian civil servants. He also tried to enlarge the spheres of activity and the powers of the General Assembly. But Gorst's regime was of too short duration, owing to a mortal illness, for him to remodel the administration. His work was sabotaged by a new generation of Egyptian nationalists, and his liberal efforts were consequently discredited among his more conservative countrymen. The problem created for the British by the rising tide of nationalism in Egypt is dealt with later in this chapter. But one must bear in mind that nationalist agitations proved fatal to Gorst's great experiment after the tragic assassination, in 1910, of the Coptic Prime Minister, Boutros Ghali Pasha. When Lord Kitchener succeeded Gorst, he introduced several reforms, including the Legislative Assembly already mentioned, which might in time have resulted in an increased measure of representative government. But further experimentation was rendered temporarily impracticable by the outbreak of the First World War.

The other grievance, forever aired by Egyptians, was that the British neglected education. They did not neglect it entirely: they kept slowly increasing the educational budget; they extended the system of school inspection – catching even some of the Muslim religious schools, the *kuttabs* of the mosques, in a far-flung net; they raised the standards in the school system; and they took the momentous forward step of initiating a system of primary instruction in

Arabic.[10] But they could not and did not attack the principles of the Muslim religious schools, or touch the famous University of al-Azhar and its 20,000 students. The British themselves have regretfully admitted that the Ministry of Public Instruction was but a stepchild of the government. In the beginning there was little money for any but purely material advancement, at least until the Egyptian government became solvent. The money that was available was devoted primarily to the Ministry of Finance, to irrigation and the development of agriculture, to the customs, the police, prisons, and sanitation, and to other similar reconstructive work. Moreover, once the pattern of priorities was set, it was difficult to change it, even after the revenue began to exceed necessary expenditure by a comfortable margin.

But there was a further, more basic reason for the British reluctance to develop and expand education in Egypt. This reason touched their basic philosophy of indirect government in a Muslim country. Since the Occupation policy was to improve the lot of the Egyptians as long as the British remained, and since the regime was intended and acknowledged to be merely transitory, British administrators held that they should do nothing to change the religious character and the cultural pattern of this Muslim country. No fundamental improvements in education could be undertaken without violating this principle. To widen significantly the educational horizon of the whole Egyptian people, to force British training on the teachers of Egypt's youth, or to expand and modernize the school curricula would be to bring about a radical change in the character of Egyptian schools. This the British could not and would not undertake. They took the position that any such innovations, any changes in the content and extent of Egyptian education had to come after Egypt had reasserted its independence, not during a period of tutelage.

A very special aspect of the educational problem was the perpetuation of French cultural influences. From the days of the Napoleonic occupation, French had been the language of diplomacy, of govern-

---

[10]   Milner, *op. cit.*, pp. 391-392. For an illuminating discussion (and criticism) of education during the British Occupation see Humphrey Bowman, *Middle East Window* (London, 1942), Part II, "Egypt 1903-1911," pp. 35-82. Bowman served in, or was director of, the several departments of education in Egypt, the Anglo-Egyptian Sudan, Iraq, and Palestine between 1903 and 1936. He makes the statement (p. 48) that "the percentage of total expenditure on education [in Egypt] between 1907 and 1912 never rose above 3.4 percent . . ."

ment, and of the higher strata of society. In many upper-class families it was even the language of the home. After the inauguration of the Mixed Courts, French legal concepts were paramount, and French became the linguistic vehicle of justice. The principal secular law-school was French, and all the state-supported schools – as distinct from the religious schools – were patterned on the French system. For years after the establishment of the British Occupation, British officials administered French law in Arabic, taught French law in English, and argued French law in French. And British officials even corresponded with each other officially in French. Until 1904 the Mixed Courts remained a center for the maintenance of French judicial and linguistic influence. After 1904, Germans replaced the French in opposition to the British in the Mixed Courts, but German culture failed to displace French culture in the hearts and manners of upper-class Egyptians.[11]

The prolonged Anglo-French rivalry also failed to dislodge Egyptians from their allegiance to France. In fact, once the British had become entrenched in the financial and political spheres, Egyptians clung even more firmly to a culture that offered them spiritual satisfaction and a counterpoise to undue or unwelcome British influences. It was only when the veiled protectorate dropped its veil that Egyptians slowly turned after 1914, for practical reasons, toward the English language and the cultural influences of Britain.[12]

Two historical events had stirred educated Egyptians profoundly. The first was the English Revolution of 1688, and the second was the French Revolution. Of the two, the French Revolution was much closer to them and more dramatic. Its repercussions, intellectual and social as well as political, had spread eastward from France, had brought Napoleon Bonaparte with his army and his savants to the shores of Egypt, and had provided Egyptians with slogans that were

[11]   See Jasper Yeates Brinton, *The Mixed Courts of Egypt* (New Haven, Conn., 1930), pp. 53, 58, 147 (note 4), 386; Colvin, *op. cit.*, p. 238.
[12] Early in the 20th century, however, a small group of Egyptians had become admirers of the British and their institutions. The lawyer Ahmad Fathi Zaghlul, brother of the better-known Sa'd Zaghlul (later the leader of the Wafd Party) was a discriminating translator of many European historical and political works. His writings "led to a cult of British education," notably his translation of E. R. Demolins' *A quoi tient la superiorité des Anglo-Saxons*. See Jamal Mohammed Ahmed, *The Intellectual Origins of Egyptian Nationalism* (London and New York, 1960), p. 46.

applicable to Egyptian life. The call to *Liberté* was directly relevant
and hallowed by the rebellion of Arabi's day. *Egalité*, it is true, had
little genuine meaning for the Egyptians of the 19th century; but
Fraternité instantly struck a responsive chord in the breasts of all
Muslims because their religion had always strongly emphasized the
concept of brotherhood.

Until after the First World War, Egyptians formed an essentially
two-class society. The great mass of impoverished peasants did not
count intellectually or socially, and they were immune to foreign influences. The rise of an indigenous, self-centered middle class was
long obstructed by the presence of an expanding population of commercial foreigners in Egypt. But the tiny upper-class elite was relatively wealthy, internationally educated, and intellectually mobile. Its
members, all of them bilingual or trilingual, responded to every intellectual wind that blew from the Continent.

The political isolation of Egypt, after it became autonomous within the Ottoman Empire during the 19th century, and later when the
country was relatively insulated from its Muslim neighbors by the
British Occupation, had a marked influence upon the development
of the Egyptian people. They were daily torn between two worlds, that
of the Muslim East and that of the Christian West. In times of stress
they turned first to one and then to the other. They maintained their
spiritual and religious affiliations with the Muslim world of the Ottoman Empire, but they sought material advancement through the pa-
tronage of western Christian powers. Egyptian leaders often seemed
to be vacillating because every action they took had to be weighed in
the light of its repercussions in Constantinople, London, or Paris as
well as in Cairo. Some Egyptian nationalists were prone to play one
government, or its representatives, off against another; and but few
of them had unalterable convictions as to the most effective means of
promoting nationalist policies in Egypt. Some nationalists were frankly opportunist in the sense that they had to be prepared to adopt the
most likely measures, at any given time, to achieve their ends. But
their ultimate goals remained constant. With their Arab neighbors
there was but little community of thought and no community of experience, at least after the 1870's. Egyptian nationalist eyes became
politically myopic, so far as the Arab world was concerned; and yet
the nationalists remained sensitive to Arab trials and tribulations in

Lebanon and Syria, Tunisia, Morocco, and elsewhere. But only on the Egyptian stage could they act and play their self-appointed parts.

For the first fifteen or twenty years of the British Occupation the nationalist movement was quiescent and its supporters were apathetic. There were no untoward incidents whatever, and Egyptian officials worked harmoniously with English Advisers in the urgent tasks of rehabilitation and reconstruction. Arabi Pasha and the military nationalists were discredited. They had failed, and their failure had demonstrably led to the foreign occupation of Egypt. But the national movement did not die with those who lost their lives on the field of Tel el-Kebir. The older generation of nationalists had lost hope; and the rising generation, after 1882, was mesmerized by unprecedented ease and prosperity. This period of nationalist torpor, however, could not last indefinitely. A breath of faith and hope had filled all hearts, a national idea had been born. But a capable leader was needed to recreate and revitalize the national movement.[13]

The 20th century ushered in a new generation of Egyptian nationalists, with different characteristics. When they came of age, the ardent impulses of the first period of nationalism burned bright once more. This new group both nurtured and transformed the nationalist spirit of the early 1880's, and it inaugurated what has been called the era of "journalistic nationalism."

One of the most ironic turns of fortune in the experience of British administrators was the way in which a genuinely liberal policy boomeranged against Cromer's "benevolent despotism." Under the Occupation, Egyptians received the right, along with foreigners, to enjoy the democratic traditions of freedom of speech and freedom of the press. When British domination made the Egyptian nationalists politically impotent, they found an outlet for their frustration in an unfettered press. In 1898 Cairo alone had fifty newspapers in the Arabic language, and nearly two hundred journals and newspapers were then being published throughout Egypt. During the last five years of the century about five hundred Egyptian newspapers and periodicals were founded. Most of them were ephemeral, but those which disappeared were often replaced by others.[14]

[13] See M. Sabry, *La genèse de l'esprit national égyptien (1863-1882)* (Paris, 1924), p. 228.
[14] Landau, *op. cit.*, pp. 104, 109; also George Young, *Egypt* (London, 1930), pp. 178-181.

The French press in Egypt, which conducted a lively propaganda campaign against the British Occupation in the 1880's and 1890's, stimulated Egyptian journalists and often gave material assistance to their newspapers. For instance, the editor of one of the most vituperative anti-British Arabic newspapers was a Frenchman.

The moving spirit of this second period of Egyptian nationalism was Mustafa Kamil Pasha, a typical example of the polished, highly educated, French-oriented Egyptian Muslim gentleman. He was born in Cairo in 1874 and was therefore a child during the period of the Arabi Rebellion. His father had been a staff officer to Said Pasha and was the chief engineer of Dakahliya Province under the Khedive Ismail. Mustafa Kamil was proficient in Arabic and trained in both law and journalism. Through the generosity of a relative this personable young man was enabled to go to France to continue his law studies in Paris and Toulouse.[15] While in France, Mustafa Kamil was introduced to Parisian literary circles by the politician Deloncle. He formed a warm friendship with Mme. Juliette Adam of the *Nouvelle Revue*, and he became acquainted with Pierre Loti and Commandant Marchand, of Fashoda fame, as well as a whole coterie of French Anglophobes.

After returning to Egypt, Mustafa Kamil dedicated the remaining years of his life to the cause of Egyptian nationalism. He was a genuine admirer of French culture, and he acquired in France a considerable knowledge of propaganda techniques and methods of party organization. His love of France was coupled with a flaming detestation of British rule, and upon his return to Egypt he became a bitter, indiscriminate critic of the British and all their ways. This brilliant young Gallicized Egyptian was the founder of the first Egyptian party with a genuinely national program, the second National Party – named after its prototype of 1879, *al-Hizb al-Watani*. In addition to his activities as a party leader he took a profound interest in education and dreamed of founding an Egyptian university; he promoted an alliance between Egyptian Muslims and Copts; and he used the press as a weapon against the British administration.

[15]   A dashing, dandified photograph of Mustafa Kamil is reproduced in J. Alexander, *The Truth About Egypt* (London, 1911), facing p. 38.   For a French appreciation of Mustafa Kamil and his activities in Europe in the cause of Egyptian independence see Juliette Adam, *L'Angleterre en Egypte* (Paris, 1922), pp. 144-214.

According to a variety of Arabic sources, Mustafa Kamil's early thinking was also greatly influenced by Sayyid 'Abd Allah al-Nadim, the orator and journalist of the Arabi revolt. Al-Nadim was the one important revolutionary who failed to surrender to the British after Tel el-Kebir. After his escape and eventual apprehension (nine years later), followed by a short period of exile, 'Abd Allah al-Nadim returned to Egypt when Abbas II became Khedive. Al-Nadim thereupon founded a revolutionary periodical, which lasted for almost a year, and he sought out and established a friendship with the congenial young Mustafa Kamil. Through the eyes of his older friend the rising nationalist leader saw the events of Arabi's period; and it was through al-Nadim that Mustafa Kamil was inspired to seek an alliance with the Khedive. It was also through him that Kamil learned to appreciate the teachings of Jamal al-Din al-Afghani, the founder of the political Pan-Islamic movement.[16]

The lesson learned by Mustafa Kamil from the failure of the Arabi revolt was twofold: namely, that disunity within the educated upper class and ignorance on the part of the unlettered masses were the two greatest enemies confronting Egyptian nationalism. Consequently, in order to deliver his countrymen from the British, he worked tirelessly to organize an enlightened and responsive public opinion. He lectured constantly in Egypt, wrote countless pamphlets as well as several books, and made frequent trips to Paris and other European capitals – including London – to present the case of Egypt's nationalists. At the same time he advocated the extension of education to all Egyptians, not only through the founding of new schools, but also by emphasizing the need for free education and for technical schools. A very successful national school was founded by him, on Muslim lines, which provided courses in French and English as well as a thorough grounding in Arabic. Kamil was also the first to urge, in 1904 and after, the creation of an Egyptian university, and he solicited contributions to establish one.

After January, 1900, when he began the publication of *al-Liwa* ("The Standard"), Mustafa Kamil devoted most of his time to a propaganda campaign. This newspaper gave him unlimited opportunities to air Egyptian grievances against the Occupation regime, to magnify the wrongs, imaginary and otherwise, suffered by his fellow Egyp-

[16]   C. C. Adams, *Islam and Modernism in Egypt* (London, 1933), pp. 221-222.

tians, and to remind his readers daily of their "right" to independence. *Al-Liwa* allegedly reached a circulation of 10,000, and early in 1907 English and French editions of the paper were published as *The Egyptian Standard*.[17] The Arabic edition of *al-Liwa* was, however, an organ of political extremism and as such it never attained the reputation of the more responsible vernacular papers – even though some eminent Egyptian writers were among its contributors.

As early as 1897, Mustafa Kamil gathered round him a group of ardent nationalists, some of whom were distinguished Egyptian patriots. Ten years later, less than a year before the death of its founder, this unofficial group gave rise to a full-fledged political party. This second National Party took shape in Cairo at a mass meeting of notables, farmers, lawyers, engineers, employers, and urban workers – more than a thousand, all of whom were assembled by invitation. The National Party was fully organized in 1907 with a central committee of thirty members and as a club with nationwide branches. Mustafa Kamil, who by then had been elevated to the rank of pasha, was chosen to be its permanent president. A formal program was drawn up, of which an edited version, palatable to French political thinking, was published in *Le Figaro* on May 8, 1907. The party's full platform called for: a written constitution and the creation of a parliament to which the departmental ministers would be responsible; improvement and expansion of education, and full restoration of the teaching of the Arabic language (instead of English); gradual replacement of foreign officials by capable Egyptians; reform or modification of the Capitulations by the granting of criminal jurisdiction to the Mixed Courts; and independence for Egypt and the Sudan. The British Advisers were to be retained, but their role was to be limited to the giving of advice, not orders.[18]

A special branch of Mustafa Kamil's work was concerned with political activities among students. He found them a most responsive group, easily stirred to vociferous expressions of patriotism, untrammeled by political or other responsibilities, and prone to hero worship. From his day may be dated the chronic involvement of Egyp-

[17]   Landau, *op. cit.*, pp. 110-111; Sidney Low, *Egypt in Transition* (New York, 1914), pp. 289-290; Alexander, *op. cit.*, pp. 30, 38, 116, 118-119.
[18]   Alexander, *op. cit.*, pp. 117-118; Landau, *op. cit.*, pp. 108, 115-116, 118-119, 122-123, 134.

tian students in politics. Their strikes and demonstrations – the first of which was staged in 1906 by the entire student body of the Law School – became a serious social problem in latter-day Egypt. Kamil's encouragement of the extracurricular political activities of students established a precedent which many later politicians exploited shamelessly and to the serious detriment of disciplined and consistent advancement toward normal educational goals. Eventually the universities which were founded after the First World War became riddled with political factionalism, and even very young school children were drafted by various political parties to create partisan disturbances. Educational chaos was the result, and the formal intellectual training of more than a generation of Egyptians was prejudiced until after the Second World War, when the Government of the Revolution, recognizing the social danger inherent in such activities, debarred students from participating in political affairs.

A later development was the spread of student political activity to the Continent. Yearly congresses of the National Party were organized, in 1908 and subsequently, by Egyptians studying in Europe. The first three congresses, accompanied by a fanfare of publicity, were held in Geneva and Brussels. These European meetings all formulated resolutions, most of which embodied demands for representative institutions, for the evacuation of Egypt, and for unfettered journalistic propaganda. French Deputies and British Members of Parliament, as well as representatives of the press, were invited to attend the yearly congresses; subjects of moment to Egyptians, such as education, were seriously debated by the various committees.

With respect to one problem of his day, Mustafa Kamil found himself in a dilemma. He had to obtain effective political support for his party. In accordance with his recognition of the need for unity in Egypt, he naturally sought the support of the young Khedive Abbas Hilmi (1892-1914; also known as Abbas II). At first this seemed like a promising alliance because Abbas Hilmi, a proud and high-spirited young ruler who was far more impatient of British tutelage than his predecessor Tawfiq had been, was drawn to the magnetic young nationalist leader. But Lord Cromer made it difficult for them to work together, and Sir Eldon Gorst, when he replaced the great Proconsul, seems to have succeeded in alienating the Khedive from Mustafa Kamil Pasha. In fact, Gorst was accused by many Egyptians of driving a fatal wedge between Abbas Hilmi and the nationalists and thereby breaking the united nationalist front.[19]

Outside Egypt, Mustafa Kamil looked first to France for sympathy and assistance in undermining the British administration. But after the Anglo-French Entente of 1904 he was received in Paris with increasing coldness. It was natural therefore that he should turn for support to the Sultan of the Ottoman Empire, who welcomed his advances and rewarded him for his pro-Turkish and Pan-Islamic sympathies by making him a pasha. This rapprochement, however, made difficulties for Mustafa Pasha at home among the anti-Turkish nationalists, and it involved him in an ideological dilemma. Mustafa Kamil was a good Muslim, but he was, first and foremost, the leader of an Egyptian political nationalism patterned on the French model. He had diverged sharply from Muslim Egyptian reformers who saw salvation for Egypt only in Islamic or Pan-Islamic terms. Moreover, his desire to unify all Egyptians, Muslims, Jews, and Christian Copts alike, made any overt Pan-Islamic alliance untenable. Consequently his connections with Muslim Turks and Pan-Islamic groups had to be tenuous and often *sub rosa*. He never advocated publicly the renaissance of Muslim Egypt as an Islamic state; he strove rather for the establishment of an independent Egyptian state framed on Western political lines.

When Mustafa Kamil Pasha died, in February, 1908, he was mourned spontaneously throughout Egypt. The funeral procession was said to be one of the most impressive sights ever witnessed in modern Cairo, and the huge crowds of mourners even included many of his active political opponents. His popularity among all urban groups soon became legendary. One English observer, writing a few years later, considered Mustafa Kamil, even though his nationalism was of "the most aggressive and assertive type," to have been the ablest of the Egyptian nationalists of the time. This writer likewise paid tribute to the "literary skill and argumentative resourcefulness" of Mustafa Pasha's journalism, though he deplored the "virulence" of his abuse of all things English. Some of the articles in Kamil's *Egyptian Stand-*

[19]   Young, *op. cit.*, pp. 186, 190. Young also quotes the greatest of Egyptian newspapers, *al-Ahram*: "The killing of the nationalist movement was Sir Eldon Gorst's." See also Alexander, *op. cit.*, pp. 120, 151, 155, 178, 181-182, 185. According to all accounts, Gorst succeeded in this, whether intentionally or not, by establishing a genuine friendship with Abbas Hilmi.

ard, "if bad politics, were excellent journalism, forcible, expressive, and ingeniously calculated to rouse native passion against British influence in every shape." [20]

The National Party outlived its founder and remained a part of the Egyptian scene for decades thereafter. It had, however, perceptibly begun to weaken and decline in prestige even before Mustafa Kamil's death, owing to its irresponsible extremism and the vitriolic nature of its press propaganda. And almost immediately after the beginning of 1908 it was forced to share the nationalist stage with six other parties. It must be remembered, however, that the National Party was the first genuine party in Egypt, that it was the first in nationalist influence, and that it remained the first in the hearts of Egyptians until Sa'd Zaghlul Pasha founded the Wafd at the end of the First World War.

During the years just before and just after the death of Mustafa Kamil Pasha several events occurred, outside Egypt as well as in the country itself, that stirred the emotions of politically conscious Egyptians. The first of these events was the victory of Japan in the Russo-Japanese War of 1904-1905. The fact that one of the mightiest of Christian powers had suffered a definitive military defeat by an Oriental people had a tremendous impact on the nationalists. Egyptian Muslims also reacted sympathetically to the difficulties encountered by their suzerain, the Sultan-Caliph, vis-à-vis the Christian West. The intervention of the Powers in Macedonia, the establishing of international controls in that Ottoman province, and the capitulation of the Sultan to a naval demonstration in 1905 had repercussions that were unfavorable to the British in Egypt. Even more adverse was the effect of the Anglo-Turkish dispute regarding the frontier between Palestine and Egypt and the yielding of the Sultan to a British ultimatum in 1906. The memory of past oppression and the wrongs suffered at the hands of the Turks had been dimmed, if not obliterated, under the Occupation; the "indissoluble bond" of Islam remained.

Lord Cromer was pointedly reminded of this fact during the Turkish war scare of 1906, when he received a well-worded anonymous letter from an Egyptian Muslim. After recapitulating the blessings of

[20] Sidney Low, *Egypt in Transition* (New York, 1914), pp. 289-290. See also Alexander, *op. cit.*, pp. 139-140.

British rule – "He must be blind who sees not what the English have wrought in Egypt" – the writer went on to say:

As men we do not love the sons of Osman . . . they have trodden down the Egyptians like dry reeds. But as Moslems they are our brethren; the Caliph holds the sacred places . . . . [He] is the shadow of God, and every Moslem must leap to his call as the willing servant to his master . . . . The call of the Sultan is the call of the Faith; it carries with it the command of the Prophet. I and many more trust that all may be peace; but if it be war, be sure that he who has a sword will draw it . . . "God give the victory to Islam." [21]

On the other hand, when Muslim constitutionalists won a concession from their own autocratic government, as in Persia in 1906, or when Muslim nationalists achieved a victory, as the Young Turks did in Constantinople in 1908 (going on to depose their autocratic Sultan in 1909), constitutionalists and nationalists in Egypt were fired with hope and the spirit of emulation.

In Egypt itself, the Dinshaway incident of June, 1906, caused the first serious clash between the Occupation administration and the Egyptian peasants. A small party of British officers on a pigeon shoot, out for a day's sport at the invitation of a village shaykh, accidentally shot a peasant woman. This led to an ugly flare-up between the villagers and the British officers; blows were exchanged, and a life was lost on each side. Extremist sentiments became articulate among the British residents and the Egyptians, and the press of both camps grew almost hysterical. Many resident foreigners allegedly believed that a general massacre was in preparation. A "Special Tribunal" of three British officials and two Egyptians, presided over by a Copt, Boutros Ghali Pasha, was set up to try the case. Four of the unfortunate villagers were condemned to death, and others were sentenced to hard labor or flogging. All the sentences were executed. This incident built up a feeling of intense bitterness among all Egyptians: it was exploited by the urban nationalists and used, for years, as a war cry against British "tyranny"; and it was long resented by the peasantry as an injustice. For decades thereafter, Egyptians dilated upon the harshness of the verdict rendered against villagers who

[21]   Unsigned letter to Lord Cromer, enclosure in No. 9, Cromer to Sir Edward Grey, May 21, 1906, "Correspondence Respecting the Turco-Egyptian Frontier in the Sinai Peninsula," Great Britain, Parliament, *Accounts and Papers: State Papers*, Vol. CXXXVII, Egypt, No. 2 (1906), pp. 35-36 (Cd. 3006).

had been justifiably roused to a moment's fatal anger. Coming as it did, in a superheated atmosphere of nationalist activity, the Dinshaway affair became a turning point in Anglo-Egyptian relations – a point of no return for the British.

Into this politically surcharged atmosphere, seven Egyptian parties were born. The first, the National Party, has already been briefly described. When its founder died, Muhammad Farid took over the leadership. But the party had been Mustafa Kamil's own personal creation; it was never the same after his death. The next to be founded, in October, 1907, was the People's Party (*Hizb al-Umma*). This was a group of able patriots and political moderates, loosely organized round the liberal newspaper *al-Jarida*. Ahmad Lutfi al-Sayyid, the founder and distinguished editor of this paper, who left the National Party because of its immoderation, later became the rector of Egypt's first secular university. Another famous member of the People's Party was Sa'd Zaghlul, Minister of Public Instruction in 1906 and later Minister of Justice, who was to become the leader of the Wafd Party. The brilliant lawyer Fathi Zaghlul,[22] and several members of the Legislative Council and the General Assembly also joined in launching the People's Party, which co-operated with the reform program of the Occupation administration as long as Lord Cromer remained in Egypt. Still a third party was founded at the end of 1907, known as the Constitutional Reformers. Like the People's Party, it was organized round a newspaper. Shaykh Ali Yusuf, a member of the General Assembly, was the editor of one of Egypt's most important newspapers, *al-Mu'ayyad*. He became the leader of the Constitutional Reformers.

The politics and the patriotism of the Umma, or People's Party, has often been misunderstood or misrepresented, and at the time its policy was consistently impugned by the zealots of the National Party. But Dr. Jamal Mohammed Ahmed is convinced that "the Umma party had confidence in England and would co-operate with it in preparing Egypt for independence." The commanding personalities in the Umma Party would in themselves seem to support Dr. Ahmed's opinion. At least two of them, Lutfi al-Sayyid and Sa'd Zaghlul, had been friends and warm admirers of Shaykh Muhammad 'Abduh. It would be reasonable to conclude that they and their party

[22]   See note 12.

were actively carrying on the 'Abduh tradition – namely, to support the British, since Britain was the Occupying Power, and strive to achieve their desired reforms in Egyptian society under the aegis of an occupation that was presumably sympathetic to their objectives. But they were equally opposed in principle to the unchecked exercise of power by both the British and the Khedive. In Ahmed's words, "they wished to act as a 'third force' to check the other two." Lutfi al-Sayyid, like Fathi Zaghlul (and like Muhammad 'Abduh before them), believed in progress through evolution alone. And he was much drawn to the ideals of English Liberalism and the social utilitarianism of John Stuart Mill. The moral and intellectual endowments of Lutfi al-Sayyid made him one of the great personalities of modern Egypt, "the Teacher" and "the Philosopher" of his generation. Neither he nor Sa'd Zaghlul, who later became the pre-eminent spokesman of Egyptian political nationalism, could ever be suspected of appeasing the British. Unfortunately, however, the Umma Party became disillusioned with the British after Cromer left Egypt – in the shadow of the Dinshaway affair. Cromer had been on leave when the incident occurred, and he was retired in 1907, the year thereafter. His final report on Egypt was a shock to the Umma Party, in that he expressed disbelief in the capacity of Egyptians "suddenly" to exercise full rights of autonomy. The Umma Party was then further alienated by the policy of Cromer's successor, Sir Eldon Gorst, when he cultivated the friendship of Abbas Hilmi and thereby drove a wedge between the Khedive and the nationalists. Sa'd Zaghlul, for his part, continued to co-operate with the British Agent until 1913, when Lord Kitchener, Gorst's successor, failed to support him in one of his recurring struggles with the Khedive.[23]

Four other, relatively minor parties were established between 1907 and 1909. The National Free Party was formed round the famous Syrian-edited newspaper, *al-Muqattam*, and its membership included Dr. Sarruf and Dr. Nimr as well as other able Lebanese and Syrians,

[23]   Jamal Mohammed Ahmed, *op. cit.*, p. 70 for the quotations, pp. 71-72, 89-90, and pp. 52-55 on Sa'd Zaghlul. Cromer's report is in British document, *Accounts and Papers: State Papers*, Vol. C, Egypt, No. 1 (1907), p. 7 (Cd. 3394). See also Nadav Safran, *Egypt in Search of Political Community: An Analysis of the Intellectual and Political Evolution of Egypt, 1804-1952* (Cambridge, Mass., 1961), pp. 90-97, on Lutfi al-Sayyid. For Zaghlul's vigorous personality as Minister of Public Instruction see Bowman, *op. cit.*, p. 75.

Copts, and some Egyptian Muslims. The Party of Nobles, unlike any of its predecessors, was established primarily to support the Khedive against the growing disloyalty of the National Party under the new leadership of Farid. The Party of Independent Egyptians, founded by a Coptic lawyer, was principally a Coptic group with a sprinkling of Muslims. The Party of Young Egyptians was established in emulation of the Young Turks, with a reform program similar to that of all its predecessors.

The first three of Egypt's new parties were the most powerful and the most significant. The other four were either negligible in numerical strength, weak in leadership, or wanting in a distinctive program. In fact, all seven parties differed more in their attitude to the Occupation – in their degree of support for or hostility to the British – than in any other way. All these parties were essentially political in their programs; they took scarcely any cognizance of social or economic problems; but they all advocated educational reforms, and most of them demanded representative institutions. Several of them demanded the independence of the Sudan as well as of Egypt; and the Party of Independent Egyptians postulated "the inseparability of Egypt and the Sudan," in order to "ensure for Egypt the possession of and command of the Nile, which is the life of the country." [24] These parties were founded by politically-minded nationalists and they rose or fell, waxed or waned, with their leaders. Furthermore, all the parties represented urban groups and catered to the urban elite, which meant that they took little or no interest in the peasantry and its problems. The National Party was the only one of the seven to survive the First World War. It is noteworthy that although four of the seven parties were formed in support of the management and policies of outstanding Egyptian newspapers, no party was formed in connection with al-Ahram.[25]

[24] Article I of the program of the Party of Independent Egyptians, printed in Alexander, op. cit., p. 176. For the programs of the seven parties, some of them verbatim, see, ibid., pp. 117-118, 128-130, 132-133, 169-172, 176-178, 184-185. See also Landau, op. cit., pp. 136-147.

[25] This newspaper, from its founding in 1876, has until recently been known as a great independent daily – the "Times" of the Arab world. The present editor (1963) of al-Ahram is a distinguished journalist, Mohammed Hasanein Haikal, who is identified in the Western press as "a close friend of and unofficial spokesman for President Nasser." See Atlas, The World Press in Translation, May, 1963, p. 288.

The year 1909 was one of turbulence and disaffection in Egypt, the worst since the inauguration of the British Occupation. After the death of Mustafa Kamil his National Party had sunk further into the deep waters of extremism, and its organ, *al-Liwa*, vilified the administration unceasingly. The friendship between Sir Eldon Gorst and Abbas Hilmi had discredited the Khedive in nationalist eyes, with the result that the extremists turned against him. Some of them, eventually, demanded the deposition of the Khedive. The nationalists also fell out among themselves and attacked each other, as well as the government, in their journals.

At the beginning of that year the students of al-Azhar University went on strike against proposed changes in the curriculum. The nationalists straightway and gratuitously mixed into the affair, encouraging the students to hold out against the Shaykhs of the University. The majority of the 20,000 students of al-Azhar were sons of Egyptian peasants, and their strike accordingly had repercussions in the rural areas as well as in the cities. Ultimately, after a prolonged period of demonstrations and disturbances, the student strikers were granted a free pardon for their unprecedented lawlessness. Thenceforth the students of al-Azhar, foreign Muslims as well as Egyptians, interested themselves in nationalist politics – to the detriment of their studies and also to the detriment of law and order. Later some of the nationalists also tried to embroil in their party politics the students of the new Egyptian University, which opened in December, 1908.

In March, 1909, Gorst and the Khedivial government decided that the nationalist press had become dangerously inflammable. They revived and modified the old press law of 1881, which had fallen into disuse during the Cromerian epoch. The law, as modified, provided among other things that any newspaper might be suppressed in the interests of order, morality, and religion. The extremist section of the press, consisting of some two dozen Arabic- and European-language journals, was instantly aroused. Demonstrations and riots followed. The editor of a nationalist organ delivered a particularly fiery public oration against the government; his newspaper was promptly suppressed, and he himself was imprisoned for twelve months. This affair completed the rupture between the Khedive and the nationalists. Muhammad Farid then made several trips to Constantinople in a vain attempt to enlist the support of the Young Turks and their new Sultan for his National Party. General lawlessness increased alarmingly, as did crimes of violence. And finally, early in 1910, a tragic incident occurred that brought the country to the brink of revolution.

Boutros Ghali Pasha, the Coptic prime minister at that time, had become the new storm center. He was a man of integrity and ability, but he was unpopular with the extreme nationalists on several counts. The fact that he was a Copt would not, of itself, have made him unpopular. But that fact, coupled with his staunch support of the Occupation and the Khedive, counted against him. The nationalists, furthermore, had never forgiven Boutros Ghali for having presided over the Dinshaway tribunal, and they blamed him for the severity of the sentences then meted out. The press law was revived while he was prime minister; and he had, that same month, attended the opening of Port Sudan in his official capacity – thereby reminding Egyptians of his acquiescence in the joint rule of Britain and Egypt in the Sudan. When, in February, 1910, Boutros Ghali Pasha introduced in the General Assembly a proposal of the Suez Canal Company for a forty-year prolongation of its concession, the Assembly summarily and almost unanimously rejected the proposal on a straight nationalist vote. Two days later the prime minister was shot by a Muslim nationalist. He died almost immediately.

The terms of the proposed new Canal convention would have been very favorable to Egypt; nonetheless, the newspaper *al-Liwa* undoubtedly voiced a widespread feeling when it declared that the one hope cherished by all Egyptians was to repossess themselves of the Suez Canal.[26] To postpone the day when this hope could be realized was, at that time, unthinkable, even in return for solid material advantages.

The assassin of Boutros Ghali Pasha, a young chemist named Ibrahim Wardani, was brought to trial, sentenced to death, and executed four months later. Revelations in the course of the trial indicated that the assassination of the prime minister was but part of a wider conspiracy against the government in which a Muslim secret society was involved.[27]

---

[26] Alexander, *op. cit.*, pp. 283-284, citing *al-Liwa*.
[27] For contemporary accounts of the assassination, the trial of Wardani and the revelations at his trial, see, *ibid.*, pp. 309-323, and Sir Ronald Storrs, *Orientations* (London, 1937), pp. 83-85.

The events of 1909 and 1910 seemed at the time to spell the bankruptcy of the new British policy in Egypt. In any circumstances, it would have been very difficult for Cromer's successor to take over the reins of government. When that successor was also charged, as was Gorst, with the task of initiating a new policy, the difficulty was infinitely compounded. After a quarter of a century as British Agent and Consul-General, Cromer had come to personify the Occupation. The forcefulness of his character, and his apparent omnipotence and omniscience, had endowed "al-Lurd," long before he left Egypt, with a legendary reputation. He had overawed the Egyptians, and at the same time his accessibility to ordinary people, to the fallahin especially, had endeared him to the poor and the defenseless.

Gorst, like Cromer, was a man of integrity and high principles, but he lacked the dominating personality of his predecessor. He was far from weak, but he was self-effacing. Gorst, moreover, had been a subordinate in various ministries under Cromer. That experience had given him an intimate, personal knowledge of the people and the problems of government in Egypt, which was all to the good. On the other hand, Egyptians had grown accustomed to thinking of him as just one among many British Advisers; it was hard for them to shift mental gears and accept him as the personification of the Occupying Power. As a further complication, many members of Gorst's staff at the Agency were alienated by a policy that they neither sympathized with nor understood.

The relaxation of British controls and the opening of the door to greater Egyptian participation in the administration of the country was not a policy of Gorst's own choosing. But for various reasons the British Government indubitably felt that it would be impolitic to announce publicly the inauguration of a new policy. So the onus of implementing an unexplained change of policy had to be borne by Gorst alone. The new British Agent was bound to carry out his instructions from London, regardless of the rapidly changing climate of opinion in Egypt. When Gorst took over from Cromer, British control was being exercised primarily through government by inspection and the giving of authoritative advice. He accorded increased responsibilities to the Khedivial government and the Provincial Councils. At the same time, the advice tendered by British Advisers became noticeably less authoritative, even though the rigorous inspection of government departments and services continued.[28]

Coming so soon after the Dinshaway incident and the departure of Lord Cromer from Egypt, Gorst's liberal and lenient measures looked to Egyptians like weakness rather than liberality. The upsurge of Egyptian nationalism, which was in any case bound to come sooner or later, received quickening nourishment from the nationalist victories of the Young Turks in the government of the Ottoman Empire. And in addition, Egypt was suffering a mild economic depression. The depression was not serious, but it was of three years' duration and it served to aggravate the emotional content of nationalist self-expression. Gorst had less than four years in which to modify the Cromerian tradition. No one can say with certainty that, in the long run, the new policy might not have proved workable. At the same time, one must take account of the fact that the new demands of Egyptian nationalism would have posed serious problems for any foreign administrator, however brilliant.

In 1911, Sir Eldon Gorst was a dying man. When he returned to England, Lord Kitchener was appointed to take his place and the essential policies of Cromer's day were restored by the masterful hand of a distinguished soldier, without undue interference from London. The new British Agent and Consul-General had been known to Egyptians for nineteen years and was deeply respected by them. Kitchener had been appointed commander-in-chief of the Egyptian army in 1892. He had completely reorganized the army, and he had led Egyptians to victory, in 1898, against the Sudanese at Omdurman. It was through him, in other words, that the prestige of Egyptian arms had been restored.

Lord Kitchener, in his unaccustomed civilian role, was firm, but he was also forward-looking. He fostered the traditional rapprochement between the peasantry and the Occupying Power by meticulous attention to irrigation and extension of the cultivable area, the establishment of a Ministry of Agriculture, and protection of the fallah against foreclosure at the hands of the local moneylenders. As

[28] For a contemporary and appreciative analysis of Sir Eldon Gorst and his administration see Storrs, *op. cit.*, pp. 75-90. For a slightly different interpretation of the controversial period of Gorst's administration see G. A. Lloyd, *Egypt Since Cromer* (London, 1934), I, 65-113. For an Egyptian view of the role of Gorst and his "curious failure" see Jamal Mohammed Ahmed, *op. cit.*, pp. 72-76.

we have mentioned earlier, he also placated the nationalists by giving Egypt a new Organic Law and by inaugurating the Legislative Assembly. Kitchener's period of control as Agent was disturbed by the restiveness of Muslim nationalists during the Italo-Turkish war of 1911-1912 and the subsequent Italian penetration of the neighboring Ottoman provinces of Cyrenaica and Tripolitania – now known as Libya. But British authority in Egypt was never challenged as long as he was there. Lord Kitchener had the strength and the commanding personality to become a second Cromer. He did not, however, have the sensitivity possessed by the great Proconsul, and he lacked the intellectual drive and the versatility of both Cromer and Gorst.

The outbreak of the First World War in August, 1914, introduced many changes into Egyptian political life. Lord Kitchener was immediately transferred to the War Office in London. Then, early in November, the British declared martial law in Egypt. When the Young Turk government declared war against Great Britain two days later, the question of the juridical position of Egypt became a crucial issue. Legally all Egyptians were Ottoman subjects, and they had therefore to be regarded, technically, as enemy subjects. It accordingly became necessary to change the status of Egypt and of the Egyptians during the war, because Britain could not contemplate withdrawing from Egypt in a period of crisis; Anglo-Indian communications had to be maintained without interruption. The wisdom or expediency of outright annexation was first seriously debated in Whitehall; in the end, the urgent advice of British officials in Egypt against annexation was heeded. The British Government then decided to adopt a compromise solution and establish a protectorate.[29] This ambiguous decision at least had the merit of giving Egyptians an implicit assurance that Britain's repeated pledges to withdraw eventually from Egypt would, eventually, be honored. On December 18, 1914, Great Britain proclaimed a protectorate over Egypt. One day later, the Khedive Abbas Hilmi, who happened to be in Constantinople when the war broke out, was deposed.[30] The Khedive's

[29] For a forthright discussion of the pros and cons of annexation, and the advice of British officials in Egypt on the protectorate status see Lloyd, *op. cit.*, I, 192-198.
[30] The official version of the position of the Khedive was that he had "adhered" to the enemy. Certainly he had become a thorn in British flesh after the death of Sir Eldon Gorst. An interesting, possibly accurate inside-story of

uncle, Prince Hussein Kamil, a son of Ismail the Magnificent, was installed as Sultan of Egypt – the new title having been accorded him in recognition of the changed status of his country. Upon his death, in October, 1917, he was succeeded as Sultan by his brother Ahmad Fuad. The British Agent, in his turn, was promoted to the rank of High Commissioner. Sir Henry McMahon first served in this capacity. He was succeeded, in 1916, by General Sir Reginald Wingate, then governor of the Sudan.

In the beginning of the war, when the Turks were on the offensive, the principal Turkish objective was the reconquest of Egypt. A few Turkish units even crossed the Suez Canal, before they were beaten back by the British and Egyptians. The defense of Egypt and the Canal consequently became the keystone of Britain's policy in the Near East. Thereafter, when the Turks retreated to a defensive position in western Asia, Egypt was needed as a military base for the British campaign in Palestine. Cairo became the headquarters of a vast network of intelligence and counterespionage services, and Egypt was overrun by British and Imperial troops – at times there were as many as 200,000. As a result, nationalist activities were repressed and expressions of nationalist feeling were deceptively quiescent, at least after 1915.

The hardships suffered by Egyptians between 1914 and 1918, however, and their grievances against Great Britain at the end of the war, led to the revival of the national movement. At the same time, nonetheless, the government of Egypt, as well as its military and logistic services, co-operated loyally with the British throughout the war. And, in the words of the Milner Report, "the obligations and disabilities which it [the war] entailed upon the people were borne with patience and goodwill . . ." [31] Egyptian co-operation was note-

---

the deposition of Abbas Hilmi was published fifteen years later by Ardern Hulme Beaman, *The Dethronement of the Khedive* (London, 1929). Beaman had gone first to Egypt in 1879 as Arabic interpreter in the office of the British Consulate-General; during the First World War he worked in Egypt in counterespionage and did secret-service work. This Englishman, who undoubtedly had many subterranean sources of information open to him, strenuously denied that the Khedive Abbas Hilmi had – in the words of the British note of December 19, 1914 (to Sultan Hussein Kamil) on the protectorate – "definitely thrown in his lot with His [Britannic] Majesty's enemies."
[31] "Report of the Special Mission to Egypt" in *Accounts and Papers: State Papers*, Vol. XLII (Cmd. 1131), Egypt, No. 1 (1921), p. 10; hereafter cited as

worthy in view of Turko-German hostilities to the east and the attacks of Sanussi Beduin allied with the Turks on the Western Desert
frontier. In many ways Egypt and individual Egyptians prospered
during the Great War, but the hardships suffered by the majority of
the people, particularly the peasantry, were very real, and their grievances were not imaginary.

The discontents of the fallahin introduced an explosive new factor
into Anglo-Egyptian relations. For the first time since the beginning
of the Occupation, the peasants felt that the British had failed to
protect their interests. And as most of the demands made upon them
were issued through the channel of their own government, they grew
to resent the new Sultanate as well as the Protecting Power. Peasant
unrest stemmed from six major causes. An Egyptian volunteer Labour Corps was established which provided, when fully organized,
about a quarter of a million men recruited on a contract basis. Thousands of Egyptian laborers served outside their country, in France as
well as in Palestine and Mesopotamia. When voluntary recruiting
fell off, as it did in the later stages of the war despite the payment of
good wages, the Egyptian government undertook to supply conscripted "volunteers." The fiction that they were volunteers had to be
maintained, in view of the announcement made at the outbreak of
hostilities that Egyptians would not be required to take part in the
war against the Turks. Provincial officials were ordered to produce
stipulated quotas of conscripts, and their methods of selection were
inequitable and were not supervised by British officials. The village
officials, notably the despotically inclined ʿumdahs,[32] freely used
compulsion to get their quotas, sometimes even press-gang tactics;
they discriminated against their personal enemies, let their friends
off, and accepted bribes for exemptions and substitutions. These
methods were more than a little reminiscent of the early days of the
19th century. The manner of their selection actually caused as much
ill feeling among the fallahin as did the fact that they were required
to leave their land. Yet the services rendered by the Labour Corps

Milner Report. See also Young, *op. cit.*, pp. 221-222, citing Lord Allenby's
despatches and other official records on the reliability of the Egyptian services
during the war.

[32]   The ʿumdah is a village chief or headman, the most important official in
every village, but the lowest administrative official in the chain of command
between Cairo and the peasantry.

were "of inestimable value and indispensable to the campaign in Palestine." [33]

A Camel Transport Corps, likewise indispensable, was established, and in its service thousands of Egyptians were wounded and more than 4,000 lost their lives. The military found it necessary to commandeer animals; and this measure was bitterly resented, even though the peasants received adequate financial compensation, because camels and donkeys were indispensable for the cultivation of the land. The necessity to requisition cereals for the army in Palestine, especially wheat, also caused great discontent, not only because the foodstuffs were purchased at fixed rates lower than open-market prices, but also because of the method of their collection. As in the case of forced recruitment, provincial officials were given a free hand and they generally made a large profit for themselves – illegally, and at the expense of the peasants.

A progressive, unprecedented rise in prices, especially in corn, clothing, and fuel, caused much suffering among the poorer peasants and among the townspeople. Impoverished Egyptians, knowing nothing of over-all economic and financial problems outside their own spheres, imagined that they were being personally victimized by an unscrupulous government. For similar reasons, the controls imposed on cotton were likewise resented. Though the cotton growers were protected against speculation, they were at the same time unable to reap the profits of high prices and wartime demands for a militarily important crop. A doggerel chant of the later war years epitomized peasant discontents:

> Woe on us, Wingate,
> Who has carried off corn,
> Carried off cattle,
> Carried of camels,
> Carried off children,
> Leaving only our lives.
> For love of Allah, now let us alone.[34]

Several other causes of discontent affected adversely the whole popu-

[33] Milner Report, p. 10.
[34] Young, *op. cit.*, p. 228. For some illuminating statistics on the war years in Egypt, a few of which are given above, see, *ibid.*, pp. 209-227.

lation of Egypt. All democratic life and normal political activities were suspended in the first year of the war for the duration, even the new Legislative Assembly. There was strict press censorship, and all nationalist newspapers were suppressed. A Disarmament Act of 1917 was strictly enforced by domiciliary visits, and Egyptians resented indiscriminate disarmament as an undeserved insult. Finally, as the Delta had become a vast hospital camp as well as a military base, the authorities opened a Red Cross drive. Donations were invited on a purely voluntary basis; but collecting was entrusted to local officials, including the village 'umdahs, and all these officials were carried away by their zeal to acquire merit in the eyes of the government. In other words, compulsory donations were frequently exacted from Muslims on behalf of an organization that operated under the banner of the Christian cross. As some British writers have pointed out, a general contribution levied on war profits in the interest of war philanthropy could have achieved the same result without offending Egyptian sensibilities.[35]

The longer the war continued, the more onerous did all of these burdens become. Most Egyptians had too little comprehension of the issues at stake or of the realities of wartime needs to understand that the British were driven by dire necessity to increase their various requisitions and their demands for labor and transport services. In most cases, however, necessary war measures were less resented than the manner in which they were carried out. Their implementation ignored the sensibilities and flouted the pride of the Egyptian people.

Another type of grievance sprang from weaknesses inherent in the Occupation administration, weaknesses that had begun to develop long before 1914. The number of British officials in Egypt had increased progressively. At the beginning of Gorst's administration there were only some 300 to 400 Britishers in the public service. By 1919 more than 1,600 British officials virtually monopolized the Egyptian civil service. In comparison to this swollen corps of aliens, Egyptian officials were poorly trained and were therefore at an increasing disadvantage in competing with Britishers for the more highly paid posts. The salary disparity between the two groups, moreover, was a constant source of irritation to Egyptian officials who

---

[35] Milner Report, pp. 11-12; Young, *op. cit.*, pp. 217-218, 223-224, 226; and Amine Youssef, *Independent Egypt* (London, 1940), pp. 58-61.

had managed to obtain office. It seemed plain to them that they would be forever relegated to a secondary position in their own administration.

The increasing size of the British official community created a special problem of its own in Anglo-Egyptian relations. This homogeneous group tended more and more to lose personal touch with the Egyptians. The British had their own residential quarters; they had their own social life, sports, and playing fields; they were sufficient unto themselves. They grew, *de facto* but not as a result of conscious policy, into a separate community from which Egyptians were normally, though not wholly, excluded. The English Sporting Club on Ghezireh Island (Cairo), for instance, had one or two distinguished, bilingual Egyptian members. But in fact the two communities had little in common, socially speaking. Before the 1930's, Egyptian men – whether Muslim or Christian – did not like sports of any kind and could not have competed with Englishmen successfully. Almost all Muslim women were then still veiled; Coptic women were not veiled, but neither Muslim nor Coptic women moved outside their respective family circles. And Egyptian men were awkward in the presence of English women who circulated freely among their own countrymen and enjoyed sports. English administrators, moreover, did not generally establish any common ground of shared intellectual interests with their Egyptian counterparts. In short, fraternization did not come easily to the two communities. Moreover, even when possible, it was discouraged by the British. Fraternization could result in a degree of assimilation of the two societies, as it did so frequently in areas administered by the French, and it was difficult to draw the line between repellent aloofness and fraternization. The British were clear on one point: any degree of fraternization which approached assimilation should be avoided. Close community relations would be deleterious for the Egyptians, in the long run, because it would make more complicated the task of eventual British withdrawal from Egypt. There was finally one other problem connected with the large number of British officials in Egypt. The conviction was widespread that the quantitative increase in this group had resulted in a qualitative decline, or deterioration in calibre, because relatively fewer Britishers were outstanding personalities or even seasoned administrators.

The principal causes of grievance dated from the 19th century.[36] The basic and long-standing goals of Egyptian nationalism had been independence and the withdrawal of British troops from Egypt. These fundamental aims had never changed. The war grievances merely added a sharper edge to the persuasiveness of nationalist propaganda. Furthermore, several happenings in the war years had given the nationalists additional impetus in their campaign for independence. In the first place, the establishment of a British protectorate over the country was misunderstood by most Egyptians. Contrary to British intentions, protectorate status was interpreted as a preliminary step to ultimate annexation. In the second place, two commitments were made during the course of the war that gave Egyptians hope for the immediate solution of their own special problems. In October, 1915, the British High Commissioner in Egypt, Sir Henry McMahon, gave a qualified pledge of independence to Sharif Hussein of Mecca. This pledge had specific reference to the Arabs of the Hejaz and of the Fertile Crescent, and it did not include the Egyptians. Nevertheless, Egyptians, conscious of their co-operation with Great Britain in the war against the Turks, could not believe that their reward would be less substantial than that given to the relatively backward Arabs of Arabia.

On November 7, 1918, Great Britain and France gave a joint commitment to the peoples of the Ottoman provinces, just "liberated" from Turkish rule, to the effect that they should have national governments "deriving their authority from the initiative and free choice" of the people themselves.[37] Egypt also qualified as a province of the Ottoman Empire, though it was true that its people had been for some time free of Turkish control, and Egyptians hoped to be included in the commitment, if only because of the enunciation by President Wilson of his principle of self-determination for all peoples.

[36]   The principal Egyptian historian of the Rebellion of 1919 lists the grievances of the war years under *political, economic,* and *social* headings. He places the political grievances first, and he includes all the pre-war nationalist grievances in his list. See ʿAbd al-Rahman al-Rafiʿi, *Thawrat sanat 1919* [The revolution of the year 1919] (Cairo, 1946), pp. 3-4.

[37]   Full text of this joint "Anglo-French Declaration" of November 7, 1918, is given by George Antonius in *The Arab Awakening: The Story of the Arab National Movement* (New York, 1939), pp. 433-434, Appendix E. This text is a translation made at the time, by Antonius, from the French text officially distributed in Beirut.

The Fourteen Points outlined by the American President in January, 1918, gave enormous significance and a supposedly international sanction to the later Anglo-French joint Declaration on the eve of the Armistice.

Directly after the war ended, the nationalists returned to the surface of political life. Saʿd Zaghlul Pasha, the greatest political figure among modern Egyptians (before the Revolution of 1952), led the national movement of the postwar period and completely dominated the scene until his death.

Saʿd Zaghlul (1860-1927) was, like Arabi Pasha, of fallah stock, with all the salty humour and stalwart characteristics of the Egyptian peasant. He left his village as a boy and went to Cairo to study at the University of al-Azhar. Early in his student days he became an ardent disciple of the Muslim reformer Shaykh Muhammad ʿAbduh. After a few years, he began his official career as an assistant to Muhammad ʿAbduh on the editorial staff of the *Journal Officiel*. In this work he received literary and linguistic training, under the guidance of his mentor, and he also gained considerable insight into the social, political and economic questions of the day. The Arabi Rebellion interrupted his literary work, and he fought at Tel el-Kebir. Later, Zaghlul studied law, qualified as a judge in the native tribunals, and finally became Counsellor to the Court of Appeal. In his law work he earned the reputation of an outstanding orator and debater.

One of the last official acts of Lord Cromer was to appoint Saʿd Zaghlul Minister of Public Instruction to combat the crisis of student indiscipline in the schools – a crisis fomented by the political activities of Mustafa Kamil. Thus early in life Zaghlul was singled out by two great men, both of commanding influence in Egypt. They both recognized him as a potential leader of men; they both warmed to his integrity and his courage and his forthrightness of character. In the eyes of the Muslim-Egyptian reformer, he had the makings of a great patriot; in the eyes of the alien proconsul, he loomed as the best of the nationalists. Zaghlul proved himself to be both patriot and nationalist, although he became the target of nationalist attacks during the period of his co-operation with the Occupation authorities. A mutual antipathy grew up between him and the Francophile Mustafa Kamil, a friction reminiscent of the antagonism between Kamil and Muhammad 'Abduh.[38] As Minister of Education, Zaghlul Pasha was also a member of the General Assembly. When the government proposal to extend the Suez Canal Concession came up for debate in 1910, he offered an able defence of the proposal. After the assassination of Boutros Ghali Pasha, Zaghlul became Minister of Justice; eventually he was elected vice-president of the new Legislative Assembly established under Lord Kitchener.

Zaghlul's long experience in Egyptian public affairs bridged the Arabi revolt, the Cromerian era, and the period of journalistic nationalism before the First World War. Until the war he labored, in the 'Abduh tradition, to initiate administrative reforms in co-operation with the Occupation government. Because he had known the best of Cromerism – that is to say, he had known the outstanding English and Scottish administrators and engineers who inaugurated the material renaissance of his country – Zaghlul remained loyal to the Occupation. His first disillusionment with the alien regime became articulate under Kitchener.[39] He resigned as Minister of Justice in 1912, but he did not turn against the British until after the establishment of the Protectorate. And his open breach with the Occupation government did not occur until after the war, when a declaration of policy from the British Foreign Office made it plain to him that London intended to perpetuate the Protectorate.

As soon as the armistice was signed, in November, 1918, Zaghlul Pasha made his first move on behalf of Egyptian independence. He called upon the British High Commissioner, then Sir Reginald Wingate, to request permission to lead a nationalist delegation to London to take up with the British Government the problem of the status of Egypt in the postwar world and, at the same time, to put forward a program for "complete autonomy." Wingate sought permission from the Foreign Office, but Zaghlul's request was turned down. The refusal, based on the technical ground that the British Government could deal only with accredited representatives, finally and decisively alienated all the nationalists. And when subsequently an Egyptian ministerial delegation was invited to London, it refused to go alone, without the moral support of Zaghlul's delegation. The British Government felt unable to retreat from its original position, so neither

[38]   See, below, p. 127.
[39]   See, above, pp. 75-76 and note 23 on the Umma Party and Zaghlul.

delegation went to England. It is true that the British were then preparing to cope with many other problems, notably those of the Paris Peace Conference. It is also true that, owing to these preoccupations, they failed to grasp the full gravity of the Egyptian crisis. Had they done so, it seems likely that they would have found a formula to meet the crisis. The Egyptians for their part realized that all political questions raised by the war were to be decided by the victorious Great Powers at a forthcoming peace conference, and for that very reason they demanded a hearing. Any Egyptian patriot who had failed to press for a favorable solution of Egypt's problems, at that critical moment in their history, would have been, as Lord Lloyd later admitted, a "traitor" to his country.[40]

Sa'd Zaghlul and some of his close friends had formed a committee, or delegation (al-Wafd al-Misri, "the Egyptian Delegation"), from among members of the suspended Legislative Assembly, in anticipation of negotiations with Great Britain. This delegation, thenceforth known as the Wafd, issued its first proclamation directly after it was refused permission to go to London under Zaghlul's leadership. The proclamation appealed for a public mandate in order to achieve the complete independence of Egypt by legal and peaceful means. Copies circulated throughout Egypt, and thousands of signatures were obtained in its support. The Wafd, which asserted that it represented the whole nation, was not constituted as a formal political party until 1924. Before that time, however, it had already been efficiently organized as an executive committee; it had vested extensive powers in its president, Zaghlul Pasha; it had taken a vigorous stand for constitutional government; and since 1918 it had led the movement for independence.[41]

In the first months of 1919, Zaghlul and the Wafd were busy organizing public opinion in Egypt. Their goal was to unify all Egyptians, of every creed and class, in a movement for independence. By March of that year, the Zaghlulists had become uncomfortably hostile to the British; their propaganda activities and demonstrations had, in the eyes of many Britishers, assumed menacing proportions.

[40] Lloyd, op. cit., I, 290-292.
[41] For more detailed information on the Wafd see Ernst Klingmüller, Geschichte der Wafd-Partei (Berlin, 1937), pp. 14-45; Landau, op. cit., pp. 148-168; and Youssef, op. cit., pp. 55-106.

Zaghlul and his closest associates were, consequently, arrested and deported to Malta, in the hope that their removal would lead to the collapse of the Wafd. Instead, within a week the response to Zaghlul's deportation was a nationwide rebellion against the British in Egypt.[42] Without the restraining hand of Zaghlul, the nationalist lid blew off, and for the first time violence intruded upon the scene.

The nationalist spirit had been kept alive in the schools during the war, and the various war grievances had fused the interests of many groups in the nation. The deportation of the Wafdist leaders canalized these currents of dissatisfaction into a genuinely national movement. So effective was Wafdist leadership that the fallahin joined the urban nationalists in anti-British action; Muslims and Copts stood solidly together; and even the women of Egypt, of all classes, joined in unprecedented public demonstrations.

During the first weeks of the rebellion, Egyptians made concerted and systematic efforts to disrupt communications all over the country and to isolate the towns. Cairo itself was cut off, briefly, from railway and telegraphic communication with either Upper Egypt or the Delta. There was some organized pillaging; there were a few isolated, brutal murders; there were many acts of violence against British soldiers. The second phase of the rebellion, in April, 1919, took the form of general strikes and the complete dislocation of public business. The strikes were initiated by lawyers and students, and they were finally joined by transport workers and government officials.

When the rebellion first broke out in March, 1919, the British commander-in-chief, Field Marshal Lord Allenby, was in Paris at the Peace Conference. He was immediately sent back to Egypt as Special High Commissioner to restore law and order and to maintain the protectorate. The first phase of the rebellion had been sternly repressed, even before he reached Egypt. Soon after his arrival, therefore, Allenby determined upon a policy of conciliation. Egyptian affairs returned briefly to a state of normality, so far as was

[42]   On the rebellion of 1919 and Zaghlul Pasha see: Milner Report, *passim*; Amir Boktor, *School and Society in the Valley of the Nile* (Cairo, 1936), pp. 93-98; Young, *op. cit.*, pp. 229-261; and, of course, ʿAbd al-Rahman al-Rafiʿi, *op. cit.*, *passim*. Also: C. P. Issawi, *Egypt at Mid-Century* (London and New York, 1954), pp. 47-50; Rashed el-Barawy, *The Military Coup in Egypt* (Cairo, 1952), pp. 51-58; and Nadav Safran, *op. cit.*, pp. 101-107.

possible under martial law. Zaghlul and his associates were released and allowed to go to Paris. Eventually, they also went to London.

Meanwhile the Wafd, in co-operation with the numerous Egyptian associations on the Continent, mounted an intense propaganda campaign to lay their cause and their case before the bar of international public opinion. They published countless pamphlets and documentary "white books" giving their version of the long history of Anglo-Egyptian relations and the "repeated pledges" from the lips of British statesmen to withdraw from Egypt. The Wafd bombarded the Peace Conference with these publications, circulated them in London and Rome as well as in Paris, and addressed a multitude of letters and telegrams to supposedly influential persons.

In the face of these difficulties, the British Government, late in 1919, sent a special mission to Egypt under the chairmanship of Viscount Milner. Its terms of reference were, "To enquire into the causes of the late disorders in Egypt, and to report on the existing situation in the country and the form of the Constitution which, under the Protectorate, will be best calculated to promote its peace and prosperity, the progressive development of self-governing institutions, and the protection of foreign interests." Unfortunately for the mission, as soon as it became known in Egypt that the continuation of the protectorate was envisaged, the nationalist rebellion entered upon a third phase. The line taken in this phase was passive resistance: the mission was boycotted, and Egyptians refused to co-operate with any British officials.

The Milner mission was composed of six very able and distinguished men, most of whom knew Egypt well. Milner himself had served under Cromer in the 1890's. When writing its report, in 1920, the mission showed courage and honesty as well as a remarkable degree of independence. The "Milner Report" began by examining the causes of unrest in Egypt and gave an impartial summary of Egyptian grievances before, during, and after the war. It freely admitted that Egyptians had good reason to be confused by a situation that had been "abnormal" since 1882; that nationalists were "able to point to a long series of declarations by British statesmen disowning the idea of annexing, or even permanently occupying, the country"; and that Egyptians had been explicitly assured "that their national status was not changed for the worse by the Protectorate." Perhaps the most penetrating criticism of British policy was made in the statement: "We have never honestly faced the Egyptian problem, and our neglect to do so is in a measure responsible for the present situation." [43]

In the section devoted to an account of the nationalist movement and Egyptian aspirations, complete independence was admitted to be their goal: "To all outward appearance, independent opinion was solidly Nationalist. And in our judgment it is likely to remain so." These words gave a clear warning for the future, as did the Report's estimate of the strength of the nationalist movement: "Nationalism has, for the time being at any rate, established complete dominance over all that is vocal and articulate in Egypt. From the Princes of the Sultan's family down to the children of the primary schools, the men of property, the professional men, the religious teachers [of al-Azhar], the *literati*, the journalists, the students and school-boys have all, more or less willingly, been swept into the Nationalist movement. Most serious of all, perhaps, it now permeates the official class and the upper ranks of the army." [44]

In commenting on the Wafd, the "remarkable organisation" under the leadership of Zaghlul Pasha, the Report was careful to point out that this group did not consist mainly of extremists – and was thus unlike the National Party (the *Hizb al-Watani*), which was "the real revolutionary and anti-British party." In the judgment of the mission, the fact that Zaghlul and his associates had been drifting steadily into a more anti-British position was owing to the British attitude, "which seemed to them to present a blank negative to all their hopes." [45]

Small wonder, when it came to drafting its policy recommendations, that the Milner mission departed from its terms of reference. In view of their findings, the members of the mission could not have done otherwise. Their Report recommended the abandonment of the Protectorate in favor of a bilateral treaty of alliance between Britain and Egypt, with appropriate safeguards for imperial communications and the protection of foreign interests and communities.

The Report of the Milner mission caused much soul-searching in London, and there were those who condemned it as an impolitic

[43] See Milner Report, p. 8, for all quotations.
[44] *Ibid.*, p. 16.
[45] *Ibid.*, p. 18.

surrender to Egyptian nationalism. But, happily for the Egyptians, there were others who believed with the members of the mission that the fulfillment of Britain's long-standing promise of self-government for Egypt could no longer be postponed. Conciliatory counsels finally prevailed, especially after Lord Allenby threw his influential support to the new policy proposed by the Milner mission. The problem that remained, however, was to draft the terms of a settlement that would satisfy Egyptian nationalists and at the same time safeguard legitimate British and European interests in Egypt.

Zaghlul Pasha had accepted in principle the suggested treaty relationship, when he was in London in the summer of 1920. Had the British Government immediately accepted the recommendations of the Milner mission, it is likely that a mutually acceptable Anglo-Egyptian treaty would have been signed at that time. But six months elapsed before treaty negotiations were begun with the government of Sultan Fuad, and during those critical months rebellion continued to smoulder. In May, 1921, serious riots broke out in Alexandria, and European and Greek residents suffered heavier losses of life and property than did the British. The consuls of Italy, France, and Greece protested against the treatment of their nationals and emphasized the need of adequate protection for the foreign communities under any proposed treaty relationship.[46]

In July, 1921, the British initiated treaty negotiations with Prime Minister Adli Yeghen Pasha, a moderate nationalist. But the climate of opinion, in the aftermath of the Alexandria riots, was no longer propitious. Britain was more preoccupied than ever with the need to protect foreign interests in Egypt. The nationalists, for their part, had been given time to realize that, though a generous gesture had been made by Britain, the terms of the proposed treaty spelled less than complete independence for Egypt. And by that time, they had ma-

---

[46] The findings of the Military Court of Enquiry into the Alexandria riots (of May 23, 1921) indicated that the rioting had not been spontaneous. In the judgment of the Court, the mobs had been organized and controlled; they had acted "under the direction of men with whistles." The Court made a special point of recalling the similar riots of 1882 and commented on the elements of xenophobia endemic in Egyptian mobs. The Court took note of the fact that the French, Italian, and Greek consuls, in their protests, asserted that they could "never consent to their [nationals] being protected by a force composed exclusively of Egyptians." See *Accounts and Papers: State Papers*, Vol. XLII, Egypt, No. 3 (1921), pp. 266-267 (Cmd. 1527).

neuvered themselves into a position from which there was no retreat. Zaghlul Pasha, who had refused earlier to co-operate with Adli Pasha, raised insurmountable difficulties for the prime minister. When a deadlock developed between the Egyptian government and the Wafd, political demonstrations and disorders were resumed. The British finally felt obliged to ban all political activity in the country. Zaghlul Pasha defied the ban. He and his principal Wafdist associates were thereupon deported for a second time. But with Zaghlul out of Egypt, no one could control the nationalists. The old story seemed about to repeat itself: another open rebellion was imminent.

Faced with a fresh crisis and a solemn warning of impending disaster from the High Commissioner, the British Government took a courageous decision. The fruitless negotiations were abandoned, and British statesmanship produced an unprecedented political formula to deal with an Imperial emergency. The new formula was a unilateral declaration of independence for Egypt, with certain inevitable reservations. The full text of this brief declaration of February, 28, 1922, which gave Egypt a new status in the postwar world, was as follows:

Whereas His Majesty's Government, in accordance with their declared intentions, desire forthwith to recognise Egypt as an independent sovereign State; and

Whereas the relations between His Majesty's Government and Egypt are of vital interest to the British Empire;

The following principles are hereby declared:—

1. The British Protectorate over Egypt is terminated, and Egypt is declared to be an independent sovereign State.
2. So soon as the Government of his Highness shall pass an Act of Indemnity with application to all inhabitants of Egypt, martial law as proclaimed on the 2nd November, 1914, shall be withdrawn.
3. The following matters are absolutely reserved to the discretion of His Majesty's Government until such time as it may be possible by free discussion and friendly accommodation on both sides to conclude agreements in regard thereto between His Majesty's Government and the Government of Egypt:—
    (a.) The security of the communications of the British Empire in Egypt;
    (b.) The defence of Egypt against all foreign aggression or interference, direct or indirect;
    (c.) The protection of foreign interests in Egypt and the protection of minorities;

(d.) The Soudan.

Pending the conclusion of such agreements, the *status quo* in all these matters shall remain intact.[47]

For the next fourteen years the history of Anglo-Egyptian relations was the story of repeated efforts to negotiate a treaty of alliance within the framework of this declaration. This objective was not accomplished until the summer of 1936, when mutual fears of Italian aggression in Abyssinia drove the British and the Egyptians temporarily into each other's arms.

Directly after Lord Allenby communicated Britain's declaration of February, 1922, to Sultan Fuad, Egyptians addressed themselves to the task of formulating a constitution and establishing representative institutions. The Sultan immediately took the title of King Fuad, and entrusted his government with the task of drafting a constitution. Whereupon a commission, appointed by the Council of Ministers, soon set to work and chose the Belgian constitution of 1830-1831 for its working model.

The fourteen months that elapsed between the unilateral declaration of independence and the proclamation of the constitution, on April 20, 1923, demonstrated clearly the continuing instability of the situation in Egypt. During those months the lines of future political struggle were clearly marked out, as well as the direction of nationalist pressures against both the King of Egypt and the British. Zaghlul Pasha was not released from internment and allowed to return to his country until after the constitution commission had completed its task. Serious nationalist outbreaks were thus avoided. But the exclusion of Zaghlul Pasha from an opportunity to assist in the work of reconstruction led to three important developments in Egyptian politics. In the first place, the King, who was autocratically inclined, obtained wider powers under the constitution than he would otherwise have been able to secure. In the second place, the Wafd emerged as the greatest political force in permanent opposition to the Palace. Thirdly, the Sudan became the chief bone of contention in Anglo-Egyptian relations.

[47] "Declaration to Egypt," Enclosure 2 in Document No. 35, *ibid.*, Vol. XXIII, Egypt, No. 1 (1922), pp. 29-30 (Cmd. 1592).

The Sudan had been deliberately excluded from all negotiations regarding Egypt, because its status (as a condominium) had been defined by the Anglo-Egyptian convention of January 19, 1899.

The situation was roughly this: the Wafdists, in Zaghlul's absence, refused to make their peace with the British. They likewise turned against King Fuad for his so-called traitorous co-operation with Britain. The King was caught between the two fires of the Wafd and the British. He wanted to become independent of both, but he was bound to co-operate with the British to a certain extent, at least until a formal Anglo-Egyptian treaty of alliance should be signed. At one point in the drafting of the constitution, the King laid claim to the title of "King of Egypt and the Sudan." Such a designation was obviously incompatible with the fourth reservation of the declaration of February, 1922. So the King had, after much diplomatic pressure, to abandon his dual claim. In yielding this point to the British, he was forced to take a stand against the Wafd on a very sensitive nationalist issue. In such a manner, therefore, the triangular struggle that developed between the King, the Wafd, and the British was born in 1923.

The exclusion of most of the nationalists from participation in and responsibility for the work of the constitution commission resulted in yet another complication. So great was the frustration and the bitterness thus engendered that a secret terrorist organization took shape and inaugurated a campaign of political assassination. The British, who had cleared the field for the constructive efforts of moderate co-operating nationalists, became the target in a new hate campaign; and British officials consequently were the principal victims of assassination.

The constitution of 1923 provided for a hereditary monarchy under the dynasty of Muhammad Ali. It also provided for a bicameral Parliament, a Senate and a Chamber of Deputies, and for ministerial responsibility to Parliament. Islam was established as the religion of the state, but freedom of worship was guaranteed and minority rights were adequately protected. Individual liberties – such as equality before the law, inviolability of property and domicile – were guaranteed. But freedoms of the press and of assembly, though likewise guaranteed, were loosely defined and contingent upon the necessity to protect society. The executive power belonged to the King and his ministers, who were his appointees. The legislative power was to be exercised by the King conjointly with the Senate and the Chamber of Deputies. The King had a suspensory veto and the right to prorogue or adjourn Parliament. The King also appointed two fifths of the senators. The other three fifths of the senators were elected. The senatorial term of office was for ten years, half being renewable every five years. The Chamber of Deputies was elected for five years. The popularly chosen senators and all the deputies were elected by universal male suffrage. The principle of indirect election for the Chamber of Deputies, provided for under a separate electoral law, became a bone of contention between the Palace and the Wafd after 1924.[48]

Zaghlul Pasha returned to Egypt in time for the first elections. The Wafd had already denounced the new constitution as giving too much power to the King; but under Zaghlul's leadership it contested the elections and gave overwhelming proof that the Wafdists were far stronger in the country than the co-operating nationalists. In these first elections, which were held between September, 1923, and February, 1924, the Wafd won 90 per cent of the votes and secured 188 out of 215 seats in the Chamber of Deputies.[49] Zaghlul Pasha accordingly took office as the first prime minister of the Kingdom of Egypt, and a few months later he established the Wafd as a formal political party.

The Wafd was and remained the only efficiently organized party in the country, with committees or branches in the remotest villages. So total, even totalitarian, was its discipline that the Wafd gradually took on the characteristics of a dictatorship in Egyptian political life, and it swept the fallahin remorselessly into its urban wake. In the process of becoming a dictatorship, the Wafd also became a truly national party, through its ideal of building a united, secular state – a state in which all Egyptians should have equal rights and duties, and in which nationalism should be dissociated from religion. For the next twenty years the Copts rallied loyally to the standard of the Wafd. Makram Ebeid Pasha, the most influential personality in the party after Zaghlul Pasha, was a leader of the Coptic community. As long as he supported the Wafd, which was until the Second World War, the Copts gave their wholehearted support to the Wafdists. But

[48] For the text of the Egyptian constitution see Helen Miller Davis, *Constitutions, Electoral Laws, Treaties of States in the Near and Middle East* (Durham, N. C., 1947), pp. 19-38. See also Young, *op. cit.*, pp. 265-267, and Landau, *op. cit.*, pp. 60-63.

[49] Young, *op. cit.*, p. 270; Landau, *op. cit.*, pp. 64, 167.

when Makram Ebeid finally broke with Mustafa al-Nahhas Pasha, Zaghlul's successor as head of the Wafd, the party split and the Wafdists were irremediably weakened. Until Zaghlul's death in 1927, and after, his residence was known as "The House of the Nation." His wife, the daughter of the most distinguished Muslim prime minister of Lord Cromer's day, was a leading feminist, with great influence in the party counsels.

The Party of Constitutional Liberals, which had been founded by Adli Pasha at the end of 1922, headed Egyptian opposition to the Wafd with a progressive program for social, educational, and economic reforms. Many of the Constitutional Liberals were men of integrity and ability, but their party never commanded anything like the popular backing of the rival Wafd Party.

It fell to the lot of Zaghlul to go to London and undertake the first treaty negotiations with Britain after the founding of the Kingdom of Egypt. He was optimistic at first, because of the supposed friendliness of the new Labour ministry in England. But, as Zaghlul was prepared to make no concessions, and as he demanded the withdrawal of British troops and the complete independence of Egypt and the Sudan, the negotiations were foredoomed to failure. Their failure led indirectly to the tragic crisis of November, 1924, which was caused by the assassination of Sir Lee Stack in the streets of Cairo. In his person, Stack had become the focal point of anti-British rancor, because he was both the governor-general of the Sudan and the sirdar, or commander-in-chief, of the Egyptian army. When Zaghlul returned empty-handed from London, an extremist nationalist group assassinated Stack. This political crime, for which Zaghlul swiftly and feelingly expressed sorrow, caused a complete breach between London and Cairo.

On the afternoon of Sir Lee Stack's funeral, Lord Allenby delivered a devastating ultimatum to the Egyptian government. The British required an apology, "condign punishment" of the criminals, an indemnity of 500,000 pounds, the prohibition of all political demonstrations, and the withdrawal of all opposition to the British protection of foreign interests in Egypt. The ultimatum contained two further demands: that the government of Egypt should order within twenty-four hours the withdrawal from the Sudan of all Egyptian officers and troops, and that it should "notify the competent department that the Sudan Government will increase the area to be irrigated at Gezira [in the Sudan] from 300,000 feddans (acres) to an unlimited figure as need may arise." [50] In an accompanying statement to Zaghlul Pasha the British Government expressed its conviction that this brutal murder of Stack was the "natural outcome of a campaign of hostility to British rights and British subjects in Egypt and Sudan." It added: "Your Excellency was warned by His Majesty's Government little more than a month ago of the consequences of failing to stop this campaign, more particularly as concerned the Sudan" – where Egyptian nationalists had been promoting mutinies among their Sudanese troops.

This ultimatum made it clear that the British proposed to lift the Sudan, once and for all, out of the arena of Anglo-Egyptian politics. The result, however, was quite otherwise. The two demands of the ultimatum concerning the Sudan frightened all Egyptians, including even the fallahin, by the implied threat of future interference with the flow of Nile water into Egypt. Thenceforth Egyptians were adamant in demanding the independence of Egypt and the Sudan, believing that their prosperity and even their security necessitated the unity of the Nile Valley under the control of Egypt.

Zaghlul Pasha was eventually cleared of all direct complicity in this and preceding crimes of political assassination, but he was forced to resign. His successor in office accepted all seven demands of the ultimatum, though not until after pressure had been put on the Egyptian government by the British military occupation of the Alexandria Customs.[51] A very troubled political period followed, with cabinet crises succeeding one another while the country continued to demonstrate its loyalty to Zaghlul Pasha and the Wafd. The real tragedy with respect to Egypt lay in the later political repercussions of the British ultimatum and the chaotic effects which were a by-product of the harsh terms imposed upon Egyptians at the dawn of their first democratic experiment. Representative government suffered a setback before ever it had a chance to become firmly established in the country.

[50] Text of the ultimatum of November 22, 1924, in Hurewitz, *op. cit.*, II, 130-131.
[51] The Customs receipts were the principal source of revenue of the government of Egypt.

The intransigeance of the Wafdists gave King Fuad an excuse to interfere in the orderly development of constitutional government. New political parties were formed, including a Union Party subservient to the King. Fuad tried repeatedly to whittle down the rights of Parliament and to rule through coalition governments without the support of the elected deputies. Undue pressures were applied to the electorate, and election results were faked by unscrupulous politicians. Finally in 1930, after the Wafd had brought about the failure of the third Egyptian attempt to negotiate an Anglo-Egyptian treaty, King Fuad repudiated the Wafd, revoked the constitution of 1923, proclaimed a new constitution and a new electoral law, and inaugurated a five-year period of royal dictatorship.[52] Eventually, however, the popular demand for constitutional government was so urgent that, in December, 1935, the King officially restored the constitution of 1923.

The first postwar decade was a period of social and economic, as well as of political, unease. The initial result of the war years had been an evanescent prosperity and great inequalities of wealth. A very small urban group had made huge fortunes out of British military expenditures. But the vast majority of Egyptians had suffered from food shortages, owing in part to the requisitioning of grains and

[52] In March, 1930, Mustafa al-Nahhas Pasha, prime minister and successor to Zaghlul as head of the Wafd Party, led a delegation to London to make a fresh attempt to negotiate an Anglo-Egyptian treaty. The subsequent Henderson-Nahhas negotiations achieved rapprochement on the solution of all Egyptian problems, but they broke down completely over the Sudan. Nahhas, entirely ignoring the 1899 Convention, held that Egyptian sovereignty over the Sudan was undivided and that the immigration of Egyptians into the Sudan should be unrestricted. — With respect to Egyptian interests in the Nile, the British Government had adequately reassured the Egyptians in an exchange of notes on January 26, 1925, a couple of months after the ultimatum. And a Nile Waters agreement, signed on May 7, 1929, had officially satisfied the Egyptian government concerning its vital interests in the river. But the Egyptians never forgot their consternation over Article 6 of the ultimatum of November 22, 1924, and the fears which it had bred. – For an interesting account of the whole period, 1924-1938, see Marcel Colombe, *L'Evolution de L'Egypte, 1924-1950* (Paris, 1951), pp. 9-76. For detailed treatment of the same period see *Oriente Moderno* and the *Annual Survey* of the Royal Institute of International Affairs; see also Royal Institute of International Affairs, Information Department Papers, No. 19, *Great Britain and Egypt, 1914-1936* (London, 1936).

animals and in part to the decline of imports from Europe. General consumer shortages, also owing to British military requirements and the decline in European imports, had contributed to stimulate the growth of new local industries. These in turn had resulted in labor problems, accompanied by an unprecedented stimulus to urbanization. The abnormal profits of the later war years had also led to an extravagant building boom in Cairo and Alexandria. Prices skyrocketed; and so did the price of urban and rural land. Rents accordingly rose some sixty to one hundred per cent, but profits therefrom went to the landlords, not to the fallahin. The one war profit in which the peasants, at least a great number of them, shared was the cotton boom. By 1920, cotton was selling at twelve times its prewar price.

When the war ended, however, a long period of deflation set in, and general prosperity declined rapidly. This was not a steady or consistent process of decline; it was shown rather in three great waves of depression, in 1921, 1926, and 1931. The 1931 depression was a delayed reaction to the great American crash of 1929-1930. And as 85 per cent of the agricultural exports of Egypt were cotton, rural prosperity was largely responsive to violent fluctuations in world cotton prices.

The First World War stimulated the beginning of industrialization in Egypt. The need of the country for a greater degree of self-sufficiency, the need for a more diversified economy, was brought home to Egyptians by shipping problems during the war years. Moreover, a number of new local industries were founded in response to the requirements of British military personnel. In 1920 the Bank Misr was established, with a total authorized Egyptian capital of more than four million pounds. In course of time, the Misr Bank owned twenty companies and developed an empire of subsidiary industrial and commercial enterprises.[53] These subsidiaries manufactured cotton, silk, woolen, and linen textiles and clothing, cigarettes, cement, soap, and vegetable oils; they also were engaged in fisheries, marble quarrying, shipping, insurance, printing, and the motion-

[53]   The National Bank of Egypt, founded in 1898, remained the central bank of the country. – For a table giving an annotated list of the Misr group of companies see Rashed el-Barawy, *The Military Coup in Egypt* (Cairo, 1952), pp. 61-63.

picture industry; and Misr Air operated local and regional airlines. The development of these companies, which the Bank Misr helped to found, was slow until after 1930, when the expiration of existing international commercial agreements made it possible for the government to initiate a policy of moderate protection for infant industries. A further impetus was given to industrialization by the establishment, in 1922, of the Egyptian Federation of Industries, representing industrialists. The Federation, which started with some fifty members, built up a membership of 430 and a capital of LE 120,000,000 by 1937.

Most of the early industrial ventures languished or actually failed after the war, owing to the renewed competition of foreign products. A clue to this fact is given by the foreign trade figures: whereas in 1924 Egypt had a favorable trade balance of more than fifteen million pounds, by 1926 this had turned into an adverse balance of trade of more than nine millions.

Major industrial development was long retarded by the lack of coal and iron. Egypt had no coal available for industrial enterprises;[54] and the first iron field was not discovered until 1938, in Upper Egypt. No official survey of industrial production was made before the Second World War. When the first industrial census was taken in 1944, the total number of factories then producing consumers' goods was estimated at 22,220, and these factories employed only 316,144 workers.

The rise of a middle class was a phenomenon of the late 19th and early 20th centuries. But, as the factory figures indicate, the industrial middle-class was wholly negligible until the Second World War. The bourgeoisie of the prewar period, and until well into the 1930's, was primarily commercial and clerical. The commercial middle class, in great part foreign, was a prosperous group. The white-collar middle class, on the other hand, formed a marginal economic group of educated Egyptians. It was composed of the intelligentsia and the civil service, chiefly clerical officeholders. The white-collar middle class was destined to grow rapidly with the expansion of secular university training after 1925, when the Egyptian University was metamorphosed into a state university. The civil service and educational

[54] Egypt's first known coal field was reportedly discovered in the Sinai Peninsula in 1959.

institutions readily absorbed the white-collar middle class during the first postwar decade. But it was not long thereafter before the supply of university graduates and white-collar workers exceeded the demand for their specialized services; and eventually white-collar unemployment showed signs of becoming acute.

Egypt's gravest problem of the mid-20th century began to emerge in the first postwar decade, namely overpopulation. The problem was not fully identified, however, until the middle of the century, when improved statistical services proclaimed to all the world that about 20,500,000 persons (in 1951) were trying to gain a livelihood on some six million acres of cultivated land, and that the population of Egypt was then mushrooming at the rate of about 300,000 per year. This rapidly expanding population is compactly crowded along the fertile banks of the Nile and in a few scattered, less fertile oases. The The further fact that population was increasing at a rate greater than the increase of agricultural productivity would be alarming in any country; but where, as in Egypt, the inelasticity of the cultivable land poses a problem of its own, apprehension mounts with each passing year. In this state, double the area of France, about 97 per cent of the country's 386,000 square miles was still desert in 1951. It has been estimated that even when the new high dam and reservoir is completed across the Nile, south of Aswan, with its new system of barrages and distributing canals, only two million more acres will be reclaimable from the desert. The Nile waters, though very bountiful, are not inexhaustible; they cannot economically be diverted too far from the river's banks to irrigate the encompassing deserts. The only rainfall in Egypt is along the Mediterranean coast, and that is scanty.

The relation between the rigidly limited supply of cultivable land and Egypt's expanding population constitutes a unique demographic problem. In 1882, the first real census of the country gave a figure of slightly more than 6,800,000 for the total population of Egypt.[55]

[55] The statistics on this and the following pages are taken from tables in A. E. Crouchley, *The Economic Development of Modern Egypt* (London, 1938), pp. 256-258; from Crouchley's two chapters on the war and the postwar years; and from relevant chapters in Issawi, *op. cit.*; Wendell Cleland, *The Population Problem in Egypt* (Lancaster, Penna., 1936); Doreen Warriner, *Land and Poverty in the Middle East* (London, 1948); British Department of Overseas Trade, *Report on Economic and Commercial Conditions in*

The population of Cairo was then recorded at almost 375,000, and there were nearly 91,000 foreigners in the country. By 1917, the total population had increased to more than 12,700,000, the population of Cairo was close to 800,000, and about 206,000 foreigners were living in Egypt. The census of 1927, which is now believed to have underestimated the population, gave the figures of 14,217,864 for the total population, 1,064,567 for the population of Cairo, and 225,600 for the resident foreigners. Between 1882 and 1927, the cultivated area of Egypt only increased from about 4,758,000 acres to slightly more than 5,544,000.

The productivity of Egypt is nevertheless far greater than these figures would seem to indicate. Owing to the modernizing of the country's irrigation system, two, and in some places three, crops a year can be grown on the same land, so that the crop-bearing area greatly exceeds the amount of land under cultivation. In 1927-1928, the crop area exceeded the cultivated area by some 3,091,625 acres. Egypt's population was concentrated in the cultivated area, and its population density was estimated, for the 1930's, at approximately 1,045 persons per square mile – almost double that of Belgium, the most densely populated country in Europe. The birth rate and the death rate in Egypt are among the highest in the world, as is also the rate of infant mortality. In the interwar years the Egyptian birth rate averaged 42 per thousand, the death rate averaged 27 per thousand, and the infant mortality rate averaged 160 per thousand live births.[56] In 1927, two thirds of the total population was under thirty years of age. The total picture began to improve after 1927, but no significant changes occurred until after the establishment of the Ministry of Social Affairs in 1939, when public health services, sanitation, and co-operatives were made available to a greater number of people and rural social centers were founded to elevate the standard of living of the peasantry.

Egypt (London, 1937); and the *Annuaire statistique* of the Government of Egypt (1949-1950).

[56] In the light of more recent and comparative statistical studies, it has been suggested that these reported averages may have been underestimated by as much as 11 per cent, 14 per cent, and 23 per cent, respectively. Issawi, *op. cit.*, p. 55, quoting Clyde V. Kiser, "The Demographic Position of Egypt," in *Demographic Studies of Selected Areas of Rapid Growth*, ed. F. W. Notestein (New York, 1944).

The rural community of Egypt, the fallahin, constituted about eighty per cent of the total population during the interwar years. Historically, the fallah has suffered from poverty, ignorance, disease, and undernourishment. And after the war, the fallah family sank still deeper into the slough of misery and indebtedness. There were various reasons for the deterioration of their already low standard of living, most of which have already been mentioned in connection with the pressures of the war years. But a principal reason was the progressive reduction in the size of the average landholding. In 1930, a mere 7 per cent of the total number of landowners owned about 70 per cent of the land of Egypt. About 12,800 landlords owned 50 or more acres of land, whereas more than one and a half million families owned less than an acre. As the annual income per acre then averaged about LE 24, out of which the fallah had to pay about one pound and a half in taxes and another pound for seed and fertilizer, the average peasant family had to eke out a bare subsistence by working part-time as laborers or tenants on another farm. The annual expenditure of a family of five was estimated, in 1931, at from LE 23 to LE 27.

Peasant poverty was accentuated by absentee landlordism and the mounting indebtedness of the small landowner. And the illiteracy of 90 per cent or more of the fallahin, combined with the above factors, made the peasant class as a whole very slow to adopt relatively costly agricultural machinery. Moreover, the traditional skill of the fallah in the use of his time-honored agricultural implements, combined with the cheapness of labor, also contributed to retard technical improvements in agriculture.

Finally, the worsening plight of the fallahin was compounded by the advancing menace of disease. Some authorities hold that 95 per cent of the peasants were afflicted by a variety of eye diseases, particularly trachoma. The peasants in addition suffered chronically from all the afflictions associated with malnutrition and insanitary living conditions. Fallah families lived in mud huts, and half of their living space was shared with their livestock. They slept on straw pallets or old blankets. They existed on a diet of ground-maize bread and onions, together with a small quantity of sugar, tea or coffee, vegetables, and cheese made from water-buffalo milk; once a week at most they ate meat. In general they were forced, for financial reasons, to sell most of the eggs, milk, and butter produced on their farms.

The squalor of village life before the advent of the rural social center was epitomized in the following poignant story told by an Egyptian author. A court case came up in one of the remote country districts. As told by the legal officer in the case, the presiding judge was trying a peasant for breaking the law:

"You are charged with having washed your clothes in the canal!"

"Your honour – may God exalt your station – are you going to fine me just because I washed my clothes?"

"It's for washing them in the canal."

"Well, where else could I wash them?"

The judge hesitated, deep in thought, and could give no answer. He knew very well that these poor wretches had no wash basins in their village, filled with fresh flowing water from the tap. They were left to live like cattle all their lives, and were yet required to submit to a modern legal system imported from abroad.

The judge turned to me and said, "The Legal Officer. Opinion, please."

"The State is not concerned to inquire where this man should wash his clothes. Its only interest is the application of the law."

The judge turned his glance away from me, lowered his head, shook it, and then spoke swiftly like a man rolling a weight off his shoulders: "Fined twenty piastres. Next case." [57]

Paradoxically, the most acute health problem of the peasants in recent times has stemmed from a notable agricultural reform. Extension of the crop area has been brought about by a significant change in the old Pharaonic or "basin" system of irrigation. This method of impounding the annual flood waters of the Nile and then allowing the water to drain off when the flood subsides – after having deposited its precious load of silt – has been progressively replaced by a new method of "perennial" irrigation. Under the new system, the flood water is stored behind high dams, the year round, and its distribution is regulated by a scientifically planned chain of canals. A reserve of water is also maintained against years of "low Nile flood." Four fifths of the cultivated land of Egypt has been converted to perennial irrigation since the end of the 19th century, and the fields are watered at regular intervals (every two or three weeks) throughout

[57]   Tewfik el Hakim, *Maze of Justice* (London, 1947), pp. 20-21. Twenty piastres are equal to one fifth of an Egyptian pound.

the year. This method of irrigation supports two or more crops annually instead of one, as under the old system.

A variety of fresh technical problems were thus created for the farmer, such as undue salinity of the soil, from inadequate drainage, and soil impoverishment, from overcropping. These developments forced Egyptians to undertake costly drainage projects and to procure expensive chemical fertilizers to compensate for the loss of Nile mud (silt) which, under the old system, used to be spread so lavishly and so effortlessly over their cultivated land. But a far worse difficulty, totally unforeseen, has been created for the peasantry. About 85 per cent of the rural population has become the victim of a serious health problem. Two parasitic intestinal diseases, bilharziasis and ankylostoma, spread by the presence of microscopic snails in fresh-water drainage canals, are prevalent wherever perennial irrigation has displaced basin irrigation. The mortality rate of the fallahin has not been appreciably increased by these diseases, but the general health of the rural community is deteriorating because of their debilitating effects, which result in loss of vitality and lowering of the work capacity of the peasants thus infected.

The fallah has but few joys to compensate him for all the ills his flesh is heir to. A large family is one of these joys, for children are a source of pride and affection – they are blessed in the sight of Allah. Children also are an economic asset, a form of insurance, because they share the work of the farm; even very young children can work in the cotton fields. In his ignorance of economic theory and demographic statistics, the average peasant fails to realize the connection between a large family and agricultural underemployment.

The fallah works extremely hard for only a grudging reward. But still today, as from time immemorial, the life-giving Nile flows by his door and the warm sun of Egypt shines daily on his meager stretch of ancestral soil.

The popular nationalist agitation for the solution of political and economic problems did not comprise the full measure of Egypt's response to the penetration of Western ways. Simultaneously a movement was taking shape which looked to the regeneration of Egyptian society in terms of a reaffirmation of the spiritual traditions of Islam. The political and religious ingredients of both movements were requisite for the launching of the Muslim Brotherhood in 1928. The religious problems raised by the modernization of Egyptian society, and the Islamic reform movements of the late 19th and early 20th centuries, will now be discussed.

III

ISLAM IN MODERN EGYPT

Much has been said in the preceding pages concerning the changes produced in Egypt by foreign political and economic pressures. It is now necessary to stress the general continuity of Egyptian life under those pressures, and the widespread resistance of the indigenous population to change. Since more than nine tenths of the Egyptian people were Muslims, Egypt had indissoluble links with the Arab-Turkish society outside its borders; and its Islamic life continued without interruption, deeply rooted in the past. But inasmuch as the country enjoyed a partial political insulation from the rest of the Ottoman Empire, first on account of the autonomous position of its rulers after the middle of the 19th century, and secondly as a result of the British Occupation after 1882, Egyptian Muslims had built up certain immunities from the encircling pressures of the Ottoman world. And the nature of Egyptian resistance to the West gave the Muslims of Egypt an opportunity for self-expression and made it possible for genuine movements of reform and modernism to develop among them.

Islam is a total way of life based on a comprehensive system of religious law. As dogma became rigid in the Arab world, after the founding of the four schools of orthodox law in the 8th and 9th centuries A.D., the lives of orthodox sedentary Muslims were thenceforth lived within a framework of inexorable legal rigidity.[1] After the Ottoman Turkish conquest of the 16th century, the peoples of the Otto-

---

[1] Dr. Kenneth Cragg has kindly called my attention to the fact that the development of rigidity in dogma was probably due, primarily, to the reaction of the orthodox Ashʿarites (between the early 10th and mid-11th centuries) against the Muʿtazilite rationalists.

man Empire, Turks and Arabs alike, gradually became socially static
and spiritually enervated. Later, during the 18th and 19th centuries,
as Sir Hamilton Gibb has pointed out in his penetrating studies on
modern Islam,[2] two simultaneous developments took place in the
Muslim regions of the Arabs and the Turks.

In the first place, the Ottoman Empire was being subjected to
mounting external pressures by the expansion of western Europe.
Political and economic pressures had their concomitant intellectual
implications, so the Islamic world of the day was slowly penetrated
by Western thought and ideas. As a consequence all exposed Ottoman territories were gradually infiltrated, from their peripheral edges,
by a complex of Western influences stemming mainly from France,
Britain, and Italy. This in turn meant that Arab society, living torpid-
ly within the oppressive political framework of the Ottoman Empire,
was likewise in process of infiltration. And the Western influences
that reached the Arab coastlands eventually began to penetrate unevenly into the interior of the Arab world. Western and Ottoman influences together combined to undermine the moral and religious
fibre of Arab society, already weakened by centuries of demoraliza-
tion. The social standards and religious practices of Arab Muslims
became corrupted – to the extent that their rigid code of behavior
and of religious thought was breaking down under foreign influence.

In the second place, even before these modern foreign penetrations
had become generally perceptible, the austerities of early Islam had
given way to laxities in conduct, though not in law. Primitive pagan-
ism, moreover, had reasserted itself in the Beduin society of Arabia
and a subterranean crisis was in the making in the heartland of
Islam. The first modern movement for Islamic regeneration came
from the sandy depths of 18th-century Arabia, born of an alliance
between Muhammad ibn 'Abd al-Wahhab, a theological scholar, and
the powerful Sa'udi family of the Nejd. This, the first Wahhabi movement, like the later Wahhabi revival of 20th-century Saudi Arabia,
was founded on the puritan fundamentalism of the Hanbalite school,
most literalist of all the four Sunni or orthodox schools of Islam, and

---

[2] H. A. R. Gibb, *Modern Trends in Islam* (Chicago, 1947) and, notably,
chap. x, on "Islam in the Modern World," of his *Mohammedanism: An Historical Survey* (London, 1950).

on the fundamentalist and anti-Sufi (i.e, anti-mystic) teachings of Ibn Taymiyah, the 14th-century religious leader.

The earliest stated objective of the first Wahhabi campaign, launched and led by the Arabs of central Arabia, was to purify Islam, to cleanse Arab society of its laxities, and to restore the Islamic ideal in all its original austerity and simplicity. The Wahhabis in fact initiated a three-pronged movement. They instituted a revolt against the recrudescence of all pre-Islamic pagan practices – notably the revival of primitive animism as well as the worship of saints, tombs, and relics. They led a revolt against the Muslim scholastics, against rationalism, and against all forms of modernism – particularly new social customs such as the use of silk and tobacco. And lastly, they rebelled against the pervasive mystic teachings of the Sufis. The moral religious campaign of the Arabian Wahhabis soon took on political overtones. It finally developed into a full-fledged military campaign against the Turks. The Ottoman Sultan then called upon his Egyptian vassal, Muhammad Ali Pasha, to collaborate in suppressing the rebellion in Arabia. Egyptian armies crushed the Wahhabi revolt, but some individual Egyptians responded to Wahhabi puritanism. Fruitful seeds were sown in the Muslim soil of Egypt, seeds which bore fruit eventually in a new movement for Islamic reform.

The conditions of life in central Arabia were, obviously, not analogous to those in Egypt. But the problems of reform in Sunni Islamic society, whether in Arabia or in Egypt, were strikingly similar. Owing to the intimate connection between theology and law in Islam, the modern orthodox Muslim could not solve his contemporary problems without recourse to the Koran and to the Sacred Law (the Shari'ah), a law inescapably rooted in Koranic principles and precepts.[3]

Egypt in the mid-19th century was ripe for change, and its doors – that faced toward the west as well as toward the east – were opening, however slowly, to a gathering tide of Western influences. As has been explained in the preceding chapters, modernism first came to Egypt in the wake of General Bonaparte's conquering army. Napoleon Bonaparte led a cultural as well as a military invasion in 1798, and when he left Egypt the cultural tide, bringing revolution-

---

[3] For one of the most illuminating studies on this interesting subject see Duncan B. Macdonald, *Development of Muslim Theology, Jurisprudence and Constitutional Theory* (New York, 1926), especially pp. 66-67.

ary ideas as well as some of the scientific and technical achievements of Western civilization, continued to flow from France into Egypt. Muhammad Ali Pasha, the founder of modern Egypt, welcomed this westernizing trend. During the first half of the 19th century he built up his strength with French technical aid and succeeded in destroying the local Mamluk rulers as well as in loosening the political hold of the Ottoman Sultan on Egypt. But in so doing he opened the door to further pressures from the West. The later assault upon Egypt, which began as a commercial and financial invasion of the Egyptian economy, led to the building of the Suez Canal by the French, and culminated in the British Occupation in 1882. British controls established at that time were primarily political and financial; but cultural pressures were inevitably associated with the inauguration of Western forms of administration in Egypt and with the concomitant modernization of life, albeit at the uppermost levels of Egyptian society.

Westernization has been indissolubly linked with power, and this power in the past has brought its benefits with strings attached, under conditions that bound the recipients of those benefits to the chariot wheels of Western empires. The continued presence of the British in Egypt, in the role of protector of Western interests, constituted a cultural threat to the whole Egyptian community. Every old society is naturally resistant to change, owing to a well-developed instinct for self-preservation. Social and economic change, moreover, is strongly resisted by any tradition-bound society wherein is embedded a rich assortment of religious-minority communities – as in Egypt. Islamic law had accorded a special position and certain local autonomies to its various Christian and Jewish minorities; time consecrated their place in Egyptian life, and a peculiarly complex and rigid social pattern consequently emerged. Change of whatever sort threatened to upset the precarious balance established in the whole matrix of that society. Furthermore, where, as in Egypt, the ruling majority is Muslim, any threat to the community represents a challenge to the Faith. When, therefore, the Shari'ah and the Muslim way of life were challenged by the changes implicit in modernism and Western secularism, the whole Islamic community felt itself to be threatened.

Egypt's western door had been forced open by an alien dynasty of westward-looking rulers, the dynasty of Muhammad Ali. The founder of the dynasty and his descendants had been aided and abetted in their program of modernization by a relatively small, though increasingly powerful, community of Western foreigners. But between them all they were capable of influencing or altering only the upper crust of Egyptian society. The will to change the basically medieval conditions of life in Egypt had to come from inside the country, from an awakening of the long-oppressed masses. A static society had to be roused to the need for self-development in a changing world. And inasmuch as more than ninety per cent of the Egyptian people were Muslims, the call to regeneration had to come from a Muslim reformer who was close enough to the people to understand their needs. At this critical time in their history Egyptian Muslims were fortunate to find a champion, a Muslim religious leader of compelling intellectual and moral stature.

This leader and reformer was Shaykh Muhammad ʿAbduh, an Egyptian peasant by origin, a devout Muslim, and a graduate of al-Azhar – most celebrated of all Muslim universities. A man of the people, he fully recognized the dimensions of the problem posed for the Muslim Egyptians of his day.[4] The modernization of life, along Western lines, had been embarked upon by the government of the Khedive – in the generation before him and with the help of the *non*-Muslim communities of Egypt: i.e., the Copts, the Greek and Syrian Christians, the Armenians and the oriental Jews, as well as the increasingly powerful communities of resident Europeans. The vast Muslim majority could not safely, or for its own sake, be left too far behind.

Three courses of action were open to a Muslim reformer in the 19th century. He might try to lead the Muslim community back to puritan fundamentalism – after the manner of the Arabian Wahhabis. He might try to make his peace with Western-based modernism – in a way that would lead to a gradual breakdown of Islamic institutions through secularization. Or, he could attempt to reformulate and re-

---

[4]   C. C. Adams, *Islam and Modernism in Egypt* (London, 1933), includes an authoritative biography of Shaykh Muhammad ʿAbduh, chaps. ii-iv. This book is a classic that has not been superseded. Adams relies heavily upon works by Muhammad Rashid Rida and Mustafa ʿAbd al-Raziq, and also makes use of the journal *al-Manar*, the periodical of the ʿAbduh movement or circle, which contains much information about Muhammad ʿAbduh and the texts of many of his countless articles. The journal was edited by Shaykh Rashid Rida.

interpret the basic principles of Islam in the light of modern rationalist thought – in an effort to reconcile orthodox Islam with the requirements of modern progress. Muhammad 'Abduh perceived clearly these three choices, and he made the third. Perhaps he did not foresee, with equal clarity, the full magnitude of the battle that would have to be fought against the forces of secularization. But in any case he chose to lead his co-religionists toward modernism, and at the same time he tried unfalteringly to preserve the framework of Muslim orthodoxy. He dedicated his whole life to the regeneration of Islam and to the reformation of Egyptian society. In so doing he provided the yeast for the later ferment of reform in 20th-century Egypt.

Shaykh Muhammad 'Abduh, when he came to grips with the problems posed by modernization and progress in 19th-century Egypt, turned for guidance – as had Muhammad ibn 'Abd al-Wahhab before him – to the primary sources of the Islamic religion. But the crucial difference between the two points of view was this: whereas the Wahhabi "reformer" was merely a puritan fundamentalist, essentially a reactionary, seeking vindication in the Koran and the *Sunnah*[5] for the preservation of a static society and a rigid legal system, the Egyptian reformer sought diligently for *new light* in the Koran and the Sunnah and tried to find in them answers to every question posed by the new requirements of living in a rapidly changing world.

If the Egyptian people were fortunate to find a fearless leader in Muhammad 'Aduh, he for his part was fortunate to come under the spell of Sayyid Jamal al-Din al-Afghani in his early, formative years. Until his death, Muhammad 'Abduh acknowledged the greatness of his debt, spiritual and intellectual, to this famous teacher who came into his life at a moment when the young Egyptian was just beginning to comprehend the full dimensions of the reform program needed in Egypt. Jamal al-Din al-Afghani, the founder of the Pan-Islamic

[5]   The Sunnah is the whole corpus embodying the record of the deeds, the words, and the judicial decisions of the Prophet Muhammad – i.e., the custom, or the usage, of the earliest Islamic community. Most of the Sunnah was first handed down by oral transmission. When the Sunnah was recorded in writing, as it all was eventually, it came to be known as the Hadith (each individual *hadith* contained a text with a statement of the "chain of authorities," the *sanad*, on which it rested). The Sunni, or Sunni Muslims, are so called because they are followers of the Sunnah.

movement, visited Egypt in the 1870's in the course of his missionary travels through the Islamic world. Once established in Egypt, he gathered around him a receptive group of Egyptians – Muslim liberals and intellectuals – who sat at his feet and became his devout disciples. To them all, and Muhammad 'Abduh was the most distinguished among them, Jamal al-Din expounded his new politico-religious philosophy. Egyptian Islamic modernism, in contradistinction to the secular modernist movement in Egypt, was born in these gatherings and in the discussions presided over by this inspired Muslim teacher. The fundamentals of the Pan-Islamic movement, as taught by Jamal al-Din, included a dual program: the rigorous purification of religious belief and practice – not necessarily along strictly fundamentalist lines – and the political union of all Muslims in defense of Islam.

When Sayyid Jamal al-Din al-Afghani finally left the country at the command of the Khedive, Shaykh Muhammad 'Abduh assumed the Muslim leadership in Egypt. But Muhammad 'Abduh, even though he later worked closely with Jamal al-Din in Paris, was not in full agreement with him on all points. Shaykh Muhammad was a man of different temperament and practical experience; and experience taught him the wisdom of being a gradualist. In addition to being a revered teacher and a far more prolific writer than Jamal al-Din, he participated fully in the public life of his own country. Muhammad 'Abduh was one of the Ulama of the University of al-Azhar.[6] Before 1882 he was editor-in-chief of the official gazette of the government of Egypt and he later founded a literary society. During a short exile, imposed because of his association with the leaders of the revolt of 1882, Muhammad 'Abduh taught in Beirut, Lebanon, and traveled widely in Syria and in the African parts of the Ottoman Empire. He also spent a year in Paris, where he collaborated with Sayyid Jamal al-Din in publishing the first international periodical of the Pan-Islamic movement.[7] Upon his return to Egypt

[6]   The Ulama are the learned doctors, accredited in Islamic theology, law, and jurisprudence.

[7]   This famous periodical was called al-ʿUrwah al-Wuthqa [The Indissoluble Bond]. It began publication in Paris on March 13, 1884; it was suppressed on October 16, 1884. Al-ʿUrwah al-Wuthqa was the organ of a secret Pan-Islamic society of the same name. The eighteen issues of this journal "exerted a very great influence throughout the Muslim world." See Adams, op cit., p. 9 (in-

in 1888 Shaykh Muhammad ʿAbduh served as a judge, organized the first Islamic Benevolent Society, and eventually became an influential and active member of the national Legislative Council. He also devoted a great deal of time and energy to an extensive program of reform in the administration and the curriculum of al-Azhar University. Finally, a crowning honor in the last six years of his life (1899-1905), he held the office of Mufti, or Jurisconsult, of all Egypt. In this position he was the supreme official interpreter of the Law of Islam. It was in fact the multiplicity of his activities and the variety of his contacts that inspired this great Muslim with the conviction that reforms were desperately needed in every branch of Egyptian life and at every social level.

Shaykh Muhammad ʿAbduh became, therefore, an impassioned advocate of religious reform in order to achieve the total reform and regeneration of Islamic and Egyptian society. To his mind, the Prophet never intended that Islam should be static or incapable of progress. Once the true spirit of the Koran was clearly perceived, and once Islamic doctrine was intelligently restated and properly interpreted (i.e., reformulated, in the light of modern thought), he believed that the door of Islamic civilization would open to every kind of social and economic reform as well as to cultural advancement. His conviction was unshakable that Islam, if rightly understood and interpreted, could provide complete answers to every requirement of modern life.

At the same time, Muhammad ʿAbduh had the wisdom to insist upon separating the religious and political reform movements – being fully cognizant through his own experience of the distracting influence and the disruptive effects of revolutionary activities. He did not wish to achieve reform or to make changes in Egyptian life by means of war or political revolution. He perceived the pitfall of political nationalism, and he warned against the attendant dangers of xenophobia. In this outlook he proved to be more farsighted than Jamal al-Din. Their ideals and their ultimate objectives were the same, but their emphases were different and they advocated divergent paths for

cluding note 5), and pp. 178-179. See also Jamal Mohammed Ahmed, *The Intellectual Origins of Egyptian Nationalism* (London and New York, 1960), pp. 27-29.

traveling toward these distant goals. Muhammad ʿAbduh had been the Cassandra of Arabi's revolt in 1882 against the Khedive Ismail. When that military enterprise failed and brought on the occupation of Egypt by a foreign power – as he had predicted – Shaykh Muhammad was confirmed in his conviction that political change could only follow (not precede) intellectual, social, and economic change. For the sake of peace and stability in his country, and for the sake of an opportunity to work constructively for the regeneration of Egyptian society, he collaborated fully with the Occupation government. In his own words, he "estimated at its true value the freedom which it made possible."

Theologically and intellectually, however, Muhammad ʿAbduh was a revolutionary. He placed implicit reliance on the role of reason in religious thought; as a corollary, he proclaimed the necessity of reopening "The Gate of Interpretation" of the Shariʿah through restoration of the right of individual interpretation (Ijtihad).[8] He was confident that the spiritual values and the religious truths of Islam would be vindicated, rather than undermined, by reason and "science" and modern thought. Wherefore he shared with Jamal al-Din al-Afghani a tremendous enthusiasm for the modernization of education.

ʿAbduh's thinking on this issue was in the idiom of the age, typical of Western thought to which he was intellectually responsive – an age rendered buoyantly optimistic by faith in the infallibility of reason and belief in the perfectibility of man. His position in an Islamic context was roughly as follows: God (Allah) had created a universe which functioned according to divine laws. Allah had also given man a Holy Book (the Koran) for the guidance of the Faithful on earth. Furthermore, Allah had endowed man with reason and commanded him to seek knowledge. It was impossible therefore that any scientific truth which could be established by reason should be at variance

[8] Ijtihad is the right of individual (personal) interpretation of the Qurʿan (Koran) and the Shariʿah (Sacred Law) by any ʿalim. The latter word is the singular form of ʿUlama. The right of Ijtihad was disallowed in theory after the beginning of the 10th century and entirely forbidden after the 16th century. – For a revealing discussion of the modern concept of Ijtihad – its legal role in the initiation of valid changes in Islamic society, and "as a means to an ultimate consensus (Ijmaʿ)" to sanction such change – see Kenneth Cragg, The Call of the Minaret (New York, 1956), pp. 147-150.

with any of God's words; it was equally inconceivable that any scientifically established truth should lead man to contravene His commandments. If science were to uncover any seeming incompatibility, it could only mean that man had misunderstood God's meaning and misinterpreted the Koran. Hence 'Abduh's insistence upon reopening "The Gate of Interpretation." As he pointed out, with ultimate logic, the Prophet Muhammad alone was the fountainhead of authority, and he had never set a time limit to the legitimate exercise of the right of *Ijtihad*; it was the later, medieval scholastic Ulama group who had arbitrarily closed the Gate to the Interpretation of God's will as set forth in the Koran.

Possibly, as some of his critics suggest, Muhammad 'Abduh did not fully understand the true nature of scientific inquiry or the ever moving frontiers of science. Possibly also he was unaware of the full implications of free investigation. But he was a man of acute intelligence and wide knowledge. He may have made an imaginative comparison between the progressive interpretation of the Koran, in the light of modern knowledge, and the process of scientific inquiry. His very effort to understand Darwinian evolutionary theory would suggest a parallel to his mind for the diligent exercise of the reinterpretive initiative to solve the problems which confronted Muslims at the dawn of the 20th century. He might well have believed that a systematic reinterpretation of the verses (suras) of the Koran could keep pace with the new science and uncover meanings in Koranic dicta hitherto unperceived.

Certain questions raised by modern science (circa 1900) and the principles of natural law, that is to say the laws of God in human history and in nature, were, in 'Abduh's view, capable of reconciliation with the teachings of the Prophet. For example, his attempt to reconcile certain suras in the Koran with Darwinian principles of evolution and to harmonize Western concepts of natural law with phrases which occur more than once in the Koran on "the Usage, or Custom (Sunnah) of God." At all events, it was 'Abduh's "firm conviction that the spirit of Islam, as truly conceived, was tolerant of all scientific investigation." [9] Muhammad 'Abduh initiated what amount-

---

[9]   Adams, *op. cit.*, pp. 140, 142. For a somewhat different approach to Muhammad 'Abduh see Nadav Safran, *Egypt in Search of Political Community* (Cambridge, Mass., 1961), pp. 62-75. Safran, however, shares the view of

ed to a crusade for the study of the modern sciences in Egypt. "Religion will take Science by the hand," he wrote, to fulfill "God's promise to make His light complete." And elsewhere he stated that "God has sent down two books: one created, which is nature, and one revealed, which is the Koran." [10] Admittedly, ʿAbduh's knowledge of the development of science and medicine in his day was superficial, but his mind was imaginatively responsive to the need for scientific study and the uses to which it could be put. He made a valiant effort to harmonize the most significant of the new scientific principles with the relevant verses in the Koran; and, through the exercise of the right of *Ijtihad*, he rejected certain currently accepted interpretations of Koranic verses on the ground that they were post-Koranic Traditions and therefore susceptible of error.

Shaykh Muhammad ʿAbduh lost no opportunity, as a teacher, as judge and Mufti of Egypt, and as a writer, to propagate his comprehensive Islamic reform program. For the complete regeneration of Islamic society, he pinned his faith to education – better education and more of it. He ardently desired to promote education among the masses, and his long-range purpose was to train up a new generation of Muslims who would be sufficiently educated to support and carry forward the reforms which he was in process of initiating, so that Islam in general and Egypt in particular would become respected among the nations of the earth. ʿAbduh sought first to reform higher education in order to train more qualified teachers. He also advocated the socially revolutionary step of educating Muslim girls as well as boys, and he tried to improve the general position of Muslim

---

Adams and others that Muhammad ʿAbduh "liberated man from the shackles of traditional religion, reaffirmed more emphatically man's moral responsibility, and dealt a blow to the spirit of passiveness" (p. 70).

[10]   As quoted in Adams, *op. cit.*, pp. 135-136. ʿAbduh extended his arguments, or rather his plea for scientific studies, by pointing out that it was the duty of Muslims to perfect themselves in the technical sciences for the express purpose of military preparedness in defense of Islam. He cited the Koran (sura viii) and stated that "One must rival them [i.e., the peoples potentially hostile to Muslims] in our time in the manufacture of cannon and rifles, of warships and airships, and other kinds of implements of war." (*Ibid.*, p. 136). In other words, Muslims should no longer fall a prey to other nations through their own ignorance and inability to cope with them. In support of this line of reasoning ʿAbduh cited the new scientific "law" of natural selection or survival of the fittest. Fr a dscussion of ʿAbduh's views on science and the importance of scientific studies see, *ibid.*, pp. 134-143.

women. He realized that uneducated Muslim women would continue to constitute a reactionary influence in the home life of Egypt's men. He fought long and hard for the reform of al-Azhar, that this great theological center of learning might become the intellectual lighthouse (al-Manar), nor only for Egypt, but for the whole Muslim world.

As a teacher of history in Dar al-ʿUlum, as a teacher of the Arabic language and literature in the Khedivial School of Languages, and for many years as a theologian in the University of al-Azhar, ʿAbduh sought to modernize teaching methods, to de-emphasize learning by rote, and to introduce new subjects and new authors into the curriculum. In his own teaching, his emphasis was upon character development, Muslim ethics, and training in the principles of government. He based his lectures on political science primarily upon Guizot's History of Civilization;[11] but he drew upon Ibn Khaldun, the great 14th-century philosopher of history, for his concept of the evolution of Muslim society, and he added significant contributions and interpretations of his own. His method of teaching, in his lectures on Ibn Khaldun, constituted a new departure in Egypt, and he gave the first example of the use of the historical method in formal teaching. In his approach to modern critical methods, ʿAbduh was unique among Muslim scholars of his day.[12]

In 1895 Shaykh Muhammad ʿAbduh became a member and the moving spirit of the "Administrative Committee for al-Azhar," newly appointed by the Khedive. Under his leadership plans were projected for radical university reforms: plans to improve the living conditions of faculty and students alike, to raise and standardize faculty salaries, to require annual examinations of students and special examinations for teaching diplomas, to double the length of the teaching sessions (from four months of the year to eight), to improve the sanitary arrangements and install a system of running water for the ritual ablutions, to organize and expand the libraries, to change and expand the curriculum. Mathematics, Islamic history, grammatical studies, and

[11] Guizot's History was translated into Arabic about 1876, or just before that year.
[12] Adams, op. cit., pp. 39-40, 44-45. Muhammad ʿAbduh suggested, without success, the introduction of the Prolegomena of Ibn Khaldun into the curriculum of al-Azhar. Ibid., p. 71, citing the periodical of the ʿAbduh movement, al-Manar.

geography were to be added to the traditional theological subjects. A fine basic library, assembled by Muhammad 'Abduh and classified by him and his disciples, became the first central library of the University of al-Azhar. As long as Shaykh Muhammad had the active support of the Khedive, his plans prospered, because there was a group of liberal Azhar Shaykhs who supported his objectives. But when the attitude of the Khedive changed and he became determinedly opposed to a reform program for al-Azhar, 'Abduh's hands were tied. The conservative majority of Azhar Shaykhs were then enabled to block the implementation of his projected reforms, and he resigned from the Azhar Committee just before his death. Consequently most of 'Abduh's liberalizing reforms did not materialize until after the First World War, and the Azhar long remained a bastion of conservatism. Radical changes – such as the teaching of philosophy and of a European foreign language (English) – were not introduced into the curriculum until after the comprehensive reorganization of al-Azhar as a genuine university of higher studies between 1930 and 1936, under King Fuad's sponsorship. The teaching of psychology and an Oriental language were added still later, as were Islamic history, sociology, modern logic, comparative literature, and new courses in Islamic law and jurisprudence.[13] The later addition of these courses together with eventual modernization of the University represented the actual fulfillment of 'Abduh's work for the expansion and reorganization of the graduate and postgraduate curriculum of al-Azhar. And so likewise did the subsequent increase in the number of al-Azhar's preparatory Religious Institutes (elementary and secondary schools for the undergraduate colleges of al-Azhar) and their greatly expanded curricula.

[13] *Ibid.*, pp. 70-78; Bayard Dodge, *Al-Azhar; A Millennium of Muslim Learning* (Washington, D.C., 1961), pp. 150-153, Appendix VI, and chap. vii, *passim.* – The secondary-school course of the twenty-two Religious Institutes of al-Azhar included, by 1959, courses on civics, history, geography, the English language, three sciences (physics, chemistry, biology), and military training. In addition to the twenty-two Institutes for elementary and secondary education, which are "conducted as an integral part of the system of al-Azhar," there are today seventeen "Free Institutes" for elementary education which are affiliated with the Azhar. *Ibid.*, p. 159 and Appendix VI.

Shaykh Mahmud Shaltut, identified as a reform Shaykh of the Azhar in 1931 and dismissed at that time because he advocated reform, eventually became the Rector of al-Azhar six years after the Revolution of 1952. *Ibid.*, p. 148.

Throughout his life, Shaykh Muhammad 'Abduh – known to his disciples as "The Imam" – did a great deal of informal as well as formal teaching. Hundreds of Egyptians and Muslim visitors to Egypt crowded the stimulating discussion groups which he held in the evenings in his own home. His home was an open house for all who wanted to ask questions of him, or to hear his extempore lectures on Islam and Islamic problems of the day.

Ancillary to his educational activities, 'Abduh also sought popular support for his earlier efforts to inspire a renaissance of the Arabic language and literature. This could not be done without a precise knowledge of Arabic and its multitudinous linguistic nuances: "A people who does not concern itself with the niceties of its language invites the death of its intellectual life." [14] Therefore Shaykh Muhammad founded and presided over a literary society. His crusade for the re-education of Muslims – in order to equip Islamic society for the responsibilities of freedom – carried forward the pioneer work of al-Tahtawi and his early 19th-century group for the revival of correct usage of the Arabic language.

As a writer, 'Abduh was a fine stylist, and he took the lead in establishing a high standard for Arabic prose writing from the day he was appointed editor-in-chief of the official gazette of the government of Egypt. He was the author of fifteen published and a number of unpublished books, and of countless articles in the press and in periodicals; in all of them, the literary quality of his writings was exemplary. Shaykh Muhammad's published books, though principally concerned with theology, included also works on Arabic philology and rhetoric, a translation from the Persian of Jamal al-Din's famous "Refutation of the Materialists," and a "Report on Reform of the Shari'ah Courts." One of his unpublished manuscripts was a translation from the French edition of Herbert Spencer's work on education. His two major published theological works, the "Treatise on the Unity of God" (*Risalat al-Tawhid*) and his commentary on the Koran were influential and celebrated. The *Risalat*, based upon theological lectures which he delivered in Beirut while in exile from Egypt, was an exposition of the essence, or the principles, of Islam, prefaced by a critical survey of the historical development of Islamic dogma. It

[14] Jamal Mohammed Ahmed, *op. cit.*, p. 40, citing Rashid Rida on Muhammad 'Abduh, *Tarikh*, ii, 643-645.

was a succinct work, written in simple language for the purpose of illuminating Islam and making it easily comprehensible to the Muslim masses. His commentary on the Koran, though unfinished when he died, broke new ground for the religious reformers and gave many concrete examples of his wisdom and skill in the method of critical interpretation. These writings were soon translated into such languages as Urdu, Malayan, Turkish, and French.[15]

Finally, through his judicial work in the courts of the Native Tribunals, in association with European judges, Muhammad ʿAbduh gave new emphasis to the principles of equity and justice in order to promote the public weal. And as Mufti of Egypt, he gave the office added dignity and importance. His predecessors in office, as supreme official interpreters of the Law of Islam (the Shariʿah), had given an official "opinion" or decision (*fatwa*) only to government departments and upon their request. ʿAbduh, however, entertained requests for opinions from individual Egyptians and from Muslims of other parts of the Islamic world. His fatwas became famous at home and abroad, and many of them initiated reforms in Egypt that were socially or economically desirable. (The influence of two of his most important fatwas is discussed later.) His duties as Mufti included supervision of all the Shariʿah courts in Egypt, and membership in the Superior Council of the Waqfs (Religious Endowments) Administration. And immediately after his appointment as Mufti, ʿAbduh was appointed a permanent member of the Legislative Council. To all of his official duties Shaykh Muhammad gave unremitting, detailed attention and devoted service.[16] In every public office he was a notable personality. Nonetheless, public service was but one facet

[15] Adams, *op. cit.*, pp. 95, 101, 110-114, 131-133, and, for an annotated list of ʿAbduh's published and unpublished works, 271-274.

[16] *Ibid.*, pp. 79-83. Four separate judicial systems operated concurrently in Egypt before the First World War: in addition to the indigenous Religious Courts, there were Consular Courts, the Mixed Courts established in 1875, and the Native Tribunals established in 1883. *Ibid.*, p. 68 (note 4) to p. 70. Three codes, two civil and one penal, were promulgated for the Mixed Courts and the Native Tribunals to apply. "These codes represented extensive adoptions of the Napoleonic legislation, although the [two] civil codes included a number of sections drawn instead from the Shariʿa . . . It was in fact provided in the Egyptian code that no Muslim should be executed until the Mufti had been consulted as to whether the death penalty was applicable in such circumstance under the Shariʿa, while it was also expressly stated that this code must not be held to nullify any private right sanctioned thereby."

of his life's work, which was dedicated to the betterment of Islamic society as a totality.

The concrete reform projects advanced by Muhammad ʿAbduh in al-Azhar University are illustrative of the genius of the man for practical planning in execution of his purposes. When very young he had begun his career as a Sufi theologian-philosopher, a mystic detached from the world of action, and this speculative introduction to theology served him well in adult life. But once he came under the activist influence of Jamal al-Din al-Afghani, ʿAbduh lived wholly in the world of his day and acknowledged the overriding claims upon him of his Muslim contemporaries. All the resources of his great store of moral strength and intellectual vitality were mobilized in their service and dedicated to the achievement of reforms in Islamic society. He identified the problems that faced him and his people with a clear vision, and then he proceeded to work out practical measures to solve them, one by one.

The renowned English scholar E. G. Browne, an authority on Persia and the biographer of Jamal al-Din al-Afghani, paid eloquent tribute to this first Egyptian reformer at the time of his premature death. He mourned the death of Shaykh Muhammad ʿAbduh in the following words:

During my lifetime I have seen many lands and many peoples. But I have never seen one like the deceased, whether in the East or in the West. For indeed he was unique in his scholarship, unique in piety and reverence, unique in his insight and comprehension, not only of the external appearances of matters but also of their inner significance, unique in his perseverance and the sincerity of his motives, unique in his eloquence and fluency, scholar, man of practical affairs, benefactor, one who feared God and did his utmost in his service, a lover of learning and a haven to the poor and needy.[17]

Another contemporary writer said of Muhammad ʿAbduh: "He died in the midst of the breaking of the new day which his doctrines

---

J. N. D. Anderson, *Islamic Law in the Modern World* (New York, 1959), p. 22. – By the last quarter of the nineteenth century, the Shariʿah courts were "restricted to questions of personal status and family law." *Ibid.*

[17] Written in Arabic by Professor Browne to the brother of Muhammad ʿAbduh, in a letter of condolence. Quoted by Adams, *op. cit.*, p. 101, note 2.

and principles have brought to pass in the Muslim world." [18]

So long as Muhammad 'Abduh lived, the force of his personality and the prestige he commanded enabled him to head a comprehensive reform movement. But when he died, in 1905, no single leader succeeded him, and his total reform program broke up into its component parts and was carried on under the auspices of diverse reformers. For example, Shaykh Rashid Rida headed the movement for religious and theological reform, and Qasim Amin founded the feminist movement and advocated wider education for all Muslim women. Amin's book on the emancipation of woman, the first work in Arabic on that subject, was inspired by Muhammad 'Abduh.

Ardent political nationalists, who had begun to undermine the influence of the great Shaykh even during his lifetime, took over the leadership of Egypt's youth, and hot-blooded counsels prevailed. Mustafa Kamil, the fiery and influential young journalist who organized the first popular anti-British campaign, was pre-eminent among these leaders. He and Shaykh Muhammad 'Abduh were opposites in their manners as in their outlook on life, and they were mutually antipathetic. Mustafa Kamil and his group, increasingly resentful of Great Britain's continued occupation of Egypt, became skilled political agitators. They looked back for their inspiration to Jamal al-Din and his revolutionary activism, rather than to Muhammad 'Abduh and his gradualism. The latter even became discredited in their eyes because he had collaborated with the Occupation government. But they also differed fundamentally from Jamal al-Din in their emphasis on Western education and on the Western concept of nationalism. The founder of the Pan-Islamic movement had sought to revive the power and the glory of the whole Islamic world; the focus of Jamal al-Din's teachings had been concentrated upon the political rehabilitation of Islam; and his nationalism, based entirely on religion, comprised a movement to restore the dignity and the political power of all Muslims in every Muslim country.

Mustafa Kamil and his followers, on the other hand, all Western-educated, conceived of nationalism on Western lines, as based on the Egyptian people rather than on religion. Their longing for the complete and unqualified independence of Egypt became an intolerable thirst, so that gradually the universal, horizontal Pan-Islamic ideal of

[18] *Ibid.*, p. 103.

Jamal al-Din was narrowed – almost obliterated, in fact – to accommodate the exigencies of vertical Egyptian nationalism. Mustafa Kamil died prematurely, but he handed on his nationalist torch to Muhammad Farid. And eventually, after the First World War left a churning wake of bitterness and frustration, Sa'd Zaghlul Pasha became the spokesman for Egypt's nationalists. Sa'd Zaghlul had begun his political career as a disciple of Muhammad 'Abduh, and in his early years he also had collaborated with the government of the Occupation. But during the war he embraced the new nationalism, and afterward he became the founder and the distinguished leader of the Wafd Party – a party that included almost all nationalist Egyptians, and in which Muslims and Christian Copts co-operated fully and effectively.

The Egypt of 1928, however, had changed greatly in less than fifty years. The political status of Egypt was equivocal, but after 1922 it was independent in name and autonomous with respect to most of its internal affairs, though still "protected" by Great Britain and still saddled with Western judicial procedures for its foreign residents. The British Occupation had served to accelerate those social and economic changes that were a natural concomitant of Western penetration. And Egypt, historically the meeting place of Western and Eastern cultures, was in the throes of modernization – a revolutionary process that had been gaining strength and momentum from the early 19th-century days of Muhammad Ali Pasha. Egyptians, moreover, had actively collaborated in this revolution; they had – at least, many of them – met modernism more than halfway. Shaykh Muhammad 'Abduh had encouraged his countrymen to implement reforms that could best be accomplished through a gradual modernization of their society, although he stipulated that these reforms should be achieved within the framework or orthodox Islam. And the political nationalists who came after him were busy striving for the establishment of a sovereign national state – a purely Western concept.

Modernism in Egypt in the 1920's included public education, supported and supervised by the state – but paralleled by the traditional system of religious education presided over by the University Mosque of al-Azhar and the mosque schools; mechanized transportation, on land and water and in the air; and the development of intellectual communications – notably through a flourishing Arabic, French, and English press – and the use of the telephone, telegraph, and radio.[19] Most important of all, the Shariʿah, the inviolable religious law of Islam, was being supplemented by new codes of civil and criminal law based on Western models.

Strict Muslims were preoccupied by the existence of many innovations or, rather, changes in Islamic custom. The following examples of change were to them especially significant. A national bank had been founded. Its establishment was a direct result of one of Muhammad ʿAbduh's notable decisions: he had handed down a fatwa, or judicial opinion, declaring it lawful for Muslims to deposit their money in postal savings banks where it would draw interest. This was a revolutionary decision because the payment of interest by or to a Muslim had been adjudged illegal through the centuries. Most upper-class Muslim men wore European dress in the 1920's, and this change also had been first sanctioned by a fatwa of Muhammad ʿAbduh. Young Muslim women had begun to associate publicly with men – e.g., in the state university and in some of the professions – and even the older women were beginning to discard the veil.[20]

In the very important matter of child marriage, an ingenious solution of the problem had been worked out. Because the Prophet Muhammad had married Aʿisha when she was a child, child marriage was a legitimate Islamic practice. So the Egyptians, recognizing that child

---

[19] See Le Groupe d'Etudes de l'Islam, *L'Egypte Indépendante* (= Publication No. 7 of the Centre d'Etudes de Politique Etrangère) (Paris, 1938). A long section in this book (pp. 369-456) is devoted to a historical and qualitative analysis of the press in Egypt. The "variety and power" of its many newspapers is well documented. – In 1937 some 200 morning and evening dailies, weeklies and monthlies were published in Arabic in Cairo, as well as 65 papers in eight different foreign languages. In Alexandria and nine other cities 58 Arabic and 35 foreign-language papers were published (pp. 398-400). The great majority of the latter were in French. An annotated list of all the Arabic and foreign-language papers published in Egypt in 1937 is appended to the text (pp. 415-456). – For a sparkling resumé of the whole interwar period and the general repercussions of modernism on Egyptian society see Marcel Colombe, *L'Evolution de L'Egypte 1924-1950* (Paris, 1951), Part III, "L'évolution des idées et de la société de 1924 à 1944," pp. 120-221. – For an authoritative discussion of the repercussions of modernism on Egyptian Islamic life see H. A. R. Gibb, *Mohammedanism: An Historical Survey* (London-New York, 1950), chap. x, on "Islam in the Modern World," pp. 165-191.
[20] The wearing of the veil by women had been customary for centuries, but this custom actually had a social, not a religious origin.

marriage was socially undesirable in modern Egypt, decided to by-pass the issue of legality and render this custom completely imprac-tical. In 1923 it was decreed that courts must refrain from giving a hearing to any action (except a paternity claim) wherein the age of the wife was under sixteen years and that of the husband under eigh-teen years at the time of marriage, and officials were forbidden to register marriages of young people under these ages. In other words, justice was denied to people who acted contrary to what was felt to be the public good, and those who so acted did so at their own risk. In such cases all divorce, marriage-settlement, and inheritance suits were to be automatically thrown out of court. Other socio-religious questions, such as the desirability of restricting divorce, were raised and debated publicly.[21]

Ultraconservative orthodox Muslims became increasingly critical of the spate of changes and the westernizing influences that had in-filtrated the Egypt of their day. Many resisted secularizing innova-tions, and some declined wholly to accept changes that struck at their socio-religious customs. Some strict Muslims, for example, would lend money, or even deposit their money in banks, but would refuse to draw interest. The naturally conservative elements of al-Azhar, notably a majority of the elite group of theologians represented by the Ulama, had resisted the liberalism of Shaykh Muhammad 'Ab-duh. This majority never ceased to resist change, and al-Azhar re-mained a bastion of conservatism.[22]

Another strong religious group of the day, the Salafiyyah, provides

[21]   See Alfred Guillaume, *Islam* (London, 1954), pp. 166-179, for an interest-ing discussion of the whole problem of legal modernization in Egypt. See also Anderson, *op. cit., passim*, and chapters on the reconciliation of Islamic law and modern life in the Middle East, the Islamic law of marriage and divorce, and inheritance. In outlining contemporary legal trends in the Muslim world, Anderson emphasizes increasing use of the "device of refusing any judicial recognition, or enforcement" of Shari'ah principles to laws which would inter-fere with the introduction of essential reforms – e.g., prohibition of child mar-riage, polygamy, and the husband's rights to "unfettered" divorce (pp. 91, 93).
[22]   Dr. Taha Hussein, who was a student at the University of al-Azhar at the time of Muhammad 'Abduh's death, observed that "the men who mourned sincerely for the Imam did not wear turbans, but tarbushes" – in other words, his sincere mourners were to be found among the lay intelligentsia. Taha Hussein, *The Stream of Days* (London, 1948), p. 105. For further con-firmation of the unchanging outlook of the Ulama on modernism see also Gibb, *op. cit.*, p. 174.

a striking illustration of the abrasive pressures exerted by the puritan reactionaries. The Salafiyyah movement had been founded after 1905 by Shaykh Rashid Rida, devoted disciple as well as biographer of Shaykh Muhammad 'Abduh, to carry forward the religious reformation inaugurated by the latter. Under Rashid Rida's editorship the Salafiyyah reformist journal, *al-Manar* ("The Lighthouse"), espoused the Pan-Islamic program of Sayyid Jamal al-Din al-Afghani and built up a circulation from Morocco to the East Indies.[23] But Rashid Rida was driven deeper and deeper into fundamentalism, propelled initially by the shock caused him by the overthrow of the Caliphate and the laicization of the Turkish government after the First World War.[24] And by 1928 the Salafiyyah group, though holding hard to the principle of *Ijtihad* and the reopening of "The Gate of Interpretation," had admittedly become "Neo-Hanbalite." They acknowledged their spiritual affinity with the puritan Wahhabis, and they were antipathetic to Western liberalism and rationalism as well as hostile to Sufism and saint worship.

The more deeply Egypt was penetrated by westernism and by secularism, the more firmly did Muslim reactionaries oppose westernization. They took fright, closed their ranks, and sought to protect their time-honored traditions. In the opinion of some modern Egyptian Muslims, too many foreign-inspired laws were introduced into Egypt too fast for the absorbtive capacity of its peoples. The Shari'ah was in great part superseded, rather than merely supplemented, by the new civil and criminal codes. The lawmakers of the Khedivial period had been preoccupied with establishing a modus vivendi with foreign states; and even before 1914 European civil law, especially French, was being taught in the Law School. A majority of Western-educated Egyptian lawyers wrote the Egyptian constitution of 1923. The resultant social and economic changes in Egyptian life could not be absorbed, at an equal rate of speed, by the three divergent groups of intellectuals – namely, the secularized Egyptians (including many non-Muslims), the liberal Muslim reformers, and the Muslim reactionaries. Therefore systematic planning for the social and eco-

[23] *Al-Manar* was established by Rashid Rida in 1898, before the death of Muhammad 'Abduh. After the founding of the Salafiyyah group, *al-Manar*, like its editor, became increasingly fundamentalist.
[24] See, below, p. 134.

nomic needs of modern life began to give way to a form of intellectual anarchy. Muslim modernists generally made little distinction between Muslim conservatives and reactionaries. They felt that for all practical purposes both of these groups lived in the past and that there was no clear line of demarcation between them because their ideals and their objectives overlapped and complemented each other.

What really happened, intellectually speaking, was this: the political nationalists, beginning with Mustafa Kamil, irresistibly usurped the national stage. They demanded that priority for both thought and action be given to purely political and nationalist problems – and no one can deny that there was a plethora of them. The First World War, followed by the general insurrection of 1919, played into their hands. It was possible to convince almost everyone that no basic religious or social reforms could be undertaken by Egyptians until the British Occupation was ended. And simultaneously religious reformers such as Rashid Rida lost sight of the fact, constantly stressed by Muhammad 'Abduh, that no genuine reforms of any kind could be brought about without a root-and-branch overhauling of the religious law. Piecemeal legislation and palliatives were consequently introduced into Egyptian life in an effort to cope with the more out-of-date anomalies. Meanwhile the secularization of urban life proceeded rapidly. The religious reform groups concentrated more and more upon purely theological speculations, and many of them – like the Salafiyyah – were pushed farther and farther into fundamentalism. The growing Neo-Hanbalite cast of thinking of the strict orthodox Muslims was a natural result of the contemporary political preoccupations and the visible permeability of their urban society by secularization, coupled with an obsessive determination to uphold and defend the integrity of the Faith.

The net result of these conflicting tendencies was a temporary bypassing – rather than any outright rejection – of the gradualist philosophy of Muhammad 'Abduh. The total reformation of Islamic society was too difficult to contemplate in the years immediately after 1919. And, up to the period of political assuagement that followed the signing of the Anglo-Egyptian treaty of 1936, the political nationalists held the stage and commanded the loyalty of Egyptian patriots. Political action – almost any *action*, for that matter – is preferred by the young and the ardent to deliberation and slow-moving reforms.

The quality of patience is at a discount. The Egyptian generation that came of age after the First World War therefore demanded action – whether in the form of public demonstrations, fiery nationalist speeches in the Chamber of Deputies, or underground (anti-British) "plots." The teachings of Jamal al-Din al-Afghani were revived and his philosophy of political activism, interwoven with religious fundamentalism, held paramount sway. Muhammad 'Abduh, the leader who had been able to keep public attention focused, if not riveted, upon a total reform program – the reform of Islamic law and society – as a prerequisite to political regeneration, was no longer with them. His counsels of moderation were swept aside in the turmoils of 1919. His liberal rationalism was held, at least by orthodox religious leaders of the 1920's, to be a threat to the integrity of Islam. So it was that the movement which he had inaugurated to reformulate and reinterpret the principles of Islam in the light of the requirements of modern living, to reshape Egyptian Muslim society within the framework of orthodox Islam, was halted.

In 1926 Cairo became the scene of an emotionally charged crisis in Muslim world affairs. The Caliphate, an institution which had been an organic part of Islamic life for thirteen centuries, had been abruptly and unilaterally abolished by the Muslim Turks.

The Caliphate was by origin an Arab Islamic politico-religious institution founded immediately after the death of the Prophet Muhammad. Under the Umayyad Caliphs of Damascus and the early Abbasid Caliphs of Baghdad, the Islamic Arabs attained their greatest territorial dominion – from Morocco to India – and achieved cultural supremacy in what is now known as the Near and Middle East. The office of the Caliphate was essentially a political one, but the bases of the authority of the Caliph were primarily religious. The Caliphs were the "Successors" of the Prophet; they wielded the sword of Islam and were the defenders of the Faith. At the same time, the Caliphs were bound by the Sacred Law of Islam which, in theory, they could neither interpret nor modify in any respect. But since it was their responsibility to see that the Islamic Law was upheld and generally observed, they were entitled to claim unqualified obedience from all Muslims – so long as they themselves acted in accordance with the Law.[25]

[25] For a clear, brief statement on the Caliphate see, in H. A. R. Gibb (ed.),

When the Muslim Ottoman Turks conquered the Arabs in the 16th century, the Caliphate became a Turkish office and was held by Turkish Sultans for four hundred years. In 1924 Republican Turkey abolished the Caliphate and disestablished Islam as a state religion. Endless complications, technical as well as ideological, were thus created for the Muslim world community. It was decided to convoke a congress to discuss these problems and to determine the feasibility of restoring the institution of the Caliphate and the choosing of a new Caliph.

In May, 1926, a general Islamic Congress on the Caliphate (*Mu'tamar al-Khilafah*) assembled in Cairo. Thirty-eight delegates from independent Muslim countries and from Muslim communities under foreign domination debated for a week, under the presidency of the Rector of al-Azhar. One third of the members of this Congress were Egyptian Ulama; the rest came from as far away as Poland, South Africa, and the East Indies. They came, of course, most numerously from the Arab world, and Palestine alone sent half of the non-Egyptian delegates. All four Sunni (orthodox) schools of Islam participated in the work of the Congress, and a Shi'i Muslim from Persia attended as an observer.

Six questions were formulated and debated: the nature of the Caliphate, its necessity in Islam, the method of choosing a Caliph, the feasibility of restoring the Caliphate at that time, the temporary alternative if it were not feasible, and finally the method of choosing a Caliph if the delegates considered that to be a practicable step.

The consensus of the majority of the delegates was that the restoration of the Caliphate was not possible of realization at that time. The most important reasons given for this negative decision were the political weakness and disunity of Muslims, the fact that so many Islamic peoples lived under non-Muslim governments, and the further fact that many of the independent Muslim peoples were animated by a spirit of nationalism – that is to say, their political ideas tended toward national particularism rather than toward Islamic uni-

---

Whither Islam? A Survey of Modern Movements in the Moslem World (London, 1932), the Introduction by Professor Gibb, especially p. 36. For a detailed analysis of the doctrinal theory and functions of the Caliphate, according to an erudite contemporary Egyptian Muslim jurist, see A. Sanhoury, *Le Califat, son evolution vers une société des nations orientales* (Paris, 1926).

versalism. In substance, the delegates recognized that no new Caliph would have sufficient authority to maintain his primary Islamic functions as supreme head of the whole Muslim community. He would not be in a position to defend the Faith, nor would he be able to enforce the Sacred Law throughout the world of Islam. The Congress closed with a recommendation to all Muslims to remain seized of the problem, which was so vital to Islam, with a view to restoring the Caliphate whenever this should become feasible.[26]

The month following, from June 7 to July 5, another Islamic Congress was convoked, in Mecca, to try to iron out the practical and legal problems created for Muslims in the absence of a centralized Caliphate government.

Two significant comments were made on the Caliphate Congress of Cairo by contemporary scholars. Dr. Sékaly made the general statement that the congresses of Cairo and of Mecca were extremely important, each in its own way, and that they both made manifest the spiritual and intellectual malaise prevalent in the world of Islam. He added further that they both underlined existing conflicts between Muslim modernists and conservatives.[27]

Dr. Sanhoury, writing from the point of view of a sincere Muslim modernist who believed profoundly in the future of the Islamic East, commented upon the final outcome of the Cairo Congress and made some bold concrete suggestions of his own for the consideration of the Muslim world. It was plain to him that the "relative indifference" of the public to the debates of the Caliphate Congress indicated that the national idea, the concept of *la patrie*, was more compelling than the pull toward a universal Islamic government possessed of over-riding executive authority. Sanhoury himself was convinced that Islamic reforms could only be achieved within the framework of the national state, because "the social edifice should be built from the bottom up, and not from the top down." [28]

The two principal proposals of this distinguished Muslim Egyptian jurist were concrete but not possible of immediate realization. In the first place, he advocated the re-establishment of the Caliphate in as-

[26] Achille Sékaly, *Le Congrès du Khalifat (Le Caire, 13-19 mai 1926) et Le Congrès du Monde Musulman (La Mekke, 7 juin-5 juillet 1926)* (Paris, 1926), *passim* and especially pp. 55-57, 73, 88-90, 103, 105-109.

[27] *Ibid.*, p. 3.

[28] Sanhoury, *op. sit.*, p. 512, also pp. xi, xiv, 570, 572.

sociation with a Society of Eastern Nations. A restored Caliphate, as he envisioned it, would be possessed of an international juridical personality.[29]

In the second place, Sanhoury proposed that a scientific, painstaking review of the now stagnant Shari'ah should be undertaken with a view to its modernization in the light of contemporary requirements. Legal evolution and flexibility were his watchwords for the renaissance of the Sacred Law of Islam and for the rehabilitation of Muslim legal institutions. He believed, moreover, that a distinction should be made between the areas of religious and temporal law because it had become necessary, in the 20th century, for all the citizens of Islamic states, Muslims and non-Muslims alike, to live as equals under the same temporal laws.[30]

As Egyptians moved into the 1930's, four identifiable Muslim groups were in process of emerging: the ultraconservatives, the modernist-reformers, the militant reactionaries, and, last of all, the Muslim supporters of a lay or secular state.

In the first place, the older generation of strict lay Muslims became more self-consciously conservative, and a parallel fundamentalism was emphasized among the majority of the Ulama. Both of these ultraconservative groups increasingly looked askance at the avalanche of westernizing change; most of them actively resisted secularizing tendencies; and many declined wholly to accept changes that struck at their Islamic customs.

In the second place, there developed a quantitatively uncertain number of Muslim "modernists": groups and individuals who believed, as Shaykh Muhammad 'Abduh had believed, that the Islamic community has sufficient strength and flexibility to adapt itself to all the requirements of modern living in a scientific age, without losing the spiritual content of Islam. These became the modern reformers of Islam. Their objectives could perhaps be summarized thus: modernization of the legal institution to meet the needs of a changing society; belief that the Prophet never intended that Islam should be static or incapable of progress; assumption that the medieval Muslim jurists must have deviated, at least in some respects, from the true

[29] For the details of Sanhoury's plan see, *ibid.*, pp. 569-607, *passim*, and especially pp. 574-577, 597-598.
[30] *Ibid.*, pp. 539, 571-572, 578-579.

spirit of the Koran, and, therefore, from Islam. The reform of Islamic society was, therefore, to be achieved through reinterpretation of the Koran and of the Shari'ah within the framework of orthodox Islam. At the same time, they supported extensive social and economic reforms: the expansion and development of education (to be accessible to all people), and improvement of the content and methods of education; administrative and governmental reform; and the emancipation of women.

Thirdly, in contradistinction to these two opposing groups of ultra-conservative and modernist Muslims, a new development occurred to channel the forces of Islamic reaction in public life. Politico-religious associations were founded to defend Islam against the abrasive encroachments of secularization. Their founders believed that "modernism" had already gone too far in Islamic society; they were convinced that the fundamental beliefs and institutions of Islam were thereby threatened. And because they blamed Western politico-economic intrusion in their world for the westernization of their society, they became xenophobic and anti-Western. Chief among these associations was the *Ikhwan al-Muslimun*, the Muslim Brotherhood, founded in Egypt in 1928. This was a militant reactionary reform group which began life as a religious revivalist movement.

The fourth and latest development of all was the emergence of a significant group of secularists, and of these there were two very different types. The radicals of that group were represented by the young intelligentsia, notably in the state universities and the professions. Many of them became agnostic. Their agnosticism, however, did not result in any public disavowal of Islam: Arab family ties are too strong, and so is their affiliation with the whole Muslim culture and ethos. Furthermore, repudiation of Islam would make them outcasts in a religious society which holds that refusal to recognize the supremacy and the unity of the One God constitutes the only unforgivable sin.

The second type of secularists were the Muslim supporters of a lay, or secular, state. These were, for the most part, devout Muslims who thought that it would take far too long to reform and reinterpret the Sacred Law, and that time was of the essence. They believed that civil and religious affairs must be separated. Many of them were also convinced that a man's faith is primarily his own business, since all

Muslims will have to answer personally to God in the hereafter for their failures in this world. The Muslim supporters of a lay or secular state did not come to the forefront in Egyptian political life until after the Second World War and the subsequent Arab defeat in the Arab-Israeli war of 1948-1949. The humiliation of this defeat then inspired a soul-searching re-examination of their own position in the world. These Muslim Egyptian secularists became more self-consciously Arab; Egyptians for the first time began to identify themselves as Arabs. Nevertheless, they recognized the paramount need of strengthening the state in which they lived. They did not lose sight of the wider Arab world of which they were a part, nor did they waver in their allegiance to the ideal of Islamic universality and solidarity. But, for very practical reasons, Egypt claimed their immediate attention, and therefore they directed their earliest reforming zeal to the rebuilding of their own national state.

Most of the leaders of the Egyptian Revolution of 1952, including General Naguib and Colonel (now President) Abdel Nasser, belonged in this last category of Muslim secularists – the military intelligentsia, so-called, and various segments of the relatively new national bourgeoisie. In their view, the rebirth of Egypt depended upon the continued modernization of its social, political, and economic institutions. A healthy modern state that expanded economically, raised the living standards of all its people, and unified the people by guaranteeing complete freedom of worship to its religious communities would, they believed, be strong enough to stand alone in the modern world and to maintain a position of dignity and of political power. Hence the emphasis of the Revolutionary Government of Egypt on social justice as well as economic planning and development, and its transfer of the administration of all religious laws to the civil courts (for the purposes of administrative unification).

In later chapters will be described the head-on clash that eventually developed in Egypt between the leading exponents of two of the four Muslim groups identified above: the militant reactionaries of the Muslim Brotherhood, and the Muslim supporters of a secular state who established the Government of the Revolution.

The spiritual dilemma of Egypt was epitomized in four intellectually epoch-making books published in the past half-century. All four dealt forthrightly with basic Islamic concepts touching the central problems at issue between Muslim modernists and conservatives. Two of the books condemned theocracy and discussed the role of Islam in government: the first concluded that the Caliphate was not an essential Islamic institution and that it had no basis in either law or religion;[31] the other and more recent one made a strong plea for a secular state, in which religion should be left to the moral, spiritual and social spheres.[32] A third book called in question, by implication, the sacrosanct character of the Koran.[33] The fourth book, however, was a reasoned defense of Muslim conservatism. The purpose of this last book was "to preach a renewal of Islamic life, a life governed by the spirit and the law of Islam," on the grounds that Islam presented to mankind a unified and comprehensive, unique, and perfect system of life; to introduce any foreign element would be ruinous.[34] Each book created a public sensation. The first three books were confiscated and their authors were tried for unorthodoxy – eventually to be acquitted or otherwise vindicated.

Only two of these books were published before 1928, the year when the Muslim Brotherhood came into existence, but this Egyptian "battle of the books" began before the founding of the Brotherhood and continued into the period of its later activities. There can be little doubt that the sensation caused by Shaykh ʿAli ʿAbd al-Raziq's study of the Caliphate and government in Islam (1925) and by Dr. Taha Hussein's book on pre-Islamic poetry and the Koran (1926) greatly affected the thinking of Hasan al-Banna, the founder of the Muslim Brotherhood. These two books, written by Muslim intellectuals, constituted a serious challenge to Islamic conservatism. They were being widely discussed when al-Banna was a young schoolteacher, still in his early twenties. He, like other strict orthodox Muslims of his gen-

[31] Shaykh ʿAli ʿAbd al-Raziq published in 1925 his book on "Islam and the Principles of Government: A Study of the Caliphate and the Government in Islam" (see Bibliography, sec. iv).

[32] Khalid Muhammad Khalid, *From Here We Start* (Washington, D. C., 1953); originally published in Arabic, 1950 (see Bibliog., sec. iv).

[33] A study "On Pre-Islamic Poetry," by Dr. Taha Hussein, published in 1926 (see Bibliog., sec. iv).

[34] Sayyid Qutb (Kotb), *Social Justice in Islam* (Washington, D. C., 1953), p. 227; see also pp. 88, 90, 248, 276. The original Arabic edition was published at Cairo, undated, after 1945 (see Bibliog., sec. iv). Sayyid Qutb eventually became an influential member of the Muslim Brotherhood. As a journalist-ideologist he wrote many articles in defense of the ideals of the Brotherhood in the early 1950's.

eration, was fearful of the secular trend in education – particularly in the state university at Cairo. The launching of this battle of the books swept him into the new controversy between the modernists and the conservatives of Islam, and inspired him to do battle against the forces of advancing secularization.[35]

Hasan al-Banna and his generation were not only confronted by a spiritual crisis. They were also caught in all the political cross-currents of their day. The young men of 1928 inherited the memory of the ill-fated revolt of Colonel Arabi and the first Egyptian nationalists in 1882. They held in their minds and hearts the memory of the rebellion of 1919; many of them, then and thereafter, had participated in mass demonstrations for their political independence. All of these young men sought emotional security, and they craved action to assuage their spiritual unease. The moment was propitious for the founding of new movements.

Late in 1927 a society was founded in Egypt known as the Association of Muslim Youth. Less than six months later the Muslim Brotherhood was established. Thereafter the world of Islam was confronted with a proliferation of such groups, organized on the Egyptian pattern. Between 1927 and 1947 some 135 Islamic groups were established in Egypt and elsewhere. Eight of these were important religious societies, eight were politico-religious organizations, and some thirteen were related groups nominally formed for alleged social, charitable, co-operative, or vocational objectives. It is noteworthy that before 1927 the Muslim community of Egypt had boasted only a single Benevolent Society. Heyworth-Dunne has drawn up a selected list of these societies, or associations, and has given some interesting information concerning them. He characterized them all in the following words: "The main tendency of most of these Islamic societies is to bring the community back to the *Sharīyah* and away from Westernism."[36]

---

[35] A number of refutations of the books by ʿAli ʿAbd al-Raziq and Dr. Taha Hussein were published by serious scholars. Outstanding among these was Muhammad al-Khidr Hussein's criticism of the former (published in 1926) and two criticisms of the latter, one by Mustafa Sadiq al-Rafiʿi (1926) and one by Muhammad Ahmad ʿArafah (1932). The criticism by ʿArafah was edited and commented upon by Rashid Rida.

[36] J. Heyworth-Dunne, *Religious and Political Trends in Modern Egypt* (Washington, D. C., 1950), p. 111, also pp. 9, 30, 84, 89-91, and Appendixes B and C (pp. 106-111).

Among the politico-religious organizations which grew into socially important movements, two deserve special mention here because
they became the principal rivals of the Muslim Brotherhood. The
Association of Muslim Youth (*Jam'iyyat al-Shubban al-Muslimin*),
more commonly known as the Young Muslim Men's Association
– the Y.M.M.A. – was founded late in 1927. It established branches
throughout the Islamic world and inaugurated an active Pan-Islamic
program in the true spirit of Jamal al-Din al-Afghani. In its early
years the Y.M.M.A. was primarily a cultural, social, and religious
organization. It launched an extensive educational program combined with relatively high-level literary activities. One of the stated
aims of the Association was to make use of the best elements of the
cultures of both East and West; its earliest goal was to reconcile
orthodox Islam with Western modernism. But as the years rolled into
the crises of Palestine and the Second World War, the Y.M.M.A.
became increasingly militant and nationalistic. The propaganda and
appeal of this organization was directed primarily to the young
Intelligentsia and the middle classes.[37]

Young Egypt (*Misr al-Fatah*), also known as the "Green Shirt
Movement," was established in 1933 by the lawyer and socialist
Ahmad Hussein.[38] Young Egypt had a comprehensive program of
social and economic reforms, and manifested great concern for the
welfare of the peasantry. In the beginning it was not, strictly speaking, a religious society, but it advocated a revival of religious training
through the University of al-Azhar and its affiliated institutes. This
was an Egyptian nationalist society *par excellence*, with the self-
appointed duty of holding a mirror to the varied glories of Egyptian
civilization from Pharoanic times to the present. In 1940 it somewhat
broadened its religious activities and propaganda and changed its
name, becoming the Nationalist Islamic Party (*Hizb al-Watani al-
Islami*).[39] Thereafter it became more and more chauvinistic; at one

[37] Most of the information on the Y.M.M.A. has been drawn from Gibb
(ed.), *Whither Islam?*, especially the chapter by Professor G. Kampffmeyer on
"Egypt and Western Asia," and from Heyworth-Dunne, *op. cit.*, pp. 11-14.
[38] Not to be confused with Dr. Ahmed Hussein who became Ambassador of
Egypt to the United States after a remarkably fruitful career in the Ministry
of Social Affairs.
[39] Heyworth-Dunne, *op. cit.*, Appendix A (pp. 103-105); Colombe, *op. cit.*,
pp. 141-144.

time it was the Muslim Brotherhood's most powerful rival. In the last years of the monarchy, after the release of its founder from his wartime internment for subversive activity, Young Egypt made its own special contribution to the anarchy of the postwar period and did much to hasten the fall of King Farouk. The organized arson and bloodshed of Cairo's "Black Saturday" (Jan. 26, 1952), is most often laid at the door of Ahmad Hussein and his organization. Young Egypt eventually changed its name a second time: before the Revolution of 1952 it became the Socialist Party.

On the eve of the founding of the Muslim Brotherhood of Egypt, which is described in the following chapters, one fact had become crystal-clear. Orthodox Egyptian Muslims, whether modernists, conservatives, or reactionaries, believed that the renaissance of the Muslim East was indissolubly linked with the renaissance of Islam. All of them were convinced of a need for capable and energetic leadership. The ideological differences between these three groups of Muslims lay in the nature of the Islamic renaissance which they envisioned. For all Muslims who deplored the secularized idea of progress, of whom the founder of the Muslim Brotherhood was one, the renaissance of Islam was conceived in purely fundamentalist, literalist terms. A revolutionary situation was therefore in the making.

IV

HASAN AL-BANNA:
THE MUSLIM BROTHERHOOD AND
ITS TEACHINGS

In this uneasy and tumultuous world, Hasan al-Banna, who was to become the founder of the Muslim Brotherhood, came of age. He was born in 1906 in the Delta province of Beheira, northeast of Alexandria, presumably in the village of Mahmudiyyah. Hasan's father, Shaykh Ahmad ʿAbd al-Rahman al-Banna, known as al-Saʿati, "the Watchmaker," was a very learned and respected Islamic scholar. The elder al-Banna was a follower of the fundamentalist Hanbalite school of the Sunni, or orthodox, sect of Islam. This fact seems to have been the all-important influence in the boy's early life; as the son of his father, Hasan was steeped from his earliest childhood in the puritan teachings of Ibn Hanbal.

In his memoirs Hasan al-Banna devotes much space to his schooling. Between the ages of eight and twelve, he attended the Rashad Religious School in his own village of Mahmudiyyah, and he seems to have been deeply influenced by the master of the school:

I benefited a great deal, I suppose, from him, may God have mercy on him. [He inspired me with] a desire to learn and a great interest in reading. I used to accompany him often to his library, which contained many valuable books, and I used to study and read for him. This library was a frequent meeting-place for scholars who discussed and debated while I listened. This direct and close attachment between teacher and student had a wonderful effect on me. I wish teachers and educators would appreciate and encourage this kind of student-teacher relationship, because it has many benefits . . .[1]

From the ages of twelve to fourteen, Hasan attended a primary

[1] *Mudhakkirat Hasan al-Banna* [Memoirs of Hasan al-Banna] (Cairo, [1949?]) I, 4-5.

school (*al-Madrasah al-I'dadiyyah*). The curricula of both schools throw considerable light on his earliest intellectual preoccupations. At the elementary school the boy memorized parts of the *Hadith*, the Islamic traditions, and studied Arabic grammar, composition, prose literature, and that most exacting of all studies, Arabic poetry. At the primary school he continued the study of religion and Arabic. No foreign languages were taught in the primary school; instead, he attended required courses on finance, real estate, and horticulture.

During these early years Hasan al-Banna started each day with morning prayers, after which he memorized passages from the Koran until it was time to go to school. When school was out, until the hour of evening prayer, he studied watchmaking in his father's shop and became much interested in this precision art. After the evening prayer he did his homework for school.

He seems to have taken a deep interest both in his classes at school and in the preparation for them. His father encouraged him to study and gave him books as presents, and also Hasan borrowed books from the library of a neighboring Shaykh for a trifling weekly payment. Stories of daring exploits and military prowess, as well as of Islamic subjects and religious devotion, were his favorite reading matter.

Between the ages of fourteen and seventeen Hasan was enrolled at the Primary Teachers School (*Madrasat al-Mu'allimin al-Awwaliyyah*) at Damanhur, a town on the railway, near his home village. While there he spent much time studying Sufi mysticism. That was a period of "absorption in Sufist sentimentalism and in worship."

When the young al-Banna was thirteen, the anti-British rebellion of 1919 broke out. Hasan's loyalty to Egypt was immediately and actively enlisted. For several years thereafter, in Mahmudiyyah and in Damanhur, he participated in strikes and demonstrations. "Despite my preoccupation with Sufism and worship, I believed that duty to country is an inescapable obligation – a holy war (*jihad*)." [2]

One of Hasan's student activities had considerable significance for his subsequent lifework as head of the Muslim Brotherhood. As a schoolboy he belonged to three different clubs, or Islamic associations. The first one, which was organized by his fellow students at the

---

[2]   *Ibid.*, p. 28.

suggestion of one of the schoolteachers, elected Hasan al-Banna its president. It was known as the "Society for Ethical Education" (*Jam'iyyat al-Akhlaq al-Adabiyyah*). All members were required to lead a strictly religious life; they had to pray regularly, and to obey God, their parents, and their elders. Its members were fined whenever they "deviated from the path of Islam" in speech or conduct. "Cursing brothers was fined one millieme, fathers two milliemes, mothers one piaster, and religion two piasters; quarreling, two piasters." [3]

Later, in thinking back to these days, al-Banna made the following pregnant comment: "There is no doubt that such an association has more influence in forming character than twenty theoretical lessons. Schools and institutions should give considerable encouragement to such societies." [4]

The members of the Society for Ethical Education became such enthusiastic reformers that they established another Muslim association which they named the "Society for the Prevention of Prohibited Actions" (*Jam'iyyat Man' al-Muharramat*). Weekly membership dues averaged between five and ten milliemes. The main function of this association was to write letters to sinners and to expostulate with Muslims who neglected their prayers or who failed to observe the month-long fast of Ramadan.

Hasan al-Banna then became the secretary of a third reform group, a benevolent society (*Jam'iyyat al-Hasafiyyah al-Khayriyyah*). This society was actively concerned in promoting the good life, according to Islamic teachings, and in condemning all who drank liquor, gambled, and indulged in other "abominations." But it had, in the words of its secretary, another significant objective, which was "to oppose the missionary activities of an Evangelical Mission which had descended on the town." This mission in Mahmudiyyah consisted of three ladies who were "preaching Christianity under the guise of medical treatment, the teaching of embroidery, and the giving of shelter to boys and girls. The struggle of the society on behalf of its cause was worthy of praise. And its cause was taken up afterwards by the Society of the Muslim Brotherhood." The example of this

[3] *Ibid.*, p. 6. There are ten milliemes in one piaster, and one hundred piasters in an Egyptian pound. One American cent equals roughly three milliemes.
[4] *Ibid.*, pp. 6-7.

Christian mission, then, furnished the germ of his later welfare program.[5]

When he was seventeen, Hasan al-Banna went to Cairo to study at the Dar al-ʿUlum, the oldest and most influential state teachers college in Egypt.[6] He graduated in 1927.

His four years in Cairo made a deep impression on the young al-Banna. For the first time, in the nation's capital, he found himself living in a cosmopolitan city; for the first time he came squarely face-to-face with the intellectual and the social problems engendered by westernization. And Hasan al-Banna reacted strongly against the subversive influences of the West. His own words on the subject are eloquent:

> After the last war and during this period which I spent in Cairo, there was an increase in spiritual and ideological disintegration, in the name of intellectual freedom. There was also a deterioration of behavior, morals, and deeds, in the name of individual freedom .... Books, newspapers, and magazines appeared whose only aim was to weaken or to destroy the influence of any religion on the masses .... Young men were lost, and the educated were in a state of doubt and confusion .... I saw that the social life of the beloved Egyptian nation was oscillating between her dear and precious Islamism which she had inherited, defended, lived with and become accustomed to, and made powerful during thirteen centuries, and this severe Western invasion which is armed and equipped with all the destructive and degenerative influences of money, wealth, prestige, ostentation, material enjoyment, power, and means of propaganda .... I remember that I was so disturbed about the threat to Islam posed by the West that I spent about half the month of Ramadan of that year in a state of great anxiety and sleeplessness. And I therefore decided upon positive action and I asked myself: Why do I not place this responsibility upon the shoulders of Muslim leaders and urge them strongly to co-operate in resisting this invasion?[7]

The positive action which al-Banna decided upon while he was still at Dar al-ʿUlum was a campaign to counteract the "wave of apostasy" which, in his judgment at least, was sweeping Egypt. For this purpose, he felt the need for writing books and articles and for es-

---

[5]   *Ibid.*, pp. 17-18.
[6]   The Dar al-ʿUlum has since been absorbed into the University of Cairo. It is noteworthy that while Hasan al-Banna was enrolled at the Dar al-ʿUlum he failed to equip himself with a knowledge of any European language.
[7]   *Ibid.*, pp. 56-59, 65.

tablishing a new periodical. Then he dreamed of founding youth groups, particularly associations of young men. And finally he sought to encourage Islamic preaching coupled with religious guidance.

Mosques alone were not adequate to convey and communicate Islamic teachings to the people . . . . I therefore thought of training a number of students from al-Azhar and from Dar al-ʿUlum to preach and to offer guidance in mosques, coffeehouses, and public places; and later to pick out a group from these students to spread the cause of Islam in villages and rural areas. And I put my idea into practice.[8]

During these years in Cairo, Hasan joined several Islamic intellectual groups and became one of the early members of the Young Muslim Men's Association, the Y.M.M.A. He also joined with a group of Ulama in the publication of a new Muslim periodical called *al-Fath* ("The Conquest").

In the year of his graduation from Dar al-ʿUlum, Hasan's class was given a special exercise, the writing of a composition. Each graduating senior was asked to discuss in his paper the ambitions of his postgraduate years and to explain how he expected to achieve them. Hasan's paper dealt in many noble generalities – such as the duty of a man to commend himself to his family and his countrymen, to place their interests above his own and to act toward them with kindness, to fight the holy war (*jihad*) for truth and general reform, and, above all, to win the approval of God. His words recall that famous verse of the Jewish prophet Micah: "He hath shewed thee, O man, what is good; and what doth the Lord require of thee, but to do justly, and to love mercy, and to walk humbly with thy God?" The young Muslim placed greater emphasis on the holy war for truth than on the virtues of humility and mercy; but the socio-religious motivations of both men were spiritually akin, and Hasan put far more emphasis on self-sacrifice in the cause of reform.[9]

Hasan al-Banna was most explicit in this paper concerning his "two greatest ambitions" after completing his education. He yearned to bring happiness to his family and friends; and he expressed determination to become a teacher and a religious guide. He proposed to dedicate himself to teach the good life, according to Islam. And he proposed to work toward this end, as a reformer, with perseverance

[8]   *Ibid.*, p. 52.
[9]   *Ibid.*, pp. 63-65. Also, Micah vi : 8.

and self-sacrifice by delivering lectures, making speeches, promoting discussions, and writing and traveling for the cause.[10]

During the year in which Hasan al-Banna graduated from Dar al-'Ulum he received a government appointment to teach school in Ismailia, the nerve center of the Suez Canal Zone. In September, 1927, he started his teaching career at the government primary school (*Madrasat al-Isma'iliyyah al-Ibtida'iyyah al-Amiriyyah*). He taught in this busy city for six years, and while there he was exposed to two European communities, both of which smacked of imperialism. British troops were stationed in the Canal Zone near Ismailia, and the French officials of the Suez Canal Company had largely taken over the city itself. He was daily offended by the sight of British uniforms on the streets and the presence of a host of non-Muslim foreign residents. The foreign community at this flourishing center of the Suez Canal Company had better jobs, and they had a higher standard of living than the underprivileged Egyptians among whom al-Banna worked. This contrast became increasingly painful to him with each passing year. The presence of British soldiers was a constant reminder of the British Occupation and the irritant of foreign domination. Al-Banna's already kindled intellectual hostility to Western influences then became crystallized into emotional xenophobia. The impact of this period is so important in Hasan al-Banna's development that it would be illuminating to give the full flavor of his reactions in his own words:

Ismailia had a wonderful inspiration. On the west was the British camp with its power, authority, and wealth stirring up sorrow and regret in every zealous patriot and urging him to re-examine this hated Occupation, which dragged Egypt into great disasters and which denied Egypt opportunities for material and moral progress. British occupation was the only obstacle in the way of Egypt's progress and the most important hindrance to Arab and Muslim unity throughout a period of sixty years.

And this elegant, magnificent, and luxurious administration office of the Suez Canal Company, having authority and influence, mistreated Egyptian employees, but was generous to foreign employees. The latter only were advanced to positions of ruling masters. [Moreover,] complete supervision of all public utilities such as light, water, and cleanliness was appropriated by the Canal Company. All services, which are ordinarily provided by municipal councils, were in the hands of the Company. Even the roads and entrances of Ismailia, which was a truly Egyptian

10   *Ibid.*, pp. 65-66.

city, were controlled by the Company, and no one could leave or enter Ismailia without the approval of the Company.

And the magnificent houses, which were widespread in all of the European quarter, were offered to the foreign employees of the Company. The Arab employees, on the other hand, lived in small and cheap homes. And all the names of the streets in the Arab quarter were written only in the language of this economic occupation. Even the mosque street was written thus, "Rue de la Mosquée". . .[11]

At the end of six years Hasan al-Banna left Ismailia. He was transferred to another government school in Cairo and he taught there continuously from 1934 to 1946.[12] The rest of his life was spent in Cairo, and his official career was that of a government schoolteacher.

Long before he left Ismailia, however, Hasan al-Banna had initiated his most important lifework. In 1928 he founded the Muslim Brotherhood (*Jam'iyyat al-Ikhwan al-Muslimin*),[13] an Islamic association that grew mightily and eventually spread its tentacles over the length and breadth of Egypt. Al-Banna tells the story of its founding in his memoirs:

I remember that in *Dhi al-Qi'dah* 1347 A.H. (March, 1928) a group of six brothers, Hafiz 'Abd al-Hamid, Ahmad al-Misri, Fu'ad Ibrahim, 'Abd al-Rahman Hasab Allah, Isma'il 'Izz, and Zaki al-Mughrabi, visited me at home. They were among those who had been influenced by my teachings and lectures. They spoke to me with emotion, confidence, enthusiasm, faith, and resolution. They said, "We have listened, we have understood, and we have been influenced, but we do not know the practical path which will lead to the glory of Islam and the welfare of the Muslim people. We are fed up with this life – this life of chains and humiliation. And now you see that the Arabs and the Muslims in this country have neither position nor respect, and their rank is even below that of servants employed by these foreigners. We have nothing to offer except our blood, our lives, our faith, our honor, and these few pennies saved from our children's sustenance. We do not know the path leading to work, nor do we know how to serve our country, our religion, and our people as you do. All we want now is to offer you what we possess in

[11]   *Ibid.*, pp. 87-89.
[12]   Ishaq Musa al-Husseini (al-Husayni), *Al-Ikhwan al-Muslimun; kubra al-harakat al-Islamiyyah al-hadithah* [The Muslim Brotherhood: The Greatest Modern Islamic Movement] (2d Arabic ed.; Beirut, 1955), p. 27. Owing to differences in the texts, I draw from both the Arabic edition and the English translation, Ishak Musa Husaini, *The Moslem Brethren: The Greatest of Modern Islamic Movements* (Beirut, 1956).
[13]   A variant of the name *Ikhwan al-Muslimun*.

order to discharge our responsibility before God and to hold you responsible before Him for us and our duties." A group which takes a sincere oath before God to live and die for His religion, to have no interest but to serve Him, is worthy of victory, though it may be small in number and poor in resources.

I was deeply influenced by their sincerity and could not elude the responsibility they passed on to me, which is what I advocate, work for, and try to make people agree upon. I was deeply touched, and I said, "May God thank you, may He bless this righteous intention, and may He lead us to virtuous work that would please Him and benefit the people. Our duty is to work, and we depend on God for success. Let us pledge ourselves before God to be soldiers for the cause of Islam, which is life for the country and glory for the people." And so it was that we took a pledge and an oath to live as brothers and to work for Islam and strive for its cause. One of them said, "What name should we give ourselves? Should we officially become an association, a club, a cult, or a union?" I answered, "None of these. Let us not be formal and official. We are brothers in the service of Islam and therefore we are 'The Muslim Brotherhood.' "

The idea came suddenly – and thus the first organization of the Muslim Brotherhood was established by these six men around this idea, in this way, and under this name.[14]

The year after its establishment, however, it was deemed advisable to give this informal group of Muslim Brothers a more formal organization. The date of the founding of the Muslim Brotherhood is therefore usually given as 1929.

At its inception the Brotherhood was in essence a religious revivalist movement – a "revitalization movement," in the terminology of modern anthropologists. It soon developed into a politico-religious action society; and eventually, as it gained political influence, it became more political than religious. Even in its latest, most political phase, however, the Muslim Brothers still clung to a religious program and frame of reference in order to sanctify their political extremism. Their slogan was always: "God is the greatest, thanks to God"; and their emblem was a Koran between two swords.[15] This was not the first modern Islamic revivalist society to be established in 20th-century Egypt, nor was it the last. But the Muslim Brotherhood was the only one of all these religious associations to become

---

[14] *Mudhakkirat Hasan al-Banna*, I, 88-89.

[15] Ishak Musa Husaini, *The Moslem Brethren*, p. 160, citing Hasan al-Banna's *Min Khutab*, 1.9.

an important political movement; and it was the only organization to combine religious missionary objectives with a carefully thought-out program of social and economic reform.

The six disciples who had gone to Hasan al-Banna and besought him to show them the practical path, to instruct them in the work that needed to be done to serve their country and their God, had confidently placed full responsibility on his shoulders for the work they sought to accomplish. He proved himself to be a leader worthy of their trust. Hasan al-Banna *was* the Brotherhood in the early stages of its development.[16] He gave his Brethren (*Ikhwan*) their group characteristics as well as their program; he inspired them with his ardor and his sincerity; and his magnetic personality attracted an ever swelling stream of adherents to the movement. Until within a few months of the end of his life, Hasan al-Banna kept the power in his own hands and personally directed the program and the policies of his organization.

The founder of the Muslim Brotherhood was well fitted to become a leader of men, not only because of his personal physical characteristics, but also because of his outstanding intellectual attainments. Furthermore, his relatively wide experience of life in Egypt, in the country village of Mahmudiyyah, in the bustling towns of Damanhur and Ismailia, and in the cosmopolitan capital city of Cairo, had brought him into contact with many men and ideas. And lastly, Hasan al-Banna's vocation as a teacher in the government school system gave him experience in administration and much practice in prying open the minds of the young.

The head of the Muslim Brotherhood was a short, robust man with a commanding presence. Yet he was reputed to be essentially modest, warm, and approachable, one who never sought to put up unnecessary barriers between himself and his followers. He had dark, penetrating eyes, and he wore a moustache and a full short beard. He dressed plainly, generally in the European style, but he always wore a *tarbush*. According to his biographer, Hasan al-Banna was possessed of exuberant vitality, almost inexhaustible energy, and a prodigious memory. He worked all day and most of the night: teaching school, writing, traveling all over Egypt to give lectures, presiding over countless meetings, and supervising all the work of the Brother-

16   *Ibid.*, pp. 25-26, 37-38.

hood. Not only during the vacations, but also on many school days, he would leave school at the end of his classes, take a train or bus to some distant town to address a meeting, and sit up all night to return to his school for the earliest morning classes. Reputedly he never forgot a name, a face, or a place.[17] Hasan al-Banna had been an exceptional student. At both the primary teachers school of Damanhur and at Dar al-ʿUlum he graduated first in his class. When he took the national competitive examination for general proficiency in education, he stood fifth in the whole of Egypt. Al-Banna himself asserted that he memorized 18,000 verses of Arabic poetry and 18,000 lines of prose for his final examination at Dar al-ʿUlum.[18]

In the opinion of those who knew him personally, including Egyptian Muslims who never belonged to the Muslim Brotherhood, its founder, al-Banna, had three outstanding qualifications for leadership. He had an extraordinary amount of personal charm and magnetism; he was a most eloquent speaker, with a degree of oratorical power that moved his audiences deeply; and he possessed an unusually good command of his native tongue. In the Arabic-speaking world, any man with the ability to express himself fluently in excellent Arabic is highly appreciated and respected.

In order to win converts to the Muslim Brotherhood, as well as to assure the wholehearted loyalty of his own Muslim Brothers, Hasan al-Banna gave careful thought to all the details of a far-flung propaganda campaign. He had studied both logic and psychology when he was a student at Dar al-ʿUlum. He was well read in the history of medieval subversive Islamic movements and in the psychological-warfare tactics of esoteric heterodox Muslim sects, such as the Ismaʿilis, and of intellectual groups such as the Brethren of Purity (*Ikhwan al-Safa*). He was conversant with their slogans, their polemic literature, and the propaganda techniques which they had employed, often with notable success, in the Arab Islamic world of their day. Hasan al-Banna was also well versed in Sufism, in the nature of the spiritual appeal of the modern Muslim Sufis and the emotional content of their evangelical mysticism. He drew upon all these sources, cleverly adapting their techniques to the modern Egyptian scene, in order to elaborate his machinery for the dissemination of

17   Al-Husayni, *op. cit.*, pp. 63, 69-70.
18   *Mudhakkirat*, I, 68; Husaini, *op. cit.*, p. 30.

Brotherhood teachings and propaganda. In the mosques and the mosque schools, in general public meetings, face to face with groups of villagers and urban workers, and in personal interviews with teachers, students of al-Azhar University, soldiers, and all Muslim Egyptians with whom he came in contact, Hasan al-Banna used every medieval and modern Muslim device to inculcate support for the principles and the objectives of the Muslim Brotherhood.

Very early in his work he trained a select group of his disciples as missionaries and propagandists, his *da'is*.[19] These became preachers and teachers and group organizers to aid him in the arduous work of reaching the hearts and the minds of Egyptian Muslims. He perfected a system of intensive personal contact to strengthen and expand the Brotherhood movement.

A high standard was set for the conduct and proficiency of the *da'is*. Hasan al-Banna required them to be knowledgeable, not only concerning religious matters, but also about the national and domestic affairs of Egypt, the general position of Islam in the world outside of Egypt, and current Islamic problems at home and abroad. In addition he exacted from them a high standard of Muslim conduct, including brotherliness toward fellow Muslims, loyalty to their own families, and strict observance of all the prohibitions of the Muslim Brotherhood with respect to dancing, theater-going, drinking alcohol, and gambling. And finally he expected them to be healthy in body and cleanly, or tidy, in appearance. Possibly al-Banna did not realize that a pre-Islamic concept, that of *mens sana in corpore sano*, was interwoven with the practical aspects of his missionary work. In any case, by insisting upon the maintenance of high personal qualifications for his agents, he furnished living examples of the ideal Muslim man.

The missionaries of Hasan al-Banna were instructed to concentrate upon disseminating Brotherhood principles in the mosques and the mosque schools and to establish branches in the villages which were then remote and far removed from the activities of competitive pressure groups. In the mosques, the *da'is*, as opportunity allowed, addressed the congregation after Friday prayers and talked to them about the Muslim Brotherhood and its ideology or gave them

---

[19]   J. Heyworth-Dunne, *Religious and Political Trends in Modern Egypt* (Washington, D. C., 1950), pp. 44-45; for much of the information on Hasan

Brotherhood views upon political or social problems of the day.

When Hasan al-Banna was transferred from Ismailia to Cairo, he was known as the Guide General (*murshid al-ʿamm*). In later years the title of Guide General came to be translated as "Supreme Guide." The change in emphasis, implicit in the more pompous and high-sounding title, may have come in part from the more complex nature of the hierarchical organization that developed after the death of the founder of the Muslim Brotherhood. But "Guide General" is a more exact translation of the Arabic, and it is also more in keeping with al-Banna's own concept of his position.

All the executive business of the organization was cleared through a central office or headquarters, known as the *Dar*. In this building the Guide General had private sessions with his personal assistants and agents, general membership meetings were held, and the master file of all Brotherhood records, most of them highly secret, was kept. The Dar was in Cairo, not far from al-Azhar University and the Royal Palace. The building was kept scrupulously clean and was equipped with a telephone switchboard with extensions to the various administrative offices.[20]

Outside Cairo a nexus of branches (*shuʿab*) was established, each with its own local headquarters or office. The branch organizations were efficiently and meticulously organized for the purpose of educating and training all of their Brotherhood members. Each branch was required to follow a strict program of activity. This included the establishment of an evening school to combat illiteracy and give comprehensive lectures on Islam; committees for charitable and social welfare work among the sick and the needy; organized physical training and athletics to promote the health of the Brothers; and the maintenance of either a group of boy scouts (*al-Kashshafah*) or a troop of "rovers" (*al-Jawwalah*) – the latter secretly trained as a paramilitary organization. Each branch was further required to have its own offices, so as to serve as a general meeting place for its members, to carry out propaganda work in the area, and to maintain a health record for every member. It was also the general duty of each branch

---

al-Banna's agents (better translated as "missionaries") and propaganda see also pp. 19-20, 43, 54, 56.

[20]   *Ibid.*, p. 17.

to "help resist all ungodly actions and corruption by every possible means." [21]

Hasan al-Banna devoted much attention to education and to village welfare work. A special committee was set up to establish primary, secondary, and technical schools, for girls as well as for boys. These all had a strong Islamic emphasis, but they were separate from the special religious schools which Muslim Brothers had opened for the teaching of the Koran. They also had special technical schools for the workers in industrial centers, and schools for the illiterate in association with every Brotherhood branch. The social service program for the villages was both flexible and experimental. A Brotherhood society was founded for the purpose of raising the standard of living in villages throughout Egypt. In one village, for example, a model farm was established; in many others the poor were fed on the "soup-kitchen" basis – sometimes as many as 600 villagers during one month. Electricity for lighting was brought to some villages; alms were collected for the poor during the month of Ramadan; help was given to the paupers and to orphaned children. In one village, cemeteries were constructed for the poor. Many mosques were built out of funds and lands donated by Muslim Brothers, and in time most of the branches had their own mosques. Some Muslim Brothers acted as arbitrators in village disputes. Some made statistical studies in certain villages with a view to giving aid to the disabled and suitable employment to the children.[22]

The activities of the Muslim Brothers were thus many and varied, since one of their objectives was to prove that Muslims could be self-sufficient and could collaborate in raising the standard of living of the whole Islamic community. Nevertheless, despite their fierce adherence to the Muslim way of life, much of their organized welfare work involved considerable dependence on Western models and techniques. Their large community projects, in addition to schools,

---

[21] *Ibid.*, p. 59. Husaini specifies the athletics as football, basketball, wrestling, and boxing (*op. cit., English ed.*, p. 58).

[22] *Ibid.*, pp. 52-53, 55-56. In these pages Husaini refers to the fact that no statistics are available on the number of schools, the number of their pupils or teachers, or the number of hospitals and dispensaries established by the Brotherhood. He does, however, cite the Brotherhood paper, *al-Ikhwan al-Muslimun* (for May and June, 1946), in noting that their dispensary at Tanta treated 3,774 patients of various religions in one year.

medical dispensaries, and scout camps, comprised half-a-dozen industrial enterprises. The latter included factories for the making of consumers' goods. All these were, for the most part, competently administered according to modern standards. The publishing of Brotherhood propaganda and newspapers led to the acquisition of printing presses. A number of commercial and industrial enterprises were carried out through a special company, and Brotherhood funds were deposited in banks and invested in bonds and shares of "big business" concerns. In 1939 Hasan al-Banna issued a lengthy report on the multifarious activities of the Muslim Brotherhood for private circulation among a select group of Muslim Brothers. This report, printed in pamphlet form, gave information on many Brotherhood affairs that was normally kept secret among the Brethren or was known only to the Guide General and his aides-de-camp. It supplied detailed information on the accounts of the organization and its publication expenses, and the names of members and number of recently established Brotherhood branches, together with notices on conference meetings and ceremonies, the scout camps and the paramilitary groups, the medical department with its network of outpatient clinics and dispensaries. A full report was also given on the special Company for Islamic Transactions, which was in the nature of a holding company for the economic and commercial enterprises initiated by Hasan al-Banna in the interests of the Brotherhood. This report also dealt with miscellaneous special projects in social welfare and in the primary schools, journalistic training, and plans for a new mosque. Lastly, considerable space was also given to a survey of Brotherhood relations with the government, with the University of al-Azhar, and with the political parties. The resumé given in this report sheds much light on the growth of the Muslim Brotherhood and on the development of its social, economic, and political program after eleven years of expansion.[23]

Unfortunately for the historian, scarcely anything has been written on the commercial and industrial undertakings of the Muslim Brotherhood, important though they were. Brotherhood publications on the subject have not as yet come to light. Al-Husayni (Husaini), probably because of the difficulty of obtaining reliable information,

[23] Heyworth-Dunne, *op. cit.*, p. 58. Unhappily the report has not been made public and it is not available to the present writer.

devotes only a couple of pages in his book to the most widely known of their enterprises and furnishes no details whatever as to their operation.

According to al-Husayni, the Muslim Brotherhood owned seven "very successful" companies. He identifies four of the seven enterprises by name: the Islamic Transaction Company (*Shirkat al-Mu'amalat al-Islamiyyah*), mentioned in the report above, with a capital investment of LE 30,000; the Muslim Press Company and Daily Newspaper (*Shirkat al-Matba'ah al-Islamiyyah wa al-Jaridah al-Yawmiyyah*), with an impressive capital investment of LE 120,000; the Ikhwan Spinning and Weaving Company (*Shirkat al-Ikhwan li al-Ghazi wa al-Nasij*), with an unspecified capital investment; and the Commercial and Engineering Company (*Shirkat al-Tijarah wa al-Ashghal al-Handasiyyah*), with a capital investment of LE 14,000.[24] These companies provided their workers with mosques, clubs, and even schools. For the first time in the history of Egypt, allegedly, workers were allowed to invest in such privately owned companies. Furthermore, the Muslim Brotherhood had a special labor department attached to its general headquarters, the Dar, in Cairo.

Hasan al-Banna stands out as a clearly marked personality, the dominant and the dominating figure in the Muslim Brotherhood. It has been far more difficult to obtain a clear-cut impression of his following, particularly of its numerical strength. When al-Banna began his extracurricular work for the Muslim Brothers, it was as a teacher, a very special kind of religious teacher. He established himself as a Master who could lead his followers to salvation, and, in the manner of the Traditional Sufi Shaykh, he received unquestioning loyalty, devotion, and obedience from his disciples. This special position he never lost.

The first Muslim Brethren were humble Egyptians: the lowliest workers, the poorer peasants, impoverished students – the undernourished and the underprivileged of all classes. They were all susceptible to inspiration coming from a revered teacher: they were the devout and the uneducated. Hasan al-Banna gave them the strong leadership of which they stood in spiritual need. From the beginning also, his fellow schoolteachers were attracted to the Muslim Brotherhood – in part, at least, because of al-Banna's perennial efforts to

[24] *Op. cit.*, pp. 104-105.

obtain higher government salaries for teachers in primary and elementary schools.

When the Guide General was transferred to Cairo in 1934, his following grew rapidly and soon began to radiate from the capital through the whole of Egypt. Before many years had passed, the members of his Brotherhood included a considerable number of students from al-Azhar; civil servants and other white-collar workers; urban laborers; some officers and many soldiers of the Egyptian army; and large numbers of the peasantry, who are by nature and upbringing religious and conservative. Hasan al-Banna even succeeded in winning many converts from the ranks of the Wafd Party, as well as from the Young Muslim Men's Association and from Young Egypt.

One of the most difficult of all tasks is to estimate the numerical strength of the Muslim Brotherhood at any given period in its history. There are three reasons for this. First of all is the fact that after the Brotherhood developed into a strong politico-religious movement it operated on the edge of, or beneath the surface of, Egyptian political life. In its later years it became subversive; during most of the war years (1940-1945) and when it was officially banned (1949-1951), it functioned as an underground resistance movement. In the second place, it was never possible for observers to differentiate clearly between the active, full-fledged members on the one hand and the affiliated members or sympathizers on the other. Thirdly, since the younger members of the Brotherhood, in the schools and universities, often felt it necessary to keep their ties a secret even from their families, the size of this important segment of the Muslim Brothers has remained uncertain.[25] Public statements as to membership and

---

[25] An interesting story was told to the author by an Egyptian official of the Department of Education in 1952. The official's son, aged eight or ten years, asked his father's permission to join a "religious group" in school, the name of which he did not know. The father gave his permission, "since it was purely religious," but pressed the boy in vain for the name of the group. When the summer holidays were approaching, the boy asked for permission to go to a scout camp with this "religious group." The father refused permission unless the boy could tell him the name of the group. When the father finally learned that his son had joined the Muslim Brotherhood, he was extremely angry and made his son withdraw immediately. – The psychology and the activities of Muslim Brothers in the universities have been made the subject of a very lively novel by P. H. Newby, *The Picnic at Sakkara* (New York, 1955).

the number of branches of the organization were occasionally made by Hasan al-Banna and later Brotherhood leaders. Such statements were suspect for the reasons given above.

Heyworth-Dunne, an Arabic scholar who lived in Egypt for some twenty years, was constrained to cite an English author and the *New York Times* for membership estimates in 1946 and 1948.[26] Professor Ishaq Musa al-Husayni, author of the most extensive history of the Muslim Brotherhood in recent times, gave some attention to this problem, but he found that reliable figures were unobtainable. In one instance he cited *al-Ikhwan al-Muslimun* (the Brotherhood newspaper) for 1946, but this journal in its turn had been obliged to rely on statistics gleaned from the London *Times*![27]

According to available sources, only the following rough estimates can be hazarded. Hasan al-Banna and six Muslim Brothers launched the movement in 1928. By 1934 there were some fifty Egyptian branches of the organization and by 1939 the fully staffed branches had increased to about five hundred.[28] In 1946, according to Hasan al-Banna, the Muslim Brothers were reckoned at half a million. Two years later a subsequent Brotherhood memorandum repeated this figure for the active membership and added another half-million supporters (or affiliated members), one million in all. The branches of the organization at that time were thought to number 1,700 to 2,000.[29] The Arab News Agency stated on December 5, 1953: "In 1948 it [the Muslim Brotherhood] was known to have over 2,000,000 members and its power has long been incalculable."[30]

When Sa'id Ramadan, a Muslim Brother official, visited the United States in October, 1953, he also reported an "estimated" two million members and 2,000 Egyptian branches. He further stated that 85 per cent of the university students enrolled in all the "Federations of Students" were Muslim Brothers.[31] In 1954 Muhammad Shawqi Zaki estimated that the number of active members of the Brotherhood stood at "more than a million," and that the branches

[26]   *Op. cit.*, p. 68.
[27]   Al-Husayni, *op. cit.*, pp. 39-40.
[28]   Heyworth-Dunne, *op. cit.*, p. 17.
[29]   These figures are from an unprinted but reliable source, which the author is not permitted to cite.
[30]   *Mideast Mirror*, December 5, 1953, p. 11.
[31]   *Middle East Report*, Vol. VI, No. 3 (October 2, 1953), p. 1.

numbered about 1,500, seventy of which were established in Cairo.[32] The central office of the Brotherhood in Cairo had its own membership registers, of course, but they were accessible only to the Guide General and his closest associates. Similarly, the branch registers were never open to the public.

The Muslim Brotherhood first spread outside Egypt in 1937. In that year branches were established in Syria (at Damascus, Aleppo, Deir el-Zor, and Latakia), and in Lebanon (at Beirut and Tripoli). In 1946 branches were established in Palestine, Jordan, and the Sudan. The Muslim Brothers claimed fifty Sudanese branches in 1952, but it is possible that some of these were merely indigenous Islamic organizations, renamed.[33] Today the strongest non-Egyptian organization of the Muslim Brotherhood is undoubtedly in Syria.[34] In Jordan there is a vigorous group, and there still are branches in the Sudan. It has proved difficult for the Brotherhood to maintain a foothold in Lebanon – partly because half of the Lebanese population is Christian. Iraq, despite the majority of Shi'i (heterodox) Muslims in its population, has branches of the Muslim Brotherhood. In Yemen there has been a strong suspicion, from time to time and particularly in 1948 when the ageing Imam Yahya was assassinated, of Brotherhood activity; but there has been no verification of the existence of an operating group in that "closed" country. Saudi Arabia, the heartland of puritan Wahhabism, has an *Ikhwan* organization of its own; the Muslim Brotherhood of Egypt has not been encouraged to establish branches there. Recently, however, this Egyptian Brotherhood has begun to reach out beyond the Arab world: to Pakistan, a Muslim country most susceptible to Pan-Islamic propaganda, and to the southern Sudan and perhaps even further into Africa.

After having summarized what details are available on the organization and the numerical strength of the Muslim Brotherhood, the next problem is to review the general ideology of the Muslim Brothers of Egypt. Their ideology is, of course, inextricably intertwined with their propaganda.

---

[32]   Author of the book *al-Ikhwan al-Muslimun wa al-Mujtamaʿ*, published in 1954; cited by al-Husayni, *op. cit.*, p. 48.

[33]   Al-Husayni, *op. cit.*, pp. 25, 39-40, 135-137, 144, 146, 149.

[34]   See, below, p. 236, n. 8.

The ideological motivation of the Muslim Brotherhood had its first source in the ardent, eloquent, forceful personality of the founder of the Brotherhood. Hasan al-Banna, like the founder of the Saudi Arabian Wahhabis, was a strict Hanbalite, extremely well versed in Hanbalite law. He proclaimed a need for the intensive purification of religious belief and practice, and he insisted upon a literal interpretation of the Koran and the Sunnah as the sole sources of doctrine and law. He later came to share with the early Wahhabis a tendency to restore the primitive concept of *jihad*: holy war in defence of Islam. In published statements, however, he repeatedly asserted that the Brotherhood did not contemplate the use of force to attain its objectives.

On the other hand, Hasan al-Banna was naturally more alive to the threat to religious orthodoxy implicit in modernization and material progress than were the Wahhabis of Saudi Arabia. At the same time he recognized the value of certain innovations, provided they were integrated within a general movement for Islamic reform. Because of the social and economic changes in modern Egyptian society, he perceived the social necessity for a reform program. In contrast, however, to Muhammad 'Abduh and like-minded modernists, he did not recognize any intellectual necessity in modern Egypt for a restatement of Islamic doctrine. A significant factor contributing to his desire for a social and economic reform program was the fact that the industrial and commercial enterprises of Egypt were largely in the hands of *non*-Muslims. To sum up: al-Banna feared the cumulative effect of change in Egyptian Muslim life, and most specifically all secularizing tendencies. He felt that Islamic modernism had gone much too far; he believed that the fundamentals of Islam were threatened – perhaps even the very existence of Islam. And lastly, as a spiritual heir of Jamal al-Din al-Afghani, founder of the Pan-Islamic movement, he placed a new emphasis on the universalism of Islam. He held all Muslims to be brothers, whether Arab or non-Arab; and he believed that all Muslims should unite to strengthen the Islamic world and to re-establish the principles and the practices of Islam in its purest form – that is, to strengthen Islam against "the encroachments of materialism."

As must be the case in any total program, particularly an Islamic one, the lines of demarcation between political, social, and economic policies were not very clear-cut. There was a good deal of over-lapping. Hasan al-Banna's political program was – inevitably, from a historical point of view – the simplest of the three, because it demanded a return to Islamic government.[35] The state was to be administered by Muslims and for Muslims – though the followers of other religious groups were to be allowed to live unmolested within the body politic. The government of Egypt was to be unequivocally established on Islamic law. All political parties were to be abolished, in accordance with the strict unitarian character of Islam, on the assumption that all Muslims should collaborate harmoniously for the welfare of the whole community.

Hasan al-Banna always maintained that the true Islamic system was essentially democratic and that Islam could provide an answer for all the ills of the modern world. He asserted that Muslims did not need to borrow political formulae or social ideas from any foreign source. He used to tell his followers that if a Communist, or a socialist, or a representative of any other politico-social system were to attempt to prove the superiority of another way of life, the line of refutation was plain: he should be told that the Muslim "has all and more," that everything demonstrably good in other systems could be readily found in Islam.[36]

When it came to spelling out specific proposals for an Islamic government, however, Hasan al-Banna was always vague. He never explained his precise intentions. Even on the all-important question of restoring the Caliphate he failed to give a clear answer. In 1938, for example, long after the indecisive Caliphate Conference held in Cairo in 1926, al-Banna made the following public statement:

The *Ikhwan* believe that the Caliphate is the symbol of Muslim Unity, and the link between the Muslim peoples. The Caliphate is a religious

---

[35] "There is no doubt that the 'religious government' is at the head of their [the Muslim Brothers'] program." Husaini, *op. cit.*, p. 62; also pp. 63, 49, 131. In the view of Hasan al-Banna and his Brethren, "Islam embraces all the affairs of men in this life and in the next. . . . It is therefore 'doctrine, worship, fatherland, citizenship, religion, state, spirituality, action, a Koran, and a sword.' " *Ibid.*, p. 62, citing Hasan al-Banna's *Min Khutab*, p. 9. Furthermore, and because of the all-inclusiveness of "the Islam of the Muslim Brothers," politics is also "an integral part of Islam and the program of the Brethren." *Ibid.*, p. 62; also pp. 24, 26, 46.

[36] Husaini, *op. cit.*, pp. 33, 40.

office to which all Muslims should give considerable thought and importance . . . .

The Muslim Brotherhood gives top priority to the restoration of the Caliphate. At the same time they believe that this necessarily requires considerable preparation, and that the direct step to the restoration of the Caliphate must be preceded by various stages. [First of all] there must be complete educational, social, and economic co-operation between all the Muslim peoples. [These steps should then be] followed by treaties, meetings, and conferences between the Muslim countries . . .[37]

Arab disunities after 1930 – coupled with the fact that Iraq, Syria-Lebanon, and Palestine-Transjordan were under the Mandatory governments of two foreign Christian Powers – made the issue of the Caliphate a delicate one. The kind of co-operation contemplated by Hasan al-Banna was scarcely feasible until after the Second World War. He had therefore to walk warily.

Vagueness on such basic issues had its drawbacks, but from the purely propaganda point of view it was perhaps wiser to demand support for a simple, grandiose, and nebulous ideal. The very vagueness of his program prevented carping critics, whether hostile or sympathetic, from fastening upon specific issues to debate them. He accordingly spared himself the embarrassment of having to refute arguments designed to expose the impracticalities inherent in his dream of restoring an outmoded system of imperial government.

In one matter Hasan al-Banna was deplorably precise and definite. He demanded that punishments prescribed by the Shari'ah for certain offences (known as *hudud*) should be restored. If this were done, judges would be constrained to mete out sentences of stoning or scourging for sexual misconduct and for drinking intoxicating liquors, amputation of the hands for theft, and varying other harsh punishments for robbery.

In coping with the triple, and often divergent, responsibilities of duty to one's country, to the larger Arab community, and to the still larger Muslim communities, Hasan al-Banna was in some ways a pioneer – breaking ideological ground without benefit of any author-

---

[37]   This quotation is from the text of a lecture delivered by Hasan al-Banna at a conference commemorating the tenth anniversary of the Muslim Brotherhood. The importance of the occasion made this one of his most important declarations on the Caliphate. This lecture was finally printed under the title *Kayfa nafham al-Islam* [*Our understanding of Islam*] (Damascus, [1949?]). The quotation is from pp. 56-57 of this pamphlet.

itative modern precedent. He was faced with the necessity of finding a workable formula that would satisfy the requirements of Egyptian nationalism, Pan-Arabism, and Islamic internationalism. How was he to integrate the universality of the latter concept with the particularity of the first and the in-between character of the second?

Western nationalist concepts with all their political trappings had been introduced into the Arab world long before the advent of Hasan al-Banna. And national states after Western models – the most jealously exclusive of which was Egypt – had been established in the Arab world under the aegis of Western powers. There was a significant difference, nevertheless, between Arab nationalism, as it developed, and Western nationalism in its home territory before it was exported to the Middle East. Arab nationalism has no trace of racism, and the modern Arab states are separated from each other by no racial barriers. Arabs, in all the Arab countries, today conceive of themselves as a "nation," one and indivisible; and Arab Muslims consider themselves part of a single Islamic community under the One Indivisible God. Hasan al-Banna attempted to solve this loyalty problem by coining some dozen Arabic terms to describe loyalty or devotion to the world of Islam, to the Islamic code of conduct, to resolute propagation of Islamic principles over the whole earth, to one's country, to one's people, to one's ancestral heritage, to one's special group in the community, to the aims and ideals of one's group, and so on. He ended by declaring that it was the duty of all Egyptian Muslims to be loyal to Egypt, loyal to the ideal of Pan-Arabism, and loyal to the ideals of Islamic internationalism – in the hope, presumably, that no conflict would ever arise between these three ideals.[38]

The practical difficulty inherent in this triple loyalty concept can readily be perceived. Hasan al-Banna assigned no priorities to these three loyalties, except that implicit in the order of their listing. In the 1930's it would obviously have been impolitic for any Egyptian to do otherwise. In those days most Egyptians, like their government, considered Egypt to be a country apart, a unique national entity. They held aloof from the problems of the Arab world around them; theirs was a mixed heritage and they revered the ancient glories of their Pharaonic civilization as much as they did the Golden Age of Islam

[38] See, below, p. 174, on *Daʿwatuna*.

in which they later participated. Many stirring events were to take place before Egyptians played a major role in Arab affairs. Intensification of the Arab-Zionist struggle over Palestine, after 1937, aroused increasing Egyptian sympathy for the Palestine Arabs; and the determination of the Syrian and Lebanese Arabs to free themselves from the heavy hand of the French Mandatory Power, during and after the Second World War, likewise stimulated a warm fraternal response in Egypt. The Arab League was nurtured and given final shape in Cairo in the spring of 1945. And the Arab-Israeli war of 1948 eventually made Egyptians active partners in the Arab struggle for independence. But it was not until after the Revolution of 1952 in Egypt that Egyptians recognized the full dimensions of Arabism and the potentiality of leadership in the Arab world. Not until 1956 did Egyptians, for the first time in modern history, declare themselves to be Arabs, "an organic part of a greater Arab entity." [39] Before that time arrived, the Muslim Brotherhood had committed itself to a struggle for power with the "secular" Government of the Revolution; and the Brotherhood was worsted, at the end of 1954, on the issue of the nature of government in Egypt. It was plain by then that the triple ideal impressed upon the Muslim Brethren by Hasan al-Banna was interpreted by the succeeding generation of Muslim Brothers as giving priority to the ideal of Islamic government (based upon Koranic Law) and Islamic internationalism, and that this ideal induced them, in the course of their struggle for power, to embark upon a subversive campaign against the government of Egypt. The details of their struggle against the military officers of the Revolution will be outlined in a later chapter of this narrative. But it deserves mention here that the Ulama of al-Azhar took the part of the Revolutionary Government against the Muslim Brotherhood.

The principal negative motivation of the Brotherhood movement in the 1930's was its aggressive determination to defend Islam against all foreign influences and encroachments. In view of the fact that the Muslim Brothers considered the progressive secularization of Egyptian life to be a threat to traditional Islamic institutions and an en-

[39] In January, 1956, the new constitution of Egypt acknowledged that Egyptians were a part of the Arab "nation" and the Arab world. See the Constitution of January 16, 1956, Preamble: "We, the People of Egypt, realising that we form an organic part of a greater Arab entity . . ." Also Part I, Article 1: "The Egyptian people are an integral part of the Arab nation."

croachment on the Islamic way of life, and in view of the further fact that all secularizing tendencies could obviously be attributed to the multitudinous impacts of the West on Egyptian society, the Muslim Brotherhood took a strong position against the westernization of Egypt. Hasan al-Banna rejected, in theory, westernism in all its forms. And yet, in his effort to make fine-spun distinctions between westernization and the legitimate modernization of Muslim life, he fell into inconsistencies. He never, for instance, resolved the problem of replacing Western-inspired laws with the Shari'ah; and he admitted that compromises between the Shari'ah and existing Egyptian laws would have to be reached. He was too realistic to condemn, as did certain of his followers, all payments of interest on capital – like a son of Europe's 16th century, he took refuge in condemning, without explicitly defining, usurious interest charges and usury. In his letter to Muslim rulers in 1936 al-Banna made one of his few concrete suggestions with respect to solving the problem of usury.[40] Later, in the 1940's, he made the following statement:

The spirit of Islam makes it obligatory that we should abolish interest immediately, and prohibit all transactions based on it . . .

Reformers in the past used to refrain from saying this, in order to avoid being confronted with the argument that abolishing interest is impossible because all economic life is based on it. But today this argument has become weak and without value because interest was prohibited and came to be [considered] the worst abomination in Russia. It is a shame that Communist Russia has preceded us toward this Islamic virtue. Interest is unlawful, unlawful, unlawful . . .[41]

Hasan al-Banna also temporized on the subject of secular education. On the one hand, he strongly advocated religious education, Islamic and Arabic studies, and the study of only a single European language; on the other, he permitted Muslim Brothers – eventually even "Muslim Sisters" – to attend the secular state universities.

He was likewise unclear as to the role of women in modern life; from him came no explicit statement on the extent to which they should be permitted to follow the professions and engage in public welfare service. A feminine branch of the Brotherhood was author-

---

[40] See, below, pp. 169-174, the analysis of al-Banna's pamphlet *Nahwa al-nur* [Toward the light].

[41] *Mushkilatuna fi daw' al-nizam Al-Islami* [Our problems in the light of Muslim institutions] (Cairo, [1948?]), p. 95.

ized during the lifetime of al-Banna and was known as the Muslim Sisters. But for long he was opposed to women's participating in public life in any way, particularly in social life and in mixed company; the Muslim Sisters were segregated as a group, even in the university, and worked separately from the men's groups. The following brief quotations give the fullest extant expression of al-Banna's opinions on the subject of women's place in the Muslim world:

The status of woman should be remedied in such a way as to assure their progress in accordance with the teaching of Islam. The problem of women, which is the most important social problem, should not be allowed to develop unchecked and under the unguided influence of self-interest [and of] eccentrics and extremists.

.   .   .   .

Self-adornment and loose conduct among women should be condemned. Women, especially teachers, students, and doctors, should conduct themselves in accordance with strict standards.[42]

The position of men and women should be improved. Co-operation and equality between them should be encouraged, and the function of each should be specified accurately.[43]

Before the Second World War, the function of each was never specified accurately. After that war, however, when various leaders of the Muslim Brotherhood were questioned publicly as to the status of women, they generally replied that woman's first responsibility was to her home and family. When pushed further, they would add that educated women made the best mothers; that it was permissible for women to be teachers of youth, especially of girls; and that it was also permissible for women to qualify as nurses and doctors – particularly in pediatrics. These professions were looked upon as a logical expansion of home activities. There was a consensus among Muslim Brothers, however, that women should not engage in politics or government; in their view men alone were qualified to govern the country and administer public affairs. Brotherhood leaders were also preoccupied with the adverse effect of bringing politics into the home lest discussions on political affairs or party politics should lead to differences of opinion between a father and a mother and thereby create dissension in the family.

[42]   *Nahwa al-nur* (Amman, 1950), p. 31.
[43]   *Bayna al-ams wa al-yawm* [Between yesterday and today] (Cairo, n.d.), p. 4.

Hasan al-Banna cheerfully made his peace with Western technology. He made personal use of modern inventions such as the press, the telephone, the radio, and the microphone, and he generally wore European dress– though he had his suits made from cloth woven in Brotherhood factories.

Hasan al-Banna, however, despite his reconciliation with Western technology, never made his peace with Western influences in Egyptian manners and morals. He laid the general deterioration of Muslim moral standards at the door of westerners because he believed that foreign residents imported and practiced, and thereby encouraged, a foreign pattern of social behavior. Brotherhood regulations were strictly enforced against gambling, dancing, attendance at theaters and films, and against the drinking of alcohol. Hasan al-Banna eventually succeeded in persuading the Wafdist leader Nahhas Pasha, when the latter was premier in a time of martial law, to issue a decree against gambling, prostitution, and the sale of alcoholic beverages.[44]

With the removal of the Muslim Brotherhood to Cairo in 1934, after Hasan al-Banna's transfer there to a government school, the *viva voce* propaganda of the Brotherhood began to be supplemented with publications. The Guide General gradually organized a press campaign, and he used funds obtained from the contributions of Muslim Brothers to set up a special press for the Brotherhood. His press published pamphlets, tracts, special reports for Brotherhood members, magazines, newspapers, and books.

One of the first books printed in the press of the Muslim Brotherhood was the first volume of a scholarly work written by the father of Hasan al-Banna, Significantly, the work was a new arrangement of the *Musnad* of Ahmad ibn Hanbal, founder of the strictest of the four orthodox schools of Islam.[45] Hasan al-Banna himself published a great number of books and pamphlets, dealing for the most part

---

[44]   See, below, pp. 182-183.

[45]   The *Musnad* of Ahmad ibn Hanbal was a six-volume collection of more than 28,000 traditions. It included the 1,700 juridical traditions collected by Malik ibn Anas in Medina (the burial-place of the Prophet and the first center of Islamic tradition). Malik (c. 715-795), a founder of one of the four orthodox schools of Islam, codified "the oldest surviving corpus of Muslim law." See Philip K. Hitti, *History of the Arabs* (London, 1946), pp. 398-399; also p. 236, note 1.

with the teachings of the Brotherhood, its activities, its aspirations, and its achievements. Al-Banna and his disciples also wrote other works, principally studies of the more theological aspects of Islam and its place in the modern world. Husaini makes the comment that no other modern Islamic movement has been "characterized by such prodigious literary output." [46]

An all-inclusive statement on the objectives of the Muslim Brotherhood was made public in a letter which Hasan al-Banna addressed to the rulers of various Muslim countries in 1936.[47] Copies were also sent to prominent Muslim leaders in the Arab world. In presenting the program contained in his letter, Hasan al-Banna pointed out clearly that he was merely outlining a program, giving only the major subject headings. He recognized that each and every one of his proposals required much study by experts in the different fields. He concluded by noting that he was well aware of the fact that his program did not offer a solution to *all* the problems of national development and progress. The plan which he proposed, admittedly, would require elaboration and its initiation would call for much patience and wisdom – it would not be an easy task. A paraphrased summary of this document, famous in the Muslim world, now follows.

The first part of Hasan al-Banna's lengthy letter is taken up with an indictment of Western civilization and an exposition of the excellences of Islam. Its tone is pacific on the whole, particularly with respect to the foreign relations of Muslim states with the West and the treatment of Christian and Jewish minorities – toward whom Islam "prescribes kindness and generosity," so long as minorities and foreigners conduct themselves peaceably and loyally toward the Muslims among whom they live. On the other hand, Hasan al-Banna makes quite a point of military preparedness on the part of all Muslims. The "Awakening Nation" depends upon a strong army, which in turn draws its strength from a healthy population. According to Hasan al-Banna, prayer and fasting are no more important in the Islamic scheme of things than are power and military preparedness.

---

[46]   Husaini, *op. cit.*, p. 50. See pp. 23-24, 49-50, and 159 for a list of principal publications by Hasan al-Banna and various other Muslim Brothers and of books about Hasan al-Banna and his organization.
[47]   *Nahwa al-nur.* This letter was eventually published in booklet form in both Cairo and Amman in 1950.

He seems also to have believed that Muslims were especially qualified to lay claim to world leadership, largely because of the ethical, just, and religious basis of Islamic nationalism.[48] Thoughts and convictions such as these naturally proved disquieting to such non-Muslims as became aware of al-Banna's pronouncements.

This pamphlet, or letter, gives general emphasis to the importance of education, especially religious and scientific knowledge. The author is quite precise about the sciences, listing botany, chemistry, geology, biology, entomology, and astronomy as being of primary value to Muslims. Emphasis is understandably given to ethics and good character as the prerequisite for success, and also to economics and to public health. But a caveat is included against the pitfalls of secularization, in the firm belief that true progress in an Islamic country cannot be divorced from religion.

Hasan al-Banna associates himself with certain current criticisms of the Ulama group: their weakness in recent times vis-à-vis oppressors and foreigners, and their willingness upon occasion to sacrifice the national cause to their own self-interest.[49] But he stoutly maintains that Islam cannot reasonably be discredited by the shortcomings of a small group of Ulama with "very limited" powers.

The second part of this revealing letter sketches a detailed program for the "practical steps" to be taken by Muslims for their own rehabilitation in the modern world. This is divided into three parts.

The first part of the program deals with political, judicial, and administrative reforms, under ten major headings. Hasan al-Banna calls first of all for the dissolution of all political parties and the reformation of the laws of the land in order to conform with the principles of Islamic jurisprudence. He advocates a strong army composed mainly of young men inspired by the Muslim concept of holy war (*jihad*); the induction of graduates of al-Azhar University into

---

[48]   *Nahwa al-nur* (Amman, 1950), pp. 9-11.
[49]   Certain critics of the Ulama had taken exception to the readiness of the Rector of al-Azhar (who held a political appointment) and the Council of Ulama as a whole to collaborate, upon occasion, with the royal government of Egypt and with the earlier Khedivial government. The still earlier co-operation of the Ulama with officials of the Napoleonic period of occupation — when they accepted representation on the council set up by Bonaparte — was held against them by these same critics. Had the Ulama refused to co-operate with the French conquerors, it was believed, they would have been better able to maintain their independence from political pressures in later years.

the army and the administration; the Islamization of the civil service;[50] supervision of the conduct of workers in the government, together with improvement of their working conditions; and the elimination of favoritism and bribery in all government jobs. A significant article in this political section urges the strengthening of ties between Islamic states, notably the Arab countries, as a preliminary step toward the re-establishment of the Caliphate.

The second and by far the longest part of al-Banna's proposed program is devoted to specific social and educational reforms. More than a third of the thirty articles enumerated in this section are concerned with the maintenance of a high standard of public morality and ethics – citizens must be held accountable for their actions and should be punished if they violate Islamic laws, in accordance with prescribed penalties. Specific prohibitions include the banning of alcoholic drinks, adultery and prostitution, gambling and night clubs, dancing and dance halls. Varying degrees of censorship of plays, songs, films, lectures, broadcasts, and all publications is urgently recommended in order to maintain unsullied the principles of Islam.

Numerous articles in this part of the program relate to the desirability of a unified educational system for Muslims and to the need for basic religious education in all schools and universities. A close working relationship between the village mosques and all village schools should be required. Study of the Arabic language and of Islamic history and culture is especially emphasized. The study of national institutions, on the other hand, is not to be neglected. Memorization of the Koran, at least in part, should still be encouraged. The question of the position of women in the new order remains unclarified. Women should be allowed to achieve progress, within the framework of Islamic custom; but co-education is condemned as un-Islamic, and a special educational curriculum for girls – different from that for boys – is considered necessary. This curriculum is not, however, spelled out. All al-Banna says is that "the curriculum for girls should be reconsidered" and that "boys and girls should have separate curricula in many stages of education."[51]

[50] Hasan al-Banna seems not to have intended that only Muslims should be eligible for civil appointments. His idea was that the spirit of Islam should be spread among government employees, and that Muslim civil servants should observe Islamic rites and customs.
[51] *Ibid.*, p. 31.

The proposed social reforms stress the need for a general public-health program – more hospitals, mobile clinics, and the training of more doctors – and concentration upon raising the standard of living in the villages. Serious attention should be given to the health, education, and recreation requirements of villagers and to raising their standard of cleanliness and improving their conduct as good Muslims.

The last part of the program deals with economic problems. Hasan al-Banna is here concerned with planning for the increased productivity of the farmer and the factory worker. To this end, he advocates aiding the workers to develop their skills, encouraging new economic projects to open up new job opportunities,[52] and exploiting more fully the natural resources at hand – notably the reclamation of waste lands and the expansion of mining industries. He is likewise desirous of improving the working conditions of agricultural and urban workers and taking cognizance of their technical as well as their social needs. He is aware of the problems of unemployment and low wages, and he advocates their control by the government. But he does not appear to have given thought, at least at that time (1936), to the relation between a low standard of living and Egypt's swiftly mounting population. One of the articles in the social section of his program specifically encourages marriage, the strengthening of the family, and a high birth-rate – presumably to increase the relative number of Muslims in the population.

A few miscellaneous articles call for special reforms. Certain time-honored customs are condemned on the ground that they are morally offensive and financially depleting. Traditional and extravagant Egyptian ceremonies connected with marriage, birth, and death are notorious examples of customs that have given rise to many abuses since the simpler days of early Islam. The stern anti-westernism of Hasan al-Banna, an ominous foreshadowing of the later xenophobia of the Muslim Brothers, is evidenced in his special exhortation to Muslims to root out all foreign influences in their home lives. Foreign nurses and teachers, alien modes of dress, and family conversation in any foreign language should all be eliminated from the home. Since the upper-class, well-to-do families were habitual offenders, in the

---

[52]   With respect to the encouragement of new economic projects, Hasan al-Banna called attention to the importance of making sure that foreign enterprises should serve primarily the national interest of the country.

eyes of al-Banna, his injunction to Arabize home life was primarily applicable to them. Many of the reforms demanded in this program seem designed to produce not merely cultural unity but cultural uniformity as well.

Hasan al-Banna shows the standard fundamentalist reaction against profits derived from interest; he condemns "usury," and he recommends that the government should take a hand in reorganizing banks and thus ensure that the banks function without running counter to this strict Muslim prohibition. The government should also set an example in repudiating usury by renouncing interest payments in connection with its own projects.[53] Al-Banna takes the position also that the public must be protected against monopolistic companies. In the matter of the charitable tithes (al-Zakah)[54] which every Muslim is traditionally expected to contribute for the public welfare, Hasan al-Banna urges reorganization of their administration; and he recommends that the Zakah revenues should be spent, in part, on charitable enterprises – such as asylums for the care of orphans, the poor, and the aged – and in part on the upkeep of the army.

This letter contains the essence of the early teachings of Hasan al-Banna, wherein his domestic and his Pan-Islamic objectives are skillfully interwoven. He proposes a charter for Muslims the world over. The emphasis of his program is on reform – on the religious, social, and economic rehabilitation of Muslims. But he also stresses Islamic power, adequately supported by military strength, and the need for dedicated Islamic leadership in the East.

The burden of Hasan al-Banna's message to the Muslim rulers is that the Awakening Nation must have hope as well as vigor, initiative as well as determination, and that Muslims are divinely equipped for world leadership. Rulers in the Islamic world should govern according to the principles he has laid down, and he promises them the full support of the Muslim Brotherhood if they accept his program. Al-Banna's statement on strengthening the ties between Muslim countries, as a step prerequisite to the re-establishment of the Caliphate,

[53]   Ibid., p. 34.
[54]   The Zakah is the third "Pillar of the Faith" of the religion of Islam. Kenneth Cragg, op. cit., pp. 150-154, has an illuminating statement on Zakat (i.e., the Zakah) "as the basis of an ideology of social responsibility [and] the institutional witness to the duty implicit in ownership" – since "to have is to share," and "Islam demands economic justice and social neighborliness."

may have been intended as a feeler outside the confines of Egypt, possibly even a tentative bid for future support toward this ultimate goal.

In 1943-1944 the Muslim Brotherhood Press in Cairo published the first edition of Da'watuna,[55] which some scholars translate as "Our Teachings" and others as "Our Propaganda Aims."[56] This pamphlet has a more specialized focus than the one summarized above, entitled "Toward the Light." Its professed aim is to publicize the goals and program of the Muslim Brothers. During a world war it was not practicable to push any proposal for the re-establishment of the Caliphate. By implication, the supposedly temporary limitations imposed on their ideal program are accepted. In any case, the pamphlet confines itself to noting that, since no Caliph exists, Muslims need a judge to arbitrate the inevitable and permissible differences of opinion in the Islamic world. The flexibility of Islam offers Muslims a basic feeling of solidarity.

The pamphlet Da'watuna contains an analysis and definition of permissible loyalties within the framework of the Muslims' overriding loyalty to Islam. The varieties of loyalty – devotion to one's country, to one's heritage, to one's own people, and so on – are tabulated in their ideal interrelationship.

Of special significance, when one considers the turmoils that confronted the Muslim Brotherhood in the decade following publication of Da'watuna, is the fact that this pamphlet divides Muslims into four categories, according to their attitudes toward the Brotherhood. First and foremost are the wholehearted believers; next, the undecided, the potential converts; thirdly, the utilitarians, who are alien to the dedicated spirit of the Muslim Brothers; and, lastly, the opponents and the skeptics, who are blind to the truth – "may God forgive them!"

The impression given by Da'watuna is that the Muslim Brothers seem convinced beyond the shadow of a doubt that they possess the right program, an all-inclusive one, and that they have faithful workers and resolute leaders to achieve their aims – in short, all the in-

[55]   The literal meaning of Da'watuna is "our call" or "our invitation."
[56]   The article by Franz Rosenthal on "The 'Muslim Brethren' in Egypt" – published in The Moslem World, Vol. XXXVII, No. 4 (October, 1947), pp. 278-291 – contains a most interesting analysis of this first edition of Da'watuna. I have used Dr. Rosenthal's translation and summary for my paragraphs on Da'watuna.

gredients of success. To their minds, Islam governs all aspects of life in this world and in the hereafter, and the Brotherhood program is Islamic in every sense of the word. They call for a united Muslim front to cope with all the social and economic problems, the intellectual heresies, the psychological weaknesses, the corrupting foreign influences that endanger the substructure of Islam.

The Muslim Brotherhood entered the field of pure journalism eight years after establishing its headquarters in Cairo. *Al-Ikhwan al-Muslimun* ("The Muslim Brotherhood") has been the name of various journals published to serve the cause of the Brethren. The first of these began publication as a bi-weekly magazine in August, 1942. After a time this magazine was issued once a week. In May, 1946, a daily morning newspaper of the same name appeared; it was continued, with some interruptions, until 1950. Ahmad al-Sukkari, a friend of Hasan al-Banna from his college days at Dar al-ʿUlum, was its first editor. He was succeeded in 1948 by Salah al-ʿAshmawi, one of the most militant of the Muslim Brothers. A little while after *al-Ikhwan al-Muslimun* ceased publication, Salah al-ʿAshmawi began to publish *al-Daʿwah* ("The Call"). But as this paper was both owned and edited by ʿAshmawi, it was not technically the official organ of the Brotherhood. After the split between ʿAshmawi and al-Hudaybi in 1953, *al-Daʿwah* sometimes reflected views that differed from those of the Supreme Guide and the Guidance Office. Finally, a monthly magazine called *al-Muslimun* was published in Cairo by Saʿid Ramadan, son-in-law of the founder of the Muslim Brotherhood. Many of the articles in this magazine were devoted to explaining the application of Muslim legal principles to the daily lives of contemporary Muslims.

In the realm of journalism the Muslim Brothers were notably inferior propagandists. The westernized press of Egypt had set a high journalistic standard for both its Arabic and its foreign-language periodicals during the present century. Brotherhood writers had so much professional competition, and were so intent upon their Islamic message, that they neglected to develop other fields of interest to attract Egyptian readers. They presented subjects of national and international interest inadequately. Articles in the Brotherhood newspapers and journals were poorly written, comparatively speaking, and given to monotonous repetitions or exaggerations. During 1946 and 1947 *al-Ikhwan al-Muslimun* was irresponsibly anti-British and xenophobic. On several occasions the paper even charged the British with deliberately introducing cholera into Egypt, and at another time with importing malaria. In November, 1946, the Egyptian government was sufficiently embarrassed by this newspaper's attacks against the British to arrest the editor, Ahmad al-Sukkari.[57]

Although Hasan al-Banna studied Western as well as Islamic propaganda techniques and professedly admired them, and although he used all the modern propaganda aids for his *viva voce* programs – such as the microphone and the radio – he seems never to have mastered the technique of modern journalism.

[57] All ideological journalism in the Arab world is of an inferior calibre; publications of the Muslim Brotherhood were no exception to the general rule. Saʿid Ramadan's monthly, *al-Muslimun*, which began publication on November 30, 1951, was, however, a relatively high-level and scholarly magazine. See Husaini, *op. cit.*, pp. 23, 159. For the titles of several other Brotherhood magazines, including one in 1954 edited by the well-known author Sayyid Qutb, see, *ibid.*, pp. 24, 50. One of the magazines in Husaini's list, the monthly *al-Manar*, was originally published by Shaykh Rashid Rida and was bought by Hasan al-Banna after the former's death in 1935 (Heyworth-Dunne, *op. cit.*, p. 96, note 60). It should be pointed out, moreover, that much of the printed material of the Muslim Brotherhood is difficult to use. Such writings or publications as are available are often vague or incomplete as to details. Furthermore, the idiom is entirely different from Western writings on similar subjects. Once the Muslim Brotherhood became politically powerful, it was by implication, and often in fact, a subversive movement. Several times between 1939 and 1954 the head of the movement was imprisoned or the organization itself was suppressed by the government. During these periods the Muslim Brotherhood operated as an underground resistance movement. And even when it was allowed to operate above ground, or barely tolerated as a dangerous and therefore marginal association, the fear or the expectation of impending suppression encouraged the Muslim Brothers to be secretive about their affairs. The organization always refrained from giving any detailed knowledge to the public concerning its activities.

V

THE HISTORY OF THE BROTHERHOOD, 1928-1952

The history of the Muslim Brotherhood falls, most logically, into two distinct parts: what one may call the constructive period, during the lifetime of its founder, from 1928 to 1949; and the period of political factionalism, from 1949 to the drastic suppression of the Brotherhood at the end of 1954. These two periods, however, must in their turn be subdivided. Between 1928 and 1936 the Brotherhood took shape and consolidated its strength. Then followed a period of expansion between 1936 and 1949, when the Brotherhood organization developed into a powerful politico-religious movement. The period of factionalism likewise falls into two parts. From the death of Hasan al-Banna, early in 1949, to the Revolution of July, 1952, the Muslim Brothers reshaped their organization and strove to regain their influence in Egyptian life. In the last part of the period of factionalism, from 1952 through 1954, the Muslim Brothers embarked upon a life-and-death struggle with the leaders of the Revolution.

From the founding of the Muslim Brotherhood until 1936, the movement was characterized almost exclusively by religious missionary activity and by social welfare work. But after 1936 the Muslim Brothers mixed into Arab affairs beyond the frontiers of Egypt. The Arabs of the Palestine Mandate had become increasingly hostile to their government, owing to the steady expansion of the Jewish National Home. In 1936 and 1937-1939 they openly rebelled against the British Mandatory government.[1] This conflict in Palestine gave

[1] The year 1936 marked the first prolonged period of Arab resistance to the British Mandatory government. In 1937 a Royal Commission made its revolutionary recommendation (in the Peel Report) for the partition of Palestine between the Arabs and the Zionists of the "Jewish National Home." Publication of the Report led to renewed violence in Palestine, and in the autumn

Hasan al-Banna an unexpected opportunity for action and expansion – an opening he was quick to seize. He gave the full moral support of his Muslim organization to the Arabs of Palestine after 1937, and initiated fund-raising campaigns on their behalf. His loyal help earned him the warm commendation of the powerful Mufti of Jerusalem, Hajj Amin al-Husseini.[2]

Hasan al-Banna's wholehearted espousal of the cause of the Palestine Arabs came at a time when new ideas were coming to the surface in Egypt. For the first time, owing to the inspiration of the Palestine Arab rebellion, the exclusive, purely Egyptian nationalism that had been advocated by Mustafa Kamil and his early 20th-century followers began to break down. A new Pan-Arab concept was formulated by 'Abd al-Rahman 'Azzam Bey, Egyptian support was gradually enlisted for a Pan-Arab movement, and Egypt was envisioned as champion of the rights of the whole Arab world.[3] Ali Maher Pasha, a sincere patriot, a staunch Muslim, and the "strong man" of Egypt between 1936 and 1940, was converted to this new concept of Egypt's place or role in the Arab area.[4] Ali Maher was in a key position to secure top-level Egyptian support for the new and significant ideal of Pan-Arabism. He and 'Abd al-Rahman 'Azzam cultivated

---

of 1937 an Arab National Conference met in Bludan, Syria, to affirm general Arab support for the Palestine Arabs and their repudiation of the proposed partition of their country. Even though the British Government refused to act upon this recommendation of the Peel Report, and eventually took a firm stand against partition (in the White Paper of May, 1939), the Arab-Zionist struggle for Palestine was marked by increasing violence after 1937.

[2] Hajj Amin al-Husseini, Mufti of Jerusalem, has long been a controversial figure in the Arab world. As a member of one of the great families of Palestine he headed one of the two most powerful Arab factions in that country. From 1936 to 1939 he actively opposed the British Mandatory government. After the British dissolved the Arab Higher Committee (of which he was the leading member), Hajj Amin left Palestine secretly, late in 1937; but he continued to give material aid and encouragement to the Palestine Arab rebellion from his refuge in Lebanon. During the Second World War he helped to spark the Iraqi revolt of 1941 against the British; and when that revolt was put down he fled, via Iran and the Balkans, to Germany.

[3] 'Abd al-Rahman 'Azzam Bey (later Pasha) was the first Secretary-General of the Arab League that was established in 1945.

[4] After King Fuad died in April, 1936, Ali Maher – one of the group of independent Pashas, without party affiliations – served as prime minister (twice) and as Chief of the Royal Cabinet during the early years of the very young and inexperienced King Farouk. He was widely respected as Egypt's first "reform prime minister."

Hasan al-Banna. They understood the strength of the militant spirit of Islam and the potential uses of a well-disciplined Islamic organization. Therefore they sought to obtain the backing of Hasan al-Banna and his Brotherhood, with its grass-roots support, for a national program that would secure to Egypt the leadership of the Arab world. Al-Banna warmly reciprocated the interest shown in him by Ali Maher, and sought to exploit it for his own ends.

The turbulent years from 1936 to the beginning of the Second World War were years of opportunity for Hasan al-Banna. The Palestine Arab rebellion of 1937-1939 was the turning point in his career, and his work on behalf of the Palestine Arabs brought many unanticipated developments in its wake – in addition to rapprochement with influential government leaders. This rapprochement gave him a hitherto unattainable personal status in Egypt, and with this new status he acquired definite political ambitions.

These ambitions were unpalatable to some important members of the Brotherhood who held that their movement should remain aloof from all political connections and that it should concentrate exclusively upon religious and social objectives.[5] Hasan al-Banna was accordingly faced, for the first time, with a serious split in the ranks of the Muslim Brotherhood. When in 1939 this opposition led to a test for the control of the Brotherhood, al-Banna sternly overrode the objections of the dissident Brothers. Thenceforth he grew more and more dictatorial, and it became increasingly obvious that he was intent upon leading a political movement.

[5] J. Heyworth-Dunne, *Religious and Political Trends in Modern Egypt* (Washington, D. C., 1950), pp. 27-28, reports this split in the Muslim Brotherhood, but gives no names, stating merely that a group of the Brotherhood's "best representatives met in 1939, and drew up an ultimatum asking their leader to dismiss Ahmad al-Sukkari because of his political tendencies, and for the immediate cessation of all political contacts in general, and with 'Ali Maher in particular." He adds that "[Hasan al-Banna] refused to accept this ultimatum and continued to have political conversations with the same groups. He dismissed those who had acted against him and threatened them with police action should they give away the secrets of the Society." In a footnote to this brief statement Heyworth-Dunne makes the point that "Some of these rebels [against Hasan al-Banna] had belonged to the Wafd and probably preferred Nahhas to 'Ali Maher . . ." He indicates, furthermore, the close relations between Ali Maher and Hasan al-Banna in the following note: "There is ample evidence to prove that the Police were protecting Hasan al-Banna, probably on instructions from a higher authority, or on account of their sympathies for 'Ali Maher . . ." (p. 88, notes 26, 27).

The active involvement of Hasan al-Banna in the rebellion of the Palestine Arabs facilitated the expansion of the Muslim Brotherhood outside Egypt. Across the Palestine bridge personal contacts were made with Muslims of the other Arab countries, and the Muslim Brotherhood won converts throughout the Fertile Crescent. But the work of the Brotherhood during this period also had other and far-reaching consequences. Hasan al-Banna dedicated the press and propaganda machinery of his organization to a relentless and often violent anti-British campaign. This campaign was based in the first instance upon support for the Arabs of Palestine, but it was soon transmuted on the home front into a campaign against the British in Egypt. In course of time a general spirit of xenophobia, derived from their Anglophobia and associated with terrorist tactics, developed among the Muslim Brothers and eventually became an integral part of their program.

By 1939 Hasan al-Banna was pre-eminent among the leaders of Islamic groups, and the Muslim Brotherhood could boast greater numerical strength and a more tightly knit organization than any rival association. More and more Egyptian politicians began to seek the active support of al-Banna.[6] And many adherents were won over

[6]   Between the end of 1940 and early 1941 the secret military organization of "Free Officers," which eventually launched the Revolution of 1952, tried to form an alliance with the Muslim Brotherhood. Colonel Anwar al-Sadat was instructed to get in touch with Hasan al-Banna, which he did. According to Colonel al-Sadat, the Muslim Brotherhood was looked upon by the Free Officers as a potentially "useful ally"; and Hasan al-Banna, a "dominating" figure on the Egyptian political scene, "had a surprising intuitive grasp of the problems facing Egypt." See Anwar El Sadat, *Revolt on the Nile*, (London, 1957), pp. 26, 29-30, 43. – According to one authoritative English observer, long resident in Egypt, Hasan al-Banna responded more than favorably to these overtures. He tried to "merge" the officers' movement into the terrorist wing of the Brotherhood. In 1942, al-Banna "proposed that the whole officer-group should join the Brotherhood, which would have meant an oath of un-questioning obedience to himself. Colonel Nasser refused..." Tom Little, *Egypt* (New York, 1958), p. 192. Mr. Little founded the Arab News Agency in Cairo (after the Arab-Israeli war) and was editor of its publication, the *Mideast Mirror*. – In 1946 and after, serious friction developed upon occasion between Hasan al-Banna and the Free Officers. It became increasingly apparent that the ideology and the terrorist tactics of the Muslim Brotherhood, and the ambitions of the Supreme Guide, were inimical to the interests of the army Revolutionary movement. *Ibid.*, pp. 248-254; see also, below, chap. vi, *passim*. Until 1947, however, the Free Officers maintained fairly close relations with Hasan al-Banna – "the only man in the Muslim Brotherhood with

to the Brotherhood from other rival organizations – members were even weaned away from the Young Muslim Men's Association and Young Egypt. The leader of the latter group, Ahmad Hussein, paid the ultimate tribute of imitation to al-Banna when he changed the name of his own organization (in 1940) to the "Nationalist Islamic Party," allegedly because he recognized the power of the Muslim Brotherhood and sought to build up the strength of his own group by insisting that it was also a *Muslim* association.[7]

The relations of Hasan al-Banna with al-Azhar University and its powerful hierarchy of mosque preachers, institute teachers, and authoritarian Ulama were equivocal. As might have been expected, this body of Muslims – with a special position to maintain and with vested interests to protect – was wary in the extreme of al-Banna and his Brotherhood. The Ulama in particular, though they recognized the value of religious fervor to Egyptian society and acknowledged the importance of a vigorous movement composed of devout Muslims, had all the traditional skepticism of an intellectual elite group toward the members of a heterogeneous popular movement wanting in intellectual discipline. Furthermore, as the power of Hasan al-Banna grew, they became jealous of the popularity of a leader whom they could not control. On the other hand, the Rector of al-Azhar held a political appointment, so that as long as al-Banna was *persona grata* with the government, al-Azhar refrained from overt hostility and never actively opposed the Muslim Brotherhood. Hasan al-Banna for his part always conciliated the Azhar, because it was a symbol and center for the expression of Muslim solidarity as well as a reservoir (at least in its lower echelons) of recruits for his movement. But he often found it difficult to counteract Azharite resentment against his influence over Azhar students and his proselytism in their midst.

---

whom we had any contact." But it is apparent from Colonel al-Sadat's account that each group was extremely wary of the other, and that each group sought to augment its own strength with the help of the other. El Sadat, *op. cit.*, pp. 43-45, 55, 61, 79-81, 83. See also, below, p. 198, note 4.

[7] Heyworth-Dunne, *op. cit.*, p. 30. For the years 1936-48, and an interesting account of Hasan al-Banna's politics during that time, see also, *ibid.*, pp. 22-48, and Marcel Colombe, *L'Evolution de l'Egypte, 1924-50* (Paris, 1951), pp. 264-269. – For the years 1936-39 see *Oriente Moderno*. Every issue of this important periodical contained a section on Egypt which drew extensively upon the Arabic newspapers of that country.

During the war, and particularly after the resignation of Premier Ali Maher in 1940, Hasan al-Banna developed an opportunistic and subtle operating technique for gaining more political power. In the presence of a strong prime minister, he played down the political aspects of his movement and insisted upon the religious character of the Brotherhood; in the presence of a weak prime minister, he debated political issues and pushed his claim for political recognition. But these tactics did not save him from temporary internment early in the war because of his too well-known anti-British propensities.[8] Even before the war his anti-British propaganda had coincided with a virulent Fascist-Nazi campaign against the British in the Middle East, and some people even thought he was working for the Italians and the Germans in the area. Like the Mufti Hajj Amin al-Husseini in Palestine, he never abandoned his demand that the British should be forced to relinquish their special position in Egypt. Hasan al-Banna and his followers dramatized to the full his persecution at the hands of the government and, consequently, he emerged from his internment stronger than ever.

In 1942, when the Wafd came to power as the result of a British ultimatum to King Farouk, the Wafdist leader, Nahhas Pasha, thought it would be politic to hold general elections. Hasan al-Banna decided that the moment was opportune to run for election to the Chamber of Deputies. He chose Ismailia, the birthplace of the Muslim Brotherhood, for his constituency. Nahhas Pasha, convinced as were all observers that the leader of the Muslim Brotherhood would win this election in Ismailia against the Wafdist contestant, sent for the Brotherhood leader and persuaded him, with some difficulty, not to run. Al-Banna, fully aware of his own strength in Egypt, but aware also of the fact that Nahhas Pasha would probably have him interned again if he refused, agreed to withdraw. He offered to give up the almost certain prospect of a seat in the Chamber of Deputies for a price: he would yield to Nahhas, provided that the prime minister would guarantee to introduce anti-vice legislation in line with the platform of the Muslim Brotherhood. As Egypt was then under

---

[8] Hasan al-Banna was imprisoned in May, 1941. According to Laqueur, al-Banna was released when the Wafd came to power, early in 1942, upon giving a promise to Nahhas Pasha to discontinue his pro-Axis propaganda. See Walter Z. Laqueur, *Communism and Nationalism in the Middle East* (New York, 1956), p. 237.

martial law, Nahhas Pasha kept his promise by issuing instructions to restrict the sale of alcohol and to prohibit prostitution and gambling. This bargain constituted a moral victory for the Brotherhood. And Hasan al-Banna was able to pose once again as a "martyr" – a man who had sacrificed himself for the Muslims of Egypt, and whose sacrifice had procured for them certain demonstrable reforms.

For a time thereafter the Muslim Brotherhood gave passive support to the Wafd Party. But Hasan al-Banna was merely biding his time for strategic reasons; his agreement with Nahhas Pasha had been in the nature of a truce rather than an armistice. As soon as the Wafdists went out of office in 1944, al-Banna joined in the current attacks against them. Makram Ebeid Pasha, a distinguished Coptic minister who had left the Wafd to establish a party of his own, gave Egyptians a great store of ammunition to use against the Wafd in his famous "Black Book" on the corruption rampant in that party. No one made more telling use of this exposure than did Hasan al-Banna. He attacked Wafdist policies and politicians in the press, and his Muslim Brothers in school and university fought the Wafdist students on the street and on the campus. Many members of the Wafd abandoned their party, and many of these seceders joined the Muslim Brotherhood.

Had the Brotherhood leader been elected to the Chamber of Deputies in 1942, his subsequent career might have been vastly different. He could have followed a conventional path to power within the framework of government institutions; his "religious association" would have become a formal political party; and he might, just possibly, have gained control of the government by constitutional means if not by a coup d'état. Having got that far, he could then have tried to establish the Islamic state which he had long advocated. But as it was, he remained outside the government; he made increasing trouble for every party leader who took office after 1944; and his Brotherhood gradually turned into a subversive organization. Al-Banna's anti-Wafd campaign became part of an inclusive plan to undermine all the political parties of Egypt. Slowly the Wafd Party began to lose its grip on the country, and, *pari passu*, the Muslim Brotherhood grew stronger – especially in the provinces. Hasan al-Banna began to think of himself as a real power in the land.

In 1947 the Muslim Brotherhood became the dominant member

of a newly established union composed of fifteen nationalist and Islamic groups or associations. Their collective programs called for the immediate "liberation" of Egypt – i.e., from the British bonds of the 1936 treaty – and for the reformation of political and social life in Egypt. In 1948 the Muslim Brothers threw themselves with fervor into the Arab-Israeli war, and Hasan al-Banna made speeches in support of the Mufti, Hajj Amin al-Husseini, and the Mufti's provisional government in Palestine.

This war, which temporarily gave activity to the Muslim Brothers outside Egypt, also gave them invaluable experience in guerrilla warfare and terrorist techniques. They learned as much from observing Israeli tactics as they did from the actual fighting in which they were engaged as dedicated volunteers.[9] When defeat in the field returned them to Egypt humiliated and embittered – as were all Egyptians who participated in the fighting against the Israelis – their bitterness was intensified by the arms scandal and other evidences of venality on the part of the Palace clique and the Egyptian government. The returning members of the Brotherhood had gained fighting experience; their fanaticism had risen to new heights; and they brought back with them enough arms and ammunition to become a grave security problem in Egypt.

Hasan al-Banna seems to have felt, more urgently than ever, that true Muslims could wait no longer to destroy the forces of secularism, to "purify" Egypt, and to establish – in his words "to restore" – an Islamic government in the country. Egyptian politicians who opposed the principles and the program of the Muslim Brotherhood, as well as Egyptians or foreigners who showed any pro-British leanings, became the targets of Brotherhood terrorist attacks, and the steady deterioration of Egyptian political life facilitated such lawlessness. The prime minister of the day, Nuqrashi Pasha, recognized the danger. Fearful that the Muslim Brotherhood contemplated the overthrow of the government after their assassination in Cairo of the police chief Amin Zaki, he decided to move against them forthwith and to break the power of their organization. In December, 1948, the Brotherhood was dissolved by proclamation under the martial law which was in effect during the Palestine war, and for some time thereafter its headquarters and branches were closed down, its pa-

9   See, below, p. 191.

pers and accounts were confiscated by the police, and its ample funds were frozen. The Muslim Brothers, who were then thought to number nearly two million, were driven underground.

Nuqrashi Pasha paid for this bold action with his life. And some seven weeks later, on February 12, 1949, Hasan al-Banna was assassinated by some supporters of the government who were not identified at the time. As Hasan al-Banna was leaving the headquarters of the Young Muslim Men's Association, he was shot down by several men who had been lying in wait for him in an automobile. It was later believed that Ibrahim 'Abd al-Hadi, who succeeded the murdered Nuqrashi as prime minister, had, with the connivance of the king, instigated the assassination of Hasan al-Banna because he was afraid to arrest him. 'Abd al-Hadi was eventually tried for this crime, in 1953, under the Government of the Revolution.

Thus ended the first phase in the history of the Muslim Brotherhood.

From the death of al-Banna until the spring of 1950, when a Wafdist government abolished martial law, the Muslim Brotherhood remained quiescent. Thousands of the Brothers had been arrested by Nuqrashi Pasha's successor in office and all but two of its leaders interned. The death of their Supreme Guide was an incalculable loss to the organization, but the Brothers used the time of their removal from the Egyptian scene to reorganize the administration of their association and to plan for the future, bleak though it then promised to be. Even in May, 1950, when the internees were all released and the Wafd Party embarked upon a policy of tentative appeasement of the Muslim Brotherhood, the movement's future was still in doubt. The released Brothers resumed their usual activities, but with great circumspection, while they awaited the issuance of a new law regulating associations: the ban against the Brotherhood was not to be lifted until the promulgation of that new law.

The Egyptian Parliament passed the Associations Law, governing the creation of societies and regulating their activities (the Societies Law, as it is sometimes called), on April 23, 1951. This law became immediately applicable to every social, religious, cultural, and literary association with a membership of more than twenty persons. Within its framework the Muslim Brotherhood was reinstated. Government supporters held that such a law was not only authorized, but was actually required under Article 21 of the Egyptian Constitution; they pointed out that they were now repairing an omission of almost thirty years' standing; and they made it plain, at the same time, that this law would have no control whatever over political parties. A seven-hour debate in Parliament indicated that this legislation was designed to inhibit organized terrorism and to prevent sedition. And the Egyptian public seemed to have no doubt that the new law was primarily intended to serve the government as an instrument of control over the Brotherhood.

During the parliamentary debate over the Associations Law, three thousand Muslim Brothers demonstrated in Parliament Square, vociferously but peaceably. According to a contemporary account, a human pyramid of Muslim Brothers raised on their shoulders orators who declared, "The Associations Law is an instrument of war against us!" and shouted such slogans as "Islam is a religion and a world!" and "Islam alone regulates all human affairs." [10] A deputation of four of the leaders was received in the Chamber of Deputies, and they presented the protests of the Brotherhood, but to no avail. When in spite of their efforts the bill became law, the Brethren were articulately resentful, and they were not in the least pacified by the reinstatement of their association under hampering restrictions.

The controls that affected them most adversely may be summarized briefly as follows: military or paramilitary affiliated groups, and the adherence of members who were legally minors, were forbidden to all associations; a burdensome system of record keeping and the right of police inspection of all papers and accounts were required of every association; and no association was to be allowed to function for any purpose not stipulated under its charter.[11] Shackled by such controls, the Muslim Brotherhood resumed its policy of hostility to the government. And in course of time it violated provisions of the

[10]   For a spirited account of this peaceful demonstration see *La Bourse Egyptienne* for April 19, 1951; see also *al-Muqattam*, Vol. 63, No. 19292 (April 24, 1951), pp. 4, 6 (especially p. 6 for the debate in the Senate). *Al-Muqattam* reported that the Chamber of Deputies passed the Associations Law by a vote of 124 for and 42 against (1 abstention), and the Senate by a vote of 98 for and 6 against. The Arabic text of the law was published in the *Journal Officiel*, No. 36, Special Supplement, April 26, 1951.

[11]   No association could "exceed the ends" for which it was created. See sections 3(f), 8, 10, 11, and 17 of Law No. 66 of April 23, 1951.

law by maintaining a paramilitary group, by expanding its stated religious and cultural aims into the political field, and by keeping secret records inaccessible the police.

Thus the Muslim Brotherhood returned to public life on the eve of a crisis in Anglo-Egyptian relations, namely, the unilateral repudiation by Egypt, in October, 1951, of the Anglo-Egyptian treaty of 1936. After this decision of Nahhas Pasha's Wafdist government, Egypt sank into a state of semi-anarchy. The Wafd government gradually became powerless to maintain internal security; guerrilla fighting against the British in the Canal Zone broke out with increasing frequency; and all xenophobic nationalist and Islamic groups felt that they had unlimited opportunities to exploit. Into this situation the Muslim Brotherhood injected itself, with all the strength of its new streamlined organization, and contributed to chaos in the land.

But a word should here be said concerning the internal affairs of the Muslim Brotherhood, before continuing with its later history.

During the period of their internment, the leaders of the Muslim Brotherhood – a small elite group composed of the men who had served as the principal aides-de-camp of Hasan al-Banna – formed a policy-making committee. It was this group that eventually emerged, after the legal reinstatement of the Brotherhood in May, 1950, as the "Guidance Office," or executive council, of the organization. They selected a Supreme Guide in October, 1950, but he was not formally "elected" until a year later. During the difficult interim period, Salah Mustafa al-ʿAshmawi, one of their most radical leaders, acted as Deputy Supreme Guide.

Even before 1949, factionalism was rife in the upper ranks of the Brotherhood. Hasan al-Banna had been able to hold in check, but not to eradicate, this development. After al-Banna's assassination, however, three factions contended for control of the Brotherhood: a conservative group headed by the late Guide's brother, ʿAbd al-Rahman al-Banna al-Saʿati; a group of extremists, or militant activists, headed by al-ʿAshmawi; and a group of able moderates headed by Dr. Hussein Kamal al-Din and Shaykh Hasan al-Baquri, a nationally recognized Islamic scholar, trained in Muslim law. The weight of political calculation was, of course, on the side of the moderates, because the Brotherhood had the difficult task of gaining the confidence of a government that had good reason to view it with suspicion. For reasons of expediency Shaykh al-Baquri and Dr. Kamal al-Din eventually persuaded the Guidance Office to choose a politically acceptable moderate as Supreme Guide of the Muslim Brotherhood.

The compromise candidate, Hasan Isma'il al-Hudaybi, was a respected judge of the Egyptian Court of Appeal. He had been the legal advisor of Hasan al-Banna as well as his loyal friend. Al-Hudaybi was formally installed as Supreme Guide on October 19, 1951. This choice, which at first seemed a happy one for the Muslim Brotherhood, did not turn out too well in the end. The election of al-Hudaybi was reassuring to the less extremist elements of Egyptian society; but the new Supreme Guide proved to be a weak leader, unable to cope with the dangerous factionalism in his own organization. He had neither the commanding personality of the founder and first Guide of the Muslim Brotherhood, nor any comparable influence among its lowlier members. A little more than two years after his election, his chief opponent within the Brotherhood, al-'Ashmawi, led a revolt against him; and later a secret terrorist group of Muslim Brothers, of whose existence al-Hudaybi stated that he knew nothing, was formed during his regime and became a threat to the life of the Government of the Revolution.[12]

Under the administration of al-Hudaybi, the organization of the Muslim Brotherhood finally developed its pyramidal structure. By November, 1953, to anticipate somewhat, its broad outlines were plainly discernible to the uninitiated. The Guidance Office, an eleven-member executive council, formed the apex of the pyramid and made all policy decisions for the organization in the name of the

[12] For an interesting account of the new Supreme Guide al-Hudaybi see Ishak Musa Husaini, *The Moslem Brethren: The Greatest of Modern Islamic Movements* (Beirut, 1956), pp. 113-114, 116, 122-124. These pages also take cognizance of the split in the Muslim Brotherhood allegedly engendered by al-Hudaybi's special relations with King Farouk. Undeniably, he was at times "close" to the Palace. Husaini also devotes a chapter to the armed Secret Organ of the Muslim Brotherhood (pp. 137-143). Husaini adopts the view that the Secret Organ was first organized by Hasan al-Banna, probably in 1940, and that al-Hudaybi discouraged the militant activities of the Secret Organ after he was elected to the office of Supreme Guide. Al-Hudaybi failed to integrate the Secret Organ with the rest of the Muslim Brotherhood (i.e., under his complete authority), but he did succeed in partly reorganizing it and giving it a new group of leaders (pp. 139, 141). The later terrorist activities of the Secret Organ may have been initiated without his specific sanction.

Supreme Guide. Its most important decisions were, however, referred to the Founders' Committee, next below it in the hierarchy of power, for approval. The members of the Guidance Office were elected annually by the Founders' Committee and were eligible for re-election. The Supreme Guide, elected by the Guidance Office for a term of two years and eligible for re-election, was the twelfth and chief member of this highest policy-making council. But his election had to be confirmed by the Founders' Committee. Once the Guide was elected, all members of the Muslim Brotherhood were required to swear allegiance to him. The Supreme Guide, reportedly, could take no important action (at least after October, 1953) without first obtaining the assent of the Guidance Office.

Next in importance to this small and powerful group was the Founders' Committee, a constituent assembly of 150 members who deliberated on general Brotherhood affairs in parliamentary fashion. This relatively large committee was a potentially powerful one – not only because it approved the choice of the Supreme Guide, elected the members of the Guidance Office, and ratified the major policy decisions made by the Guidance Office, but also because it was in personal touch with the Supreme Guide. The Supreme Guide seems to have had the right to refer proposals directly to the Founders' Committee, and if the committee approved his proposals, the Guidance Office was bound to implement them. This provision obviously opened a channel of power that could be readily exploited by a strong and influential Supreme Guide.

The next step down, below the two higher councils, was a body composed of ten regional committees which represented the Branches. The basic Branch units, variously estimated as between 2,000 and 10,000 in number, formed the base of the pyramid. These were organized pretty much as in the days of Hasan al-Banna, but they were very closely supervised by the bodies at the top of the pyramidal organization. Membership in the Branches was divided between dues-paying members and associate members who were not required to contribute. The Branches played an important national as well as local role, however, because they elected the 150 members of the Founders' Committee. For administrative convenience, the Branches were organized in regional groups, ten in all, each one of which was composed of Branch representatives approved by the Guidance Office. Each Branch elected a chief to preside over its own local business, but even the lowly Branch chief had to have his election confirmed by both the Guidance Office and his own Regional Committee. There was a single Regional Committee (or regional administrative office) for Cairo and a single one also for the second largest city in Egypt, Alexandria; there were four Regional Committees for Lower Egypt and also four for Upper Egypt. The chief of each of these committees was elected by the Branch chiefs in its own region; as in the case of the Branch chief, each Regional Committee chief had to be confirmed by the Guidance Office. Controls from the top did not stop here. A representative from either the Guidance Office or the Secretariat – the "supreme administrative office" which operated directly under the Guidance Office – was required to sit on each of the ten Regional Committees.

The Secretariat restricted its publicly known activities to paper work, but it was strategically placed to act as a listening post. On the one hand, it drew its membership from the Guidance Office and the Founders' Committee – the two highest councils of the Brotherhood, for both of which groups it prepared lengthy reports. On the other hand, it was closely affiliated with the one women's group, the Muslim Sisters Section, and with the press activities and the publications of the Brotherhood. The Supreme Guide normally presided over Secretariat meetings, and his private secretary was one of the four permanent members of this high administrative group, together with three regional representatives.

Such are the main outlines of this tightly knit Brotherhood organization. It is easy to see, even from this skeletal description, why its influence in Egypt steadily expanded, and how it was that orders issued by its supreme council, or Guidance Office, could be efficiently and rapidly executed the length and breadth of the land.[13]

Only one other group of the Muslim Brotherhood needs to be mentioned here: its unofficial military organization known as the "Phalanx of the Muslim Brethren" (*Katibat al-Ikhwan al-Muslimin*). The "Rovers" and the scout groups of Hasan al-Banna's era had been liquidated during the period of reorganization and only this single paramilitary group survived.

[13]   Much of the information on the Brotherhood organization (after 1951) is from a confidential source.

A Brotherhood publication of 1952 described in general terms the hierarchical organization of the battalions that formed the Phalanx of the Muslim Brethren. Its basic unit, the secret group or cell (*usrah*), was composed of ten people. Four of these units formed a larger group of forty, known as an *ʿashirah*; five of the larger groups formed a still larger group of 200, the *raht*; and five of the latter constituted a *katibah*, a battalion of 1,000 men.[14] This collective organization of battalions and their subdivisions was commonly known as the Phalanx, not only because its members received military training, but also in view of the more modern, secondary meaning of the word *phalanx* – namely, a group of persons banded together for a common purpose. The members of each *usrah*, or basic unit, elected their own president or leader (*naquib*) and held weekly meetings. The members brought their problems to these meetings and discussed them and their current activities. They read letters sent from headquarters and studied all matters referred to their attention. And they likewise read books on Islamic jurisprudence, the Traditions, and commentaries on the Koran.[15]

The Phalanx of the Muslim Brethren had been organized originally to enlist and train volunteers for the war against Israel in 1948. Country-wide recruiting had met with generous response, particularly on the part of students and proletarian workers. By the end of 1953, its membership was roughly estimated at five thousand. The senior members had had fighting experience in the Arab-Israeli war; many of them later saw guerrilla action against British troops in the Canal Zone during 1951-1952; and all of its members had received military training. The leader of the Phalanx, until his death in 1951, was a former major in the Ottoman army who had served in the First World War. He was assisted in the training program by a corps of retired and reserve officers of the Egyptian Army, all of them members of the Muslim Brotherhood, and by a group of students who had undergone military training in Egyptian universities.

The recruits of this paramilitary organization were reportedly not required to be members of the Muslim Brotherhood, nor were they

---

[14]   Al-Ikhwan al-Muslimun [The Muslim Brotherhood], *Qism al-Usar, Nizam al-Usar, nash ʿatuh wa ahdafuh* [The group, or cell, system: its development and aims] (1952), pp. 18-19.

[15]   *Ibid.*, pp. 22-23.

even automatically admitted to membership in the Brotherhood after joining the *Katibat*. They were, however, taught to give unquestioning loyalty and obedience to the Muslim Brotherhood and to its Supreme Guide. In addition to military drills and physical culture exercises, the recruits received instruction in the religion of Islam.

A few weeks before the Revolution of 1952, a camp was opened at Dukhaylah, near Alexandria, and thousands of youthful recruits, by report, received their basic training there. In 1953 it was rumored that a certain staff officer of the *Katibat* was engaged in organizing a secret terrorist group, allegedly without the sanction of Supreme Guide al-Hudaybi.

It has been charged from time to time that the Muslim Brothers worked between 1946 and 1952 with underground Communist cells in Egypt. The organization as a whole, with its uncompromising Islamic principles, could never have allied itself with communism. But it is, of course, impossible to say that certain individuals in the Brotherhood may not have been subverted by Communist propaganda. It also is not possible to affirm that no Communist succeeded in infiltrating Brotherhood ranks. Once in a while, when Brotherhood centers were raided by the police, Communist publications were found on the premises. But this is not conclusive evidence. The poorer, semiliterate members of the Brotherhood could have acquired such literature quite innocently, without even recognizing it for what it was; or it could equally well have been planted to discredit them with the government. There were occasions when Muslim Brothers and Communists apparently collaborated to stage destructive – usually antiforeign – incidents. "Black Saturday," with arson, murders, and looting in Cairo on January 26, 1952, was one of these occasions. It seems fairly certain that the Muslim Brothers had a dishonorable share in these black doings, along with the Socialists (led by Ahmad Hussein, of the renamed "Young Egypt" organization) and the Communists.[16] But at least some observers now think that the Communists were primarily responsible for the organized terrorism of that day. On other occasions it has appeared that a bombing or some terrorist incident was planned by Communists, with or without the active aid of the Muslim Brothers, and that Communists then contrived to plant incriminating evidence to implicate

16   See, above, p. 142.

the Brotherhood or even to give the illusion that Muslim Brothers were solely responsible for the outrage. The Brothers had a sufficiently bad record in terrorist activities to give credence to such imputations – they made credible "fall guys."

High-ranking members of the Muslim Brotherhood were split on the issue of a collective policy toward communism. Ideologically, as devout Muslims, they were all extremely antipathetic to communism. But they had no fear of it. The very strength of their religious convictions misled them into thinking that the issue was primarily one of political expediency. They believed absolutely that the armor of Islam would prove impenetrable to atheism or to materialism, and that no infidels could undermine the religious principles of devout Muslims. At the same time, the fervor of their nationalism tempted the more politically minded Brethren to use, or at least to try to exploit, any amenable group ready to hand that would help to further their political or nationalist ends.

Communist cells existed in Egypt although Communist parties under whatever pseudonyms were banned, and their members sought to establish a common cause with all nationalists by vociferously denouncing foreign "imperialism." When the Muslim Brothers considered that the time was ripe to organize a drive against the British in Egypt, the Communists manifestly had their uses. Some of the Brothers – in particular the political extremists, not excepting al-'Ashmawi – were frankly in favor of working with local Communists, or else with the Soviet Union government in Moscow. Others, including al-Hudaybi, went no further than to state that the Soviet Union need not, or should not, be regarded as the enemy of Egypt.[17]

---

[17] As late as August 18, 1953, Supreme Guide al-Hudaybi made the following statement, published in *al-Misri* on that date: "Communism is a creed founded on purely materialistic grounds. It denies all religion and recognizes no relation between man and anything else higher than that between him and his daily bread. As for Islam, it was built first and foremost on the unity of God. It related man eternally to Him in all his deeds. . . . Thus you will find the differences between Communism and Islam tremendous. Communism conflicts with Islam's principles, manners, morals and social system . . . [But] We have no reasons for hostility toward Russia as a state. As an ideal we cannot fear it if we execute the Muslim teachings as they should properly be, for then they must triumph over all other ideals." – Quoted by Husaini, *op. cit.*, pp. 145-146; see also pp. 144-147 for discussion of the attitude of the Muslim Brothers toward communism.

Like some other nationalists in the Arab world, the Muslim Brothers were too ignorant of the real nature of communism to fear it; they thought that they could play with political fire without getting burned; and – what was still more dangerous for them and for their countries – they were generally naive enough to believe that they could put out any Communist-built fire at will.

Only one thing is certain. If ever the Muslim Brothers were to grasp the real nature and the full implications of the international Communist movement, with its attendant dangers to Islamic civilization and its political threat to Muslim independence, they would inevitably agree upon a positive anti-Communist policy. The Muslim Brotherhood would become, without equivocation, an implacable and militant enemy of communism in the Islamic East.

VI

THE MUSLIM BROTHERS CHALLENGE THE
LEADERS OF THE REVOLUTION

Early in 1952 two parallel revolutionary movements were operating
below the surface of Egyptian political life: the Muslim Brotherhood,
and the secret army organization of the "Free Officers," *al-Dubbat
al-Ahrar*. The existence of the Free Officers was only suspected by
the government, however, and its top leaders were not identified by
King Farouk until it was too late to avert their coup d'état which
brought about his dethronement and exile at the end of July, 1952.
A large number of the military – many soldiers and some officers –
were members of the Muslim Brotherhood; but the Free Officers had
carefully excluded the Muslim Brothers from their top executive
committee as well as from their secret counsels.[1]

The coup d'état of the Free Officers marks the greatest event in

[1] Colonel Rashad Muhanna, who organized the abortive army revolt of 1947
and was later one of the three members of the provisional Council of Regents
(established by the Revolutionary Government in 1952 to represent the infant
King Ahmad Fuad II), was probably a Muslim Brother, although he denied
being one. He co-operated with the Free Officers, but he was never a member
of the executive committee (which became the Council of the Revolution).
Colonel Muhanna was dismissed as Regent, in October, 1952, for working
against the Revolutionary Government. In January, 1953, he was arrested for
plotting a counter-revolution, and in March he was tried in camera by the
entire Council of the Revolution and sentenced to life imprisonment. – The
reason given by General Naguib for Colonel Muhanna's plot against the Revolutionary Government was most significant in view of the struggle which had
already begun between the Revolution Command Council and the Muslim
Brotherhood: "[Muhanna] chose to conspire against us on the ground that a
secular republic would be inimical to Islam . . . Although we were . . . preparing
the ground for the establishment of a secular republic, we had no intention,
as Muhanna well knew, of dispensing with religion. Islam would continue to
be the official religion of Egypt . . ." See Mohammed Neguib, *Egypt's Destiny*
(London, 1955), p. 177, and also pp. 14, 32, 149, 150, 175-178.

the history of modern Egypt: the inauguration of the Revolution. Lieutenant Colonel Gamal Abdel Nasser, the "strong man of the Revolution," had been patiently preparing the ground for a coup d'état ever since the Abdin Palace incident of 1942, when the British forced King Farouk to accept Nahhas Pasha as premier. During the war against Israel this group gained strength and purpose. It was then, under the leadership of Colonel Nasser, that the Free Officers met behind the lines to debate their problems and discuss their objectives. Three distinct domestic goals actuated the realistic and forword-looking group of young military men who spearheaded the Revolution. In the first place, there was awareness of the serious financial crisis that faced Egypt in 1952, and a determination to save their country from approaching bankruptcy. There was, in the second place, recognition of the need for basic social, economic, and administrative reforms that would establish social justice for all Egyptians, raise their standard of living, and unite them in a general reform movement. And finally, there was an ardent desire to free Egypt from the incubus of a morally discredited king and his corrupt advisers, a desire which was coupled with a determination to root out corruption in every department of government and the public services. The Free Officers had, of course, another principal, long-range objective: to liberate their country from every vestige of British control and rid Egypt of all foreign troops. They had long shared the primary goal of Egyptian nationalism, resistance to British domination. The national humiliation of the Abdin Palace incident was doubly humiliating to the army, because the ultimatum to the king had been issued in the presence of British tanks. But the Free Officers were the first Egyptian nationalists who realized that they had first to put their own house in order and establish a strong government before they could hope to achieve full national independence.

Following the three-day bloodless coup d'état, King Farouk abdicated in favor of his infant son on July 26, 1952. Thereafter a Regency Council carried on in the name of the monarchy, until the proclamation of the Republic in June, 1953. But the actual Government of the Revolution, created immediately after the dethronement and exile of the King, was in fact a military dictatorship. The Revolution Command Council took to heart the words of Mirrit Boutros Ghali: "The problems which now face the country . . . have become so large and so grave that no solution for them can be contemplated without the intervention of government in practically all aspects of national life."[2] In December, 1952, the Egyptian Constitution of 1923 was abrogated. A fifty-man non-party committee was then appointed under the chairmanship of former premier Ali Maher, the reforming premier of the prewar period, to draft a constitution. Early in 1953 a three-year transitional period was announced, during which General Muhammad Naguib, acknowledged "chief of the Revolutionary Movement," was to exercise his powers through the twelve-man Revolution Command Council.

For the first few months the bitterest opponent of the Revolutionary Government was the Wafd Party. For its own part, the grievance of the new regime against the Wafd was due, not alone to the corrupt practices of so many Wafdists, but also to the fact that a majority of the Wafd leaders had sabotaged a reform program under the monarchy. The men of the Revolution never lost sight of the fact that they had initiated, and had dedicated themselves to, the implementation of two concurrent revolutions, one political and one socio-economic. Colonel Nasser reminded his fellow countrymen of this fact in his autobiographical booklet, *The Philosophy of the Revolution*:

Every nation on earth undergoes two revolutions: One is political, in which it recovers its right for self-government from an imposed despot, or an aggressive army occupying its territory without its consent. The second revolution is social, in which the classes of society would struggle against each other until justice for all countrymen has been gained and conditions have become stable.[3]

Immediately after the Revolutionary coup d'état, the question arose of the prospective relationship between the Muslim Brotherhood and the newly installed Revolution Command Council (hereafter referred to as the R.C.C.). The Brotherhood did not immediately throw its support to the army movement; it waited until it should receive assurances of recognition and support. In July, 1952, five days after

---

[2] Mirrit Boutros Ghali, *The Policy of Tomorrow* (Cairo, 1938, 1951; English ed., Washington, D. C., 1953); quotation from English edition, p. 16.
[3] Gamal Abdel Nasser, *The Philosophy of the Revolution* (Buffalo, N. Y., 1959), p. 36. Nasser's book originally appeared in three articles published in Egypt. The translation quoted here is the third to be published in English and is by far the most authoritative. See also Gamal Abd el-Nasser, *The Philosophy of the Revolution* (Cairo: Dar al-Maaref, n.d.), p. 23.

the inception of the Revolution, the Supreme Guide of the Muslim Brotherhood, Hasan al-Hudaybi, and the Secretary-General, ʿAbd al-Hakim ʿAbidin, were received by General Muhammad Naguib. Shortly thereafter the Supreme Guide sent a circular letter to all *Ikhwan* Branches calling upon the Muslim Brothers to support the army movement. At the same time he began to press for representation in the Revolutionary Government.

It is clear that in the beginning the Free Officers hoped to obtain the co-operation of the Muslim Brotherhood, which had become so powerful in Egypt. All members of the R.C.C., including General Naguib, had friends among the Muslim Brothers. They admired the fighting record of the Brotherhood volunteers in the war against Israel and their long-continued resistance to the former king. The R.C.C., moreover, was made up of devout Muslims who sympathized with the religious principles of the Muslim Brotherhood, even though they all refused to contemplate the establishment of theocratic government in Egypt.[4] Shortly after the inauguration of the Revolution, the new regime took several positive steps to conciliate the Brotherhood. The investigation into the assassination of the first Guide, Hasan al-Banna, was reopened. Seven of the reported eleven Muslim Brothers who had been imprisoned for terrorist activities under the royalist regime were released from jail; two of these men were serving life sentences for the assassination of the late premier Nuqrashi Pasha in December, 1948. And lastly, when General Naguib formed his first cabinet, early in September, he invited the Muslim Brother-

---

[4] For this and preceding statements in this paragraph see *Mideast Mirror*, August 16, 1952, p. 3, and January 16, 1954, pp. 1-2; also Naguib, *op. cit.*, p. 32. – For a discussion of the relations between the army and the Muslim Brotherhood see Ishak Musa Husaini, *The Moslem Brethren: The Greatest of Modern Islamic Movements* (Beirut, 1956), chap. xi, "The Brethren and the Army" (pp. 125-129); chap. xii, "The Brethren and the Revolution (pp. 130-136); and pages 147-148. According to Husaini, Colonel Anwar al-Sadat was the first liaison between the "Free Officers" and the Muslim Brotherhood (after 1940). He later became a member of the Revolution Command Council and eventually Minister of State in the Revolutionary Government, and was editor of *al-Jumhuriyyah*, the semi-official organ of the R.C.C. Several years later, ʿAbd al-Munʿim ʿAbd al-Raʾuf became the "official liaison officer" with the Muslim Brotherhood. ʿAbd al-Raʾuf was eventually won over wholeheartedly to the Brotherhood (pp. 125-126). All the above statements are corroborated by Colonel Anwar El Sadat in his *Revolt on the Nile* (London, 1957), pp. 26, 55, 80. For additional information see, above, chap. v, note 6.

hood to participate in his government. After much negotiating, the Brotherhood was invited to designate three of its members, including Shaykh Ahmad Hasan al-Baquri, for ministerial posts. Two Muslim Brothers in addition to al-Baquri were thereupon designated, but they proved to be unacceptable to the R.C.C. The Brotherhood thereafter refused to designate any other members and declined to participate in the government. Shaykh Hasan al-Baquri, however, resigned his post in the Guidance Office of the Muslim Brotherhood and became Minister of Waqfs (religious and charitable endowments) in the Naguib cabinet.

Supreme Guide al-Hudaybi also tried other pressure tactics on the R.C.C. First he sought to persuade General Naguib to promise that Egypt should have a new constitution based exclusively on Koranic principles. When this proposal was firmly rejected, al-Hudaybi then came up with an ultimatum: if the R.C.C. desired the full co-operation of the Muslim Brotherhood, they must agree to refer all proposed laws to him for consideration and approval, before such laws were made public.[5] The R.C.C. flatly refused to accord any such veto power to the Supreme Guide. Thenceforward, the Brotherhood gave passive co-operation in public to the new regime and worked against the R.C.C. in secret.

In retrospect, it is apparent that the Muslim Brotherhood misjudged the strength of the leaders of the Revolution. First in one way and then in another, they sought to take over or to control the Revolutionary movement. But they waited too long to offer their support to the new regime, and by asking too high a price for their co-operation they found themselves first rebuffed and then relegated to the side lines. And when they lost their chance to participate in the government, they began to undermine the R.C.C.

In this position of undeclared opposition, they embarked upon a dual program to build up their own power vis-à-vis the new government. First they tried to outbid the R.C.C. for popular support by proclaiming a rival reform program. Later they tried to organize a subversive movement within the army and the police forces.

During the critical first year of the Revolution, strong Brotherhood opposition could have spelled disaster for the R.C.C. There

---

[5] *Al-Jumhuriyyah,* No. 40, January 15, 1954, pp. 1, 5, 11; and *Mideast Mirror,* January 16, 1954, pp. 1-2.

were those, in both the Revolutionary and the Brotherhood movements, who believed that an alliance between the two was prerequisite to the implementation of rigorous and sweeping reforms. But, happily for Egypt, the men of the Revolution were able to cope with the competitive reform program of the Brotherhood; they soon produced a well-defined reform program of their own and lost no time in inaugurating it. The many similarities as well as the significant differences between the respective reform programs of these two groups will be discussed below.

The second feature of the Brotherhood's opposition to the R.C.C. was a different matter. Its subsequent subversive activities were destined to involve it, sooner or later, in a head-on clash with the Government of the Revolution – as came about in 1954.

Between the first of August and mid-December of 1952, Supreme Guide al-Hudaybi and members of the Guidance Office made a series of official policy statements which, taken collectively, embodied the most nearly complete declaration of principles ever made publicly by the Muslim Brotherhood.[6] These pronouncements reiterated the general Islamic principles of the Brotherhood – strict devotion to all religious duties and consistent dedication to the teachings of Islam – and proposed legislation against gambling, dancing, theaters, films, lewd magazines, and intoxicating drinks. There was, however, no insistence, as in the early days of the movement, upon restoring the severe physical punishments prescribed by the Shari'ah for certain types of crimes and moral offences. In the social and economic spheres, which attracted his earliest attention, the Supreme Guide entered the arena of practical politics and advocated a number of specific measures – though without providing any precise formulæ for their implementation.

In the social category, Brotherhood reform proposals may be grouped under education, welfare, social security, and labor legislation. Al-Hudaybi called for universal free education; he pointed out the need for an extension of all educational facilities and, specifically, for more libraries and more universities. At the same time, he stipu-

[6] The principal and most inclusive Brotherhood statement, on which my summary is based, was issued at the beginning of August. *Al-Ahram* carried the full text under the headline: "Statement of the Muslim Brotherhood on Reforms Anticipated in the New Era." Vol. 78, No. 24005 (August 2, 1952), pp. 4-11.

lated that religious education should be continued through the mosque schools, and that the village mosques in the rural areas should serve as social as well as religious and educational centers. For the poor, he demanded adequate housing and food. He likewise demanded a thorough review of the existing labor laws to ensure wage controls according to Islamic principles, a comprehensive insurance system for sickness, death, physical injury, and unemployment, as well as service and old-age pensions, and free medical treatment for the indigent. All persons were expected to work, and all laborers were to be required to pay subscriptions to trade unions.

In the economic field, the Brotherhood supported agrarian reforms, industrialization, and the nationalization of the Bank of Egypt. It advocated a land law that would set an acreage limitation on individual landholding,[7] provide for land expropriation and reclamation, enable landless peasants to buy surplus and reclaimed lands on easy terms, ensure to landlords and tenants equal shares in the produce of the land, and establish rural rent control. The Brotherhood also wanted to establish a national mint, close the Alexandria cotton exchange, and give the government control over Egypt's central bank. It called for government regulation and supervision of all other banks, "in such a way as to lead to the abolition of interest on money" – in line with the Koranic prohibition of interest; and it urged the government to set an example, in government projects, of doing business without benefit of interest payments.[8]

In the general area of social rehabilitation and egalitarianism, and in the name of justice, the Supreme Guide urged the abolition of all decorations and all titles (Pasha, Bey, etc.). He also called for the purging of all who had contributed to misgovernment and corruption under the royalist regime, and he demanded the reopening of investigations into the defective arms scandal of the Arab-Israeli war and into certain recent assassinations – notably that of Hasan al-Banna.

The Brotherhood showed keen interest in the army and in military

---

[7] In the Muslim Brotherhood statement of August 2, 1952 (see note 6, above), no acreage limitation was specified; however, when the R.C.C. denounced the Brotherhood in a long communiqué, January 15, 1954, the government stated that the Muslim Brotherhood had favored a limitation of 500 faddans on individual landholdings.

[8] *Al-Ahram*, Vol. 78, No. 24005 (August 2, 1952), p. 11.

affairs. It advocated compulsory military training in all schools and universities, stepped-up recruiting for the army, and a raise in military pay. At the same time it desired a purge and a more efficient reorganization of the police force, and the abolition of political police. In its concern that the army should be properly equipped, it also urged the government to build new factories for the production of arms and ammunition.

The Supreme Guide quite naturally issued a number of statements on foreign policy and constitutional problems. In company with all Egyptian nationalists, he demanded that the British should be made to leave the Suez Canal Base. He reiterated the oft-repeated call for the unity of Egypt and the Anglo-Egyptian Sudan and for the termination of "British imperialism" throughout the Nile Valley. Nor did he forget the Pan-Islamic role of the Brotherhood. He urged the Muslim Brothers of Egypt to maintain close contact with Brotherhood organizations in other Islamic countries, and he insisted that "colonists" (i.e., "imperialists") should be forced to withdraw from all Islamic states. At the same time, he insisted that Egypt should hold aloof from any Middle East defensive alliance, that the country should remain "neutral unless attacked," and that the government should abstain from adhering to any one "bloc of powers."

In August, 1952, the Brotherhood proposed that a representative constituent assembly should be convoked to draft a new constitution for Egypt, a constitution based on Islamic principles. And in December of the same year, al-ʿAshmawi, then a member of the Guidance Office of the Muslim Brotherhood, made a long statement to the effect that the future head of state should be chosen by the people and held accountable for all his acts – just as any other citizen. Al-ʿAshmawi also insisted that the new constitution should include a specific statement asserting that "Islam is the religion of the state." In order to make sure that this constitutional provision should become effective – i.e., not a "dead letter," as under the old constitution – he urged the inclusion of an additional statement, that "the sacred law of Islam is the source of the laws of the state." [9] At about

---

[9] *La Bourse Egyptienne*, No. 297 (December 16, 1952), pp. 6 f.: "Pour assurer à la révision constitutionnelle toutes les chances de succès, écrit M. Achmaoui dans 'Al-Daawa,' le gouvernement devrait commencer par restaurer certaines libertés: 'Il faut assurer une liberté complète de presse, de parole et de réunion, afin que le peuple puisse exprimer ses espoirs et ses désirs quant

the same time Supreme Guide al-Hudaybi is reported to have advocated that the Egyptian monarchy should be replaced by a republic.

In comparing the 1952 platform of the Muslim Brotherhood with
the actual accomplishments of the R.C.C., one is immediately struck
by the great similarity of the two reform programs. Many of the
measures advocated by both groups were in the air, so to speak —
they reflected the almost universal needs and wishes of Egyptians, or
they were the inevitable response to the overthrow of a corrupt monarchy. Other proposed measures were but an implementation or an
extension of reforms already initiated or envisioned by individual
Egyptian reformers.

In the years before the Revolution, especially after 1936, various
distinguished scholars and a few political leaders had analyzed the
unhealthy aspects of Egyptian society and government, and had begun to map a comprehensive cure for the economic and social ills
which they had diagnosed. Outstanding among these leaders were
Dr. Taha Hussein, the dynamic minister of education; Mirrit Boutros
Ghali Bey, a member of the nonpartisan scientific organization known
as the *Groupement de relèvement national*; Dr. Ahmed Hussein, of
the Ministry of Social Affairs; and Abdel Rahman Bialy Bey, founder of the Egyptian Labor Party in 1946. The little-publicized group
of reformers who organized the Ruad Society as early as 1925 had
first prepared themselves by study in European universities and then,
upon their return to Egypt, had thrown themselves with ardor into
planning and working for the social and economic betterment of their
country. Six founding members of the Ruad Society were appointed

à la constitution nouvelle. Il faut abolir la censure des journaux, au moins en
ce qui a trait à la question constitutionnelle.' En ce qui concerne la constitution elle-même, elle doit être d'inspiration islamique, estime M. Achmaoui:
'Telle doit être l'unique base de la constitution de l'Egypte islamique, dont la
population est en majorité musulmane. En conséquence, le chef de l'Etat doit
être choisi par le peuple et non imposé. L'Islam n'admet pas le régime héré-
ditaire dont les siècles ont démontré les défauts et le danger. En ce qui concerne la responsabilité du chef de l'Etat, l'Islam ne reconnaît la sainteté à per-
sonne. Le chef doit donc être directement responsable devant le peuple. Il
doit agir et rendre compte. Nous voulons que la constitution précise que
"l'Islam est la religion de l'Etat." Mais cela ne suffit point car cette disposi-
tion est restée lettre-morte dans l'ancienne constitution. Nous voulons donc
qu'on ajoute: "La sharia islamique est la source des lois de l'Etat." 'Nous
voulons que l'on garantisse la liberté d'opinion mais que l'on fasse exception
pour l'appel à l'impiété et à la licence.' "

to the first cabinet of the Revolutionary Government. The Egyptian Association for Social Studies, founded in 1937, organized the Cairo School of Social Work and conducted various experiments in rural welfare and urban problems. Ali Maher Pasha, chairman of that association, became the first premier of the Revolution in August, 1952. All these men and groups did the spadework for the reforms that were eventually carried out by the R.C.C.

The organic connection between the social reformers of the 1930's and those of the Revolution has been demonstrated in various progressive legislative enactments. For instance, an extended program of free public education, through secondary school, was actually adopted in 1950. The "development" budgets of the Revolutionary Government made it possible to allocate an increasingly large proportion of the national income to education. Literacy in Egypt increased from approximately ten per cent in 1938 to some thirty per cent in 1953, and the school population grew form 1,500,000 in 1949 to 2,300,000 in 1953. A third state university was established, in Cairo in 1950, and the construction of a fourth state university was begun in Assiut. A unique experiment in adult education was also embarked upon in 1945. The "People's University," later renamed the Institute for Popular Culture, offered courses in social science, history, music, the graphic and manual arts, journalism, and special subjects such as photography, hygiene, and social welfare. Education for the blind was also provided. All classes of Egyptians were admitted to this Institute without any prerequisites. By 1953 the Institute for Popular Culture had 16 urban centers with an enrollment of well over 15,000 men and women.[10]

A significant example of co-ordinated welfare services for the economically depressed two-thirds of the population of Egypt may be found in the Ministry of Social Affairs, established in 1939. The Fallah Department of this new Ministry, under the direction of Dr. Ahmed Hussein, planned and carried out notable reforms on behalf of the peasantry. Among its earliest pioneer projects was the launching of the rural social centers (later known as rural social welfare

[10]   For all the above statistics see Taha Hussein (Taha Husain), *The Future of Culture in Egypt* (Washington, D. C., 1954), and the pamphlet *Story of Education in Egypt*, published by the Embassy of Egypt, Washington, D. C. (1955). Supplementary statistics were kindly made available to me by the Embassy.

centers) which eventually won international recognition. Between 1941 and 1946 experimental centers were founded in eleven widely separated villages. Their marked success among the villagers determined the government to extend the project throughout all the rural districts of Egypt. By 1950, 136 rural social centers were in existence, each of which served 10,000 peasants. The peasants had first to request the organization of a rural center, and they had to agree to give land, some of their savings, and their labor for its establishment. Co-ordinated services of the Ministries of Public Health, Agriculture, and Education, combined in each case with the active collaboration of the peasantry, provided each center with interrelated programs of rural education, health, and welfare. The centers provided medical and maternity clinics and instruction in the benefits of pure drinking water and rudimentary sanitation. Agricultural advice was given and agricultural experiments were carried on through co-operative societies. The centers further provided adult education and sometimes schools, recreation grounds for the young people, assembly halls, and libraries. Thus, practically all phases of village life were affected and generally benefited. By mid-1955, 180 rural social centers were fully equipped and functioning, and many more had been started.[11]

The Labor Office, established in 1930, became a department of the Ministry of Social Affairs in 1939. Industrial and urban workers formed only a small segment of the population, but, after Egypt joined the International Labor Organization in 1936, the government gave increasing thought to improving both living and working conditions among Egyptian laborers. As early as 1933 there were labor laws regulating employment of children in industry and working con-

---

[11]   Dr. Ahmed Hussein, *Rural Social Welfare Centres in Egypt* (Government of Egypt pamphlet, Washington, D. C., 1954); Beatrice McCown Mattison, "Rural Social Centers in Egypt," *Middle East Journal*, Vol. IV (Autumn, 1951); and information from the Embassy of Egypt, Washington. After 1955, larger and more ambitious rural social welfare centers, known as "Combined Centers," were established. Each one has a school, which supplements other schools in its district, and serves an average of 15,000 peasants. The new centers numbered 250 in 1960, and more have been built since then. By 1964 it is planned that the co-ordinated services of the old and the new centers will serve about three quarters of the rural population of Egypt. See Doreen Warriner, *Land Reform and Development in the Middle East* (New York and London, 1962), pp. 197-198.

ditions for women. The Trade Union Act of 1942 gave official recognition to industrial and commercial trade unions; a decade later the government of the Revolution sanctioned a national or general federation of trade unions. By December, 1952, an entirely new labor code had been drafted by the Revolutionary Government. The right of unions to bargain collectively was recognized in the Collective Agreement Act of 1950, and after the Revolution agricultural workers were allowed to form unions and to bargain collectively. In 1946 there were 488 labor unions, with 95,538 members; by 1954, 1,120 trade unions claimed a total membership of 450,000 and there were 64 unions of agricultural workers.[12] Several self-contained "workers' cities" have been built, complete with model housing and community services for education and health. The textile workers' city of Mahalla al-Kubra, most notable of these, in 1953 had a population of 180,000. Workmen's compensation became part of the comprehensive Social Security Law of 1951, the first passed in any Arab country.

After the Revolution, the principles of social insurance (for old age, sickness, and unemployment) were affirmed, and they were eventually written into the Constitution of January 16, 1956 (Article 21). The new constitution also expressly acknowledged the right of all Egyptians to a "decent living-standard" and committed the state to attempt to provide food, housing, and health, cultural, and social services for every citizen (Article 17). An expanding program of public health services was likewise guaranteed, in acknowledgment of the right of all Egyptians to medical care (Articles 21, 56). From the inception of the Revolution, the decision was taken that public and social services should be available to all. The cost of these services is determined, as in the case of graduated taxation and tax-exemption for the indigent, according to the individual's ability to pay. In each case the ideal of social justice and equality of opportunity for all Egyptians forms the guiding principle (Articles 5, 59, 22). Furthermore, the right of all Egyptians to education, "sponsored by the State," is explicitly recognized. Elementary education is compulsory and free: "Throughout its divers stages in State schools, education is given free of charge in accordance with the limits defined by Law" (Articles 48,

[12] Abdel Raouf Abou Alam, *The Labor Movement in Egypt* (Government of Egypt pamphlet, Washington, D. C., 1955).

49, 51, 50). Laws of the Revolutionary Government, confirmed in the Constitution of 1956, regulated the relationships between workers and employers, the contractual relations between landlords and tenants, and various special matters such as the "determination of wage-scales" and the limitation of working hours; the constitution also acknowledged that "Egyptians have the right to work, which right the State will attempt to secure" (Article 52; also Articles 54, 14, 53). Finally, under the transitional Government of the Revolution, as in the new constitution, the equality of all Egyptians was established by law, and freedom of worship, "in accordance with the established usage in Egypt," was guaranteed; all Egyptians were "equal in respect of rights and obligations without discrimination on account of race, origin, language, religion or creed" (Articles 31, 43). By contrast the Muslim Brothers were principally concerned with the rights and equality of Muslims, rather than with those of *all* Egyptians. By implication at least, the Christian and Jewish Minorities would have played the role of second-class citizens under any government established by the Muslim Brotherhood.

The Agrarian Reform Law promulgated September 9, 1952, not only met but exceeded the demands of the Brotherhood. In accordance with this law, landholdings in Egypt were limited to 200 faddans (about 200 acres). Five years were allotted for the partial dispossession of an estimated 2,115 large landowners, who would be partly compensated by three per-cent government bonds. The area of land to be expropriated during the five-year period, including the land belonging to the former Royal Family, was estimated at approximately 621,500 acres – about 10.4 per cent of Egypt's total cultivated area in September, 1952.[13] It was calculated that about 1,250,000

[13]   See, in *Land Reform Law, Full Text* (Cairo, 1954), "Decree-Law No. 178 of 1952 on Land Reform." – In 1949 more than 73 per cent of the population of Egypt was engaged in agriculture, and there were 2,731,120 landowners. It was then estimated that some 2,568,816 peasants owned 2,091,486 faddans (acres), an average per peasant of 0.8 faddans. Only 2,145 people owned 1,166,341 faddans, an average of 539 faddans per person. About 58 great landlords owned 259,745 faddans, an average of about 4,478 faddans per person. See the Ministry of National Economy, Department of Statistics, *al-Ihsaʾ al-Sanawi* [Statistical Year Book, 1949/50] (Cairo, 1951), and The Higher Committee of Agrarian Reform, "Agrarian Reform in Egypt," Press Office Release No. 10 (Cairo, 1954), pp. 1-2. At that time, furthermore, approximately 1,500,-000 agricultural laborers owned no land at all; the surplus labor in rural districts was reckoned at between five and six million persons.

small farmers and their families, or approximately one ninth of the agricultural population of Egypt, would be beneficiaries of the new land law. Peasants receiving expropriated land will pay for it on easy terms, in thirty annual installments at 3 per cent annual interest, plus a small additional charge to help defray the costs of expropriation and redistribution.

Compensation for expropriated land, and conversely the price to be paid for such land by the peasantry, was fixed at ten times the annual rent, which, in turn, was calculated at seven times the land tax. Simultaneous provision was made by law that at least one co-operative society would be established in every village benefiting by the land law. in order to assist the peasants with agricultural advice and loans. These organizations were to function as producers', marketing, and consumers' co-operatives. Agricultural tenants were also aided by the Land Law of September, 1952. Rural rents were fixed at seven times the basic land tax as levied in 1945-1946. Peasants will in the future be encouraged to improve their land because they are assured, under the law, of a minimum three-year lease.

Admittedly only a small fraction of the rural population now benefit from this new land law; but the principle thus established is an earnest of good faith on the part of the Revolutionary Government, and there is promise of more to come.[14] The distribution of expropriated or "surplus" lands, begun in July, 1953, has continued with regularity since then. Land has been distributed in lots of not fewer than two or more than five faddans among peasants whose holdings did not previously exceed five faddans. Priority was given to cultivators working on expropriated land and to peasants with large families. By mid-1955 the R.C.C. had distributed 140,000 faddans to the peasantry.

The national development policies of the R.C.C. with respect to land tenure have gone hand in hand with land-reclamation projects and the exploitation of mineral resources. Between 1952 and 1955, more than twelve thousand faddans of desert land had been reclaimed; the production of cotton had been increased by 5 per cent,

---

[14]   A revised agrarian law, passed in July, 1961, further limited individual landholdings to 100 faddans. Repayment obligations were reduced, and additional safeguards were provided to aid the peasants benefiting from land distributions. *Draft of the Charter*, May 21, 1962 (Published by the Information Department of the United Arab Republic), p. 48.

wheat by 10 per cent, and rice by 70 per cent; mineral production had risen by 26 per cent, fertilizers by 46 per cent, and iron and steel by 50 per cent. The new agrarian reforms, coupled with the abolition of civilian titles (upon the establishment of the Revolutionary Government in July, 1952), have given a death blow to feudalism in Egypt. And the notable increases in national production, together with the extension of public and welfare services, have all contributed to raising the general standard of living.[15]

One would be safe in stating that as of now the Government of the Revolution has cut the ground from under the economic and social welfare program of the Muslim Brotherhood. In these spheres demonstrable reforms were initiated in the earliest days of the Revolutionary regime, and methods for continuing them have been progressively elaborated. The mounting resentment of the Muslim Brothers and their repeated complaints against the men of the Revolution are doubtless traceable to the fact that the R.C.C. had a social and economic platform so similar to their own and that, at the same time, the R.C.C. was prepared to inaugurate a practical reform program with dispatch and without benefit of Brotherhood assistance or participation. The attitude of the Brotherhood recalls the resentment voiced by Hasan al-Banna in 1939 when he was excluded from the

---

[15]   Statistics furnished by the Embassy of Egypt, Washington, D. C. See also three consecutive articles on Egypt in *The Americana Annual* for 1954, 1955, and 1956, sections headed "Finance" and "Production and Industry," by Christina Phelps Harris. – The *Draft of the Charter* of May, 1962, illustrates how far the Government of the Revolution has gone since 1954 toward implementing a program of Arab socialism in Egypt. A policy of selective nationalization, aimed at the abolition of exploitation and of large-scale private monopolies, has brought the banks, insurance companies, foreign trade, the transportation services, sea- and airports, all public utilities, and all major industries under government control. At the same time, the right to own private property has been specifically guaranteed, and the participation of private capital and enterprise in about 25 per cent of the export trade and 75 per cent of the internal trade is stipulated. The place in society of democratic farmers' co-operatives and of industrial and agricultural labor unions is strongly emphasized. The Revolutionary Government's ideal of social justice requires the control and the expansion of national production and the assumption that "planning must be a scientifically organized creative process that would meet the challenges facing our society." See, *ibid.*, p. 46 and also pp. 40, 47-48. – The nationalization of the Suez Canal Company in July, 1956, and the subsequent nationalization of French and British banks and businesses heralded the new Revolutionary policies – all of which lie outside the scope of this study.

newly founded Ministry of Social Affairs and his maintenance thereafter of a competitive welfare program in rivalry with that of the government. In 1952 the Muslim Brothers had only themselves to blame for their exclusion from the new government. That exclusion was based on the one great ideological barrier that separated them from the leaders of the Revolution. The Brotherhood had never ceased to demand the establishment of a wholly Islamic government – and this was the issue on which the two groups split irretrievably.

Before the end of 1952, General Naguib and his military associates had made it clear that they were opposed to extremism in all its forms, "fanatical Islamism" on the one hand and communism on the other. They proposed to weld a united Egypt, wherein all Egyptians, Muslims and non-Muslims alike, should exercise the full rights of citizenship, and they believed the religion of Islam "in its truest form" to be genuinely tolerant.

In furtherance of this ideal the government of Colonel Gamal Abdel Nasser eventually introduced a startling innovation in Egyptian society. Late in 1955 the government announced its decision to transfer the administration of all religious laws to the state civil courts. Current Muslim and non-Muslim religious laws were to be upheld in cases that did not contravene Egypt's modern codes of civil and criminal law – notably in matters of personal status, marriage, divorce, and inheritance. But in the interest of social unity and equality of treatment for all Egyptian citizens, the traditional autonomous religious courts, with their obsolete practices and procedures and their conflicting jurisdictions, were to be abolished. Justice was to be efficiently centralized under the supervision of the civil courts.

The concept of equality of status, the full rights of citizenship for all Egyptians, was also significantly extended to include women in the Constitution of 1956. Their political rights were guaranteed in the electoral law of March 3, 1956. The right of women to vote was, however, to be exercised optionally: voting was *not* to be compulsory for them as it was for men.

Nevertheless, despite these assaults upon the walls of custom that have stood so long between the various religious communities and between the men and women of Egypt, and despite the charges by Muslim Brothers that the R.C.C. was preparing the destruction of Islam by establishing a secularized government, the military men in power had no intention of turning their backs on the Islamic faith. They were devout Muslims, and when their new constitution was proclaimed in January, 1956, its third article declared unequivocally that "Islam is the religion of the state."

VII

THE BROTHERHOOD LOSES ITS BID
FOR POWER

The first public crisis between the Brotherhood and the Revolutionary leaders occurred after September 9, 1952, the date on which the Revolutionary Government promulgated a law regulating political parties. Under this new law, the rights, powers, limitations, and obligations of all political parties were defined in seventeen articles. The parties were to be required to make public their objectives and statutes, the names of their founders or presidents, and their financial resources; their funds were to be deposited in a publicly recognized bank. Parties were, furthermore, forbidden to own real estate; they were not to be allowed to support any military or semi-military formation; and they were to operate under the joint jurisdiction of the Ministers of Interior, Social Affairs, and Justice.

It was generally considered that the powerful and unreconciled Wafd Party was the principal target of the new legislation. The Wafdists themselves charged that the R.C.C. sought to destroy their party. At the same time, however, Muslim Brothers realized that they were caught on the horns of a dangerous dilemma. The Brotherhood was *de jure* an association, not a political party; but their organization had expanded far beyond the legal limitations of an association and had taken on *de facto* all the attributes of a political movement. The Brotherhood would have to clarify its status. But neither as an association nor as a political party could the Brethren hope for long to maintain their organization intact. Clearly, the Government of the Revolution was determined to enforce the laws of Egypt. The activities of the Brotherhood would therefore be severely restricted, either under the stipulations of the old Associations Law of 1951 or under the new law regulating political parties. For a brief while there was some talk, and a few press reports, to the effect that Fathi Radwan, Minister of State in the Naguib government, might absorb the political activist wing of the Muslim Brotherhood into his nationalist party, and that the religious and culturally minded elements of the Brotherhood would continue to operate as an association, shorn of all the attributes of a political party. This talk, however, came to nothing.

At the beginning of October, the R.C.C. was given its first clear indication that the Muslim Brotherhood might eventually prove to be an even greater danger to the new regime than the erstwhile powerful but discredited Wafd Party. General Naguib made a "triumphant tour" of the Delta country

... amid such scenes of wild enthusiasm as have never been seen in recent memory.... The name of Nahas or the Wafd was not heard even in the home village of Nahas himself, where the massed people were as fervent for General Naguib as elsewhere. In fact, on the whole tour, there was no single sign of support from the people for any of the political parties or their leaders.

There was, however, evidence everywhere of the activity of the Moslem Brotherhood. The chanting calls for General Naguib and the army were frequently interspersed with purely religious chants from organized groups of the Brotherhood and in some places there were pictures of the murdered Brotherhood leader Hasan el-Banna [sic] and cries in support of him.[1]

In October, when fifteen parties, including the Wafd, applied to be allowed to operate under the new Parties Law, the Muslim Brotherhood was one of the fifteen groups to so register. But it was plain to the government that they did so with reservations. The Brethren, however, were saved from an open clash with the R.C.C. at that time by the Wafd Party which, as it kept trying in one way and another to evade the new controls, acted as a lightning rod to divert the attention of the Revolutionary leaders from the problem of the Brotherhood. Eventually the government decided to cut the Gordian knot. On January 17, 1953, a decree law dissolved all the political parties and confiscated their funds. Simultaneously the government of General Naguib announced the establishment of a military dictatorship for a three-year period of transition. In this situation the Muslim Brotherhood summarily repudiated its registration as a political par-

[1] *Mideast Mirror,* October 4, 1952, pp. 1, 3.

ty, insisted that it was a nonpolitical association, and announced its decision to operate under the pre-Revolutionary Associations Law of April 23, 1951. The R.C.C. decided to accept this equivocal move on the part of the Muslim Brothers, though it did so with grave misgivings and soon came to question the wisdom of having allowed them to maintain their formidable organization.

Directly after the joyous celebration festivities which marked the first six-month anniversary of the Revolution, January 23-26, 1953, the government established the "Liberation Rally" as an instrument of the Liberation movement. The Rally was a single party designed to replace the dissolved political parties and pledged to support the government of the Revolution. It was hoped at first that the Muslim Brothers might be willing, for the price of their continued official existence, to co-operate with the Liberation Rally. An effort was even made to absorb them into this newly created government party. But in the words of General Naguib, the Brethren "joined it only to subvert it . . . . In the end we had to arrest a lot of their leaders in order to purge the Rally of their subversive influence." [2]

In actual fact, the Liberation Rally became the source of one of the bitterest complaints of the Brotherhood against the Revolutionary Government. Within a year some 1,200 Liberation Rally centers had been founded in Egypt, and several branch centers existed outside the country. The Rally movement was undertaking health, social welfare, and poor relief work, and its youth section was actively involved in education. The Muslim Brotherhood charged that the Rally Centers constituted superfluous and undesirable duplications of their own Branches. Presumably the Brethren felt that the government was challenging them on their own ground by offering a rival social, welfare, and educational program to the masses. At a meeting of the Brotherhood Secretariat, in February, 1953, individual Muslim Brothers were authorized to join the Liberation Rally; but it was decided that the Muslim Brotherhood would maintain its independence as an organization vis-à-vis the Liberation movement.

During the spring of 1953 the Muslim Brotherhood behaved with considerable circumspection, though it exploited every opportunity to extend its membership still further and to build up its strength. In-

[2]   Mohammed Neguib, *Egypt's Destiny* (London, 1955), pp. 209, 183, 181; in the American edition, pp. 187, 163, 161.

creasingly, the Brethren tended to endow the character of their founder, Hasan al-Banna, with messianic qualities and to sanctify his
assassination as a martyrdom. Their concepts of dedication to Islam,
purification of the spirit, and Brotherhood loyalty were notably emphasized during this period. But after the proclamation of the Republic on June 18, 1953, the Brotherhood actively resumed its subversive activities among the military, notably in the artillery branch,
and among the police and in the Liberation Rally. There was, however, no overt defiance of the government during that year.

The R.C.C., for its part, deemed it prudent to refrain from open
conflict with the Muslim Brothers for as long as possible – if only
because of the mutual devotion of both groups to the religion of
Islam. Even so, certain members of the government reportedly decided to fight guile with guile and adopted the policy of contributing
privately to the existing factional cleavage within the Muslim Brotherhood. And some members of the Brotherhood are alleged to have
tried, without success, to persuade Colonel Nasser to use his influence to prevent a split within the organization.

This cleavage finally came out into the open after the Muslim
Brotherhood held its annual elections for the Guidance Office on
October 8, 1953. As a result of these elections, five or six members
of this highest executive council were voted out of office; among
them was Salah Mustafa al-ʿAshmawi, leader of the anti-Hudaybi
faction. Hasan Ismaʿil al-Hudaybi and ʿAbd al-Hakim ʿAbidin, on
the other hand, were respectively confirmed in office as Supreme
Guide and Secretary-General. Supreme Guide al-Hudaybi's actual
authority was at the same time reported to have been curtailed considerably. Nineteen days later the group that had been ousted from
the Guidance Office staged a brief revolt under the leadership of
Salah al-ʿAshmawi, stormed the Brotherhood headquarters in Cairo,
and tried to force the resignation of the Supreme Guide. But al-
ʿAshmawi's revolt was quelled by al-Hudaybi and the new Guidance
Office within twenty-four hours after it started.[3]

[3]   Just before this internal struggle came to a head, the Brotherhood had sent
an emissary to the United States – no less a person than Saʿid Ramadan, son-
in-law of its founder, the first Supreme Guide, and editor of its Cairo monthly
magazine *al-Muslimun*. In a public statement he presented the Muslim Brotherhood to Americans as a powerful but peaceful organization, uncontroversial in
character, "basically religious," and intent upon "reconverting Muslims to the

The year 1954 witnessed the long-anticipated climax of the protracted duel between the Muslim Brotherhood and the leaders of the Revolution. The break between them was precipitated by an incident on January 12, when, at a "martyrs' day" ceremony held at the University of Cairo, Brotherhood speakers openly attacked the government. A bloody clash ensued on the university campus between a group of Muslim Brother students and a student group that was loyal to the Revolutionary movement. Among the Brotherhood speakers on that occasion was a visiting foreigner, the leader of Iran's *Fidaiyan-i Islam*. Without doubt, the presence of a hostile visitor on such a platform would have been embarrassing to the government. But the embarrassment was compounded – given perhaps even a tinge of apprehension – by the facts that the organization which he represented was a fanatical and terrorist Islamic group kindred in many ways to the Muslim Brotherhood,[4] and that its members had been responsible for the assassination of a distinguished Persian, General Razmara.

That very night of January 12 the R.C.C. decided to move against the Brotherhood. Four hundred and fifty Muslim Brothers were promptly arrested, including Supreme Guide al-Hudaybi, the whole of the Guidance Office, and Salah al-ʿAshmawi. The leader of the *Fidaiyan-i Islam* was expelled from Egypt forthwith. In a long official

---

real Islam." According to him, the Brotherhood had a four-point reform program comprising land reform, new educational programs, the raising of the general standard of living to ensure social justice "for all," and a new constitution to assure "true representation for all people." When Saʿid Ramadan was asked whether the Brotherhood had used violence to achieve its ends, he gave the following answer: "The contrary is true. Violent means have been used to stop us." *Middle East Report*. Vol. VI, No. 3 (October 2, 1953), pp. 1-2.

[4] Some observers have tended to equate the Egyptian Brotherhood with the *Fidaiyan-i Islam*, founded in Iran at the end of the Second World War. But any such comparison does less than justice to the Muslim Brotherhood. The two organizations are not really comparable, militantly Islamic and xenophobic though they both are. Unlike the Muslim Brotherhood, the *Fidaiyan-i Islam* never, reportedly, succeeded in penetrating the professions or infiltrating the state universities. This Iranian terrorist group was very loosely organized, and it operated almost entirely among the underprivileged proletariat and the nonpeasant rural elements. Moreover, it has offered no constructive program to advance the social and economic welfare of the masses, no program similar to that of the Muslim Brotherhood in Egypt. – Information on this Persian (Iranian) religious organization was given the writer by two Iranians, one a scholar and author of books on Islam, the other a journalist.

communiqué explaining its action, the government made the following significant statements:

The Muslim Brotherhood is now considered a political party and as such falls under the law dissolving all political parties ... We therefore declare, in the name of the Revolution, which bears the trust of the nation's aims, that the Supreme Guide and his followers hvae directed the activities of their organization in a manner harmful to the motherland and have profaned religion.

The Revolution will not allow the recurrence of a reactionary tragedy in the name of religion.[5]

But this was not all. The R.C.C. had decided that the moment was appropriate for reviewing, publicly, the thorny course of its relations with the Muslim Brothers and for giving a full airing of government grievances against them. The principal charges brought against the Brotherhood in this detailed communiqué revealed the full extent of the conflict between the R.C.C. and the Muslim Brotherhood and made clear the impossibility of future co-existence of the government and this organization, unless the latter changed its attitude toward the new regime.

Briefly summarized, the government charges were as follows:

1) Supreme Guide al-Hudaybi had refused to make a strong and unequivocal statement in support of the Free Officers on the first day of the Revolution;

2) The Muslim Brotherhood had exerted pressure on the Revolutionary government to establish, immediately, a wholly Muslim state in Egypt;

3) The Supreme Guide had tried to force the Council of the Revolution to give him the right to veto all new laws, in advance of their publication;

4) The Muslim Brothers had refused to participate in General Naguib's first ministry on terms acceptable to the Revolution Command Council;

5) In the important matter of the 1952 land law, the Brotherhood had favored limiting landholdings to 500 faddans, instead of approving the 200-faddan limitation decided upon by the R.C.C.;

---

[5] *Al Jumhuriyyah* [*Al Goumhouria*], Vol. 1, No. 40 (January 15, 1954), pp. 1, 5, 11; *Mideast Mirror*, January 16, 1954, pp. 1-4. – The direct quotation and some other relevant items are taken from the *Mideast Mirror*, p. 3; the subsequent summary of the communiqué is based on the cited issue of the *Jumhuriyyah*.

6) The Supreme Guide had opposed the creation of the government-sponsored Liberation Rally centers;

7) Whenever the R.C.C. had sought the co-operation of the Muslim Brotherhood, the latter had tried to impose unacceptable conditions for its support of the new regime – conditions that would have been injurious to the wider interests of all Egyptians;

8) The Muslim Brotherhood had engaged in secret subversive activities within the army and the police forces with intent to overthrow the Government of the Revolution;

9) The Muslim Brotherhood had arranged secret contacts with officials of the British Embassy, in the spring of 1953, thus indirectly strengthening Britain's hand in the current Anglo-Egyptian negotiations concerning the future of the Suez Canal Base.

These last charges were in a different category from all the preceding. Their publication could be expected to rouse Egyptian public opinion against the Muslim Brothers by implying traitorous collusion between them and a foreign "imperial" power against the R.C.C. They would at the same time tend to discredit the British, since the charges also implied that British Embassy officials were intervening in Egypt's domestic politics and even, perhaps, encouraging a subversive group against the government. Needless to say, the British were quick to disavow all secret contacts with the Brotherhood. British sources in Egypt pointed out that the Oriental Counsellor of their Embassy met and talked with prominent Egyptians as a necessary part of his work and had never made any secret of such conversations. At the time of these reported interviews, the Muslim Brotherhood was a legally recognized organization and there was "no open indication" of any serious disagreement between them and the Government of the Revolution.

The turning point in the relations between the Brotherhood and the government, according to the communiqué, came in January, 1953. After the dissolution of the political parties in that month, the Muslim Brotherhood had again raised the question of representation in the cabinet. The refusal of the R.C.C. to offer any cabinet post to the Muslim Brothers at that time had resulted in the progressive deterioration of relations between them. The Supreme Guide had even gone so far as to attack the government, repeatedly, in the press.

The government also chose this moment to reveal the source of its knowledge concerning the recent treasonable activities of the Muslim

Brotherhood. Early in June, 1953, intelligence officers had discovered that the Muslim Brothers were sponsoring three separate subversive movements: one among army officers, one among army noncommissioned officers, and one among police officers. Unknown to the Brotherhood, however, some of the army officers involved were members of the original Free Officers group that had organized the coup d'état of July, 1952. These officers had attended the secret subversive meetings in order to keep the R.C.C. fully informed of developments. They reported that the army and police officers were asked to take an oath of allegiance to the Supreme Guide and were promised generous treatment when the Brotherhood would have succeeded in achieving its aims. They also reported that a systematic attempt was made at these periodic meetings to discredit, and even to "incite hatred" against, the Government of the Revolution. At this stage of affairs the R.C.C. contented itself with issuing a warning to the Muslim Brotherhood through Salah al-ʿAshmawi, who was then still a member of the Guidance Office. But this warning went unheeded.

The suppression of the Muslim Brotherhood, the arrest of 450 Muslim Brothers, and the closing of their Branches by the government was received calmly by the Egyptian people. The country remained completely quiet. On January 17, 1954, the Minister of Interior made public the discovery of a large Brotherhood cache of arms and ammunition, hidden in the bricked-in cellar of ʿAshmawi's country estate. That same day a government official announced that the educational program of the government-sponsored Liberation Rally would include the teaching of "religious observance and orthodoxy" and would, simultaneously, "combat destructive ideologies and religious fanaticism." [6]

Meanwhile, within the R.C.C., the first serious crisis of the new regime was swiftly approaching, as the rift between General Naguib and Colonel Nasser daily widened. The public break between these two leaders of the Revolutionary movement did not occur until more than a month after the R.C.C. issued its denunciatory communiqué against the Muslim Brothers. But the top echelons of the Brotherhood must have known that the break was coming soon, and the Guidance Office had doubtless chosen its own moment to challenge the government publicly with full knowledge that the moment was a

[6] *Mideast Mirror*, January 23, 1954, pp. 1-2.

dangerous one for the R.C.C. When the break did come, at the end of February, and General Naguib was repudiated by the R.C.C. and deprived of all his government posts with a suddenness that shocked the whole of Egypt, the Muslim Brothers exploited the crisis to the full. Forty-eight hours after his arrest, General Naguib was restored to the presidency by the overwhelming pressure of popular demand, but ceremonies in honor of his restoration were marred by the bloody rioting of Muslim Brothers, Communists, and Wafdists. Then and later the Brotherhood made a career of sowing discord between President Naguib and the other members of the R.C.C. The existing disunity in the Council of the Revolution, which could no longer be concealed, made both sides peculiarly vulnerable to these tactics.

The trial of strength between General Naguib and Colonel Nasser continued behind the scenes until the middle of April, when the issue was finally decided in favor of the young colonel. During that period the Muslim Brothers were treated with deceptive leniency – until the R.C.C. once again felt sure enough of its strength to cope with them. At intervals after January 22, al-Hudaybi, 'Ashmawi, and most of the others were released, and the Brotherhood was eventually given permission to operate as a nonpolitical association – on condition that its activities were strictly confined to religious, cultural, and social affairs. But whether the Brotherhood leaders realized it or not, their organization was still suspect and was allowed to operate on probation, as it were, during good behavior. Throughout the summer of 1954 negotiations between the Egyptians and the British on the evacuation of the Canal Base were progressing favorably, and the Revolutionary Government was naturally anxious that no untoward domestic incidents should postpone or disrupt the successful conclusion of an agreement acceptable to both sides.

On October 19 the new Anglo-Egyptian treaty was signed. One week later, while Egyptians were still rejoicing in their final liberation from the last vestiges of seventy-two years of foreign occupation, the Muslim Brotherhood was so ill advised as to bring down on its head the wrath of the R.C.C. A Muslim Brother made an abortive attempt to assassinate Colonel Nasser as he was addressing a public meeting in Alexandria.

The Muslim Brotherhood, or possibly only its "terrorist wing," presumably took a calculated risk. Colonel Nasser had not as yet achieved any great measure of popularity in Egypt – partly because of the known rift between him and the universally popular General Naguib. Moreover, Egyptian rejoicing over the prospective departure of all British troops from Egyptian soil was markedly tempered by the "return clause" in the newly signed Anglo-Egyptian treaty. Under this clause, the Revolutionary Government had bound itself to make the Suez Base reavailable to British troops in case of any outside attack against any member state of the Arab League or against Turkey. The potential reavailability of the Suez Base to Great Britain and the inclusion of Turkey – a member of the North Atlantic Treaty Organization – in the agreement made it clear to Egyptians that they were still aligned with the West in the "cold war." In case of NATO involvement in a third world war, in which case Turkey might be attacked by the Soviet Union, Egypt could again be drawn into major war operations – against the will of its people. Muslim Brothers, who had publicly denounced the new Anglo-Egyptian treaty for this reason, identified themselves with many Egyptians and other Arabs who had grave misgivings about Nasser's commitment to one of the Western Powers. The Muslim Brotherhood counted, undoubtedly, upon the support of Egyptians outside its own ranks. Had Colonel Nasser been killed in their assassination attempt, the Anglo-Egyptian agreement of October, 1954, might have been invalidated. They took that gamble. But Colonel Nasser escaped entirely unharmed from the eight shots fired at him from close range, and he therefore remained in command of the situation. The R.C.C., strong in their triumphant solution of all current problems with Great Britain, felt themselves at long last to be masters in their own Egyptian house. The Revolutionary leaders decided that no occasion could be more fitting or more opportune to take resolute action against the obstructive Brotherhood organization and achieve order in their domestic affairs. They immediately took stern measures to suppress the Muslim Brotherhood once and for all.

Before the end of 1954 the R.C.C. rounded up and arrested about a thousand Muslim Brothers, including the Supreme Guide and other leaders. All of the Muslim Brothers then arrested were publicly tried, according to the indictments, for treason either against the Revolution or against members of the government. Those adjudged guilty were duly sentenced, many of them to long prison terms or to penal servitude, and six of the terrorist Brothers were executed.[7] Ample evidence was obtained in the trials to establish conclusively the existence of a secret, terrorist wing of the Brotherhood. The trials, however, brought out a great deal of conflicting evidence concerning internal affairs and divisions of opinion among the Muslim Brothers with respect to terrorist tactics. Many of the leaders gave incriminating evidence against each other. There was even disagreement as to the precise role of the Supreme Guide in the assassination plot and his position in the conspiracy against the government. Al-Hudaybi himself denied responsibility for subversive activities and repudiated policies of terrorism. Some of the evidence indicated that the Brotherhood's secret organization of terrorists had tried either to force al-Hudaybi's hand or to bypass his authority. And some of the evidence indicated that the Supreme Guide feared the R.C.C. and was afraid of continuing terrorist policies. The Brotherhood witnesses readily admitted that Colonel Nasser had more than once warned them against terrorism.[8]

The Ulama of al-Azhar University immediately sent a message of support to Premier Nasser, and the Council of Ulama of al-Azhar subsequently issued a strong statement denouncing the Muslim Brotherhood. In their statement the Ulama accused the Muslim Brothers of "deviating from the teachings of Islam," denounced them for conspiring against the security of the state, and declared that any

---

[7]   The six men who were hanged in Cairo on December 7, 1954, were Mahmud Abdel Latif, the tinsmith who tried to assassinate Colonel Nasser; Yussuf Talaat, commander of the whole Secret (terrorist) Organization; Shaykh Muhammad Farghaly, a preacher and the alleged adviser of the Secret Organization; Hindawy Dweir, head of a Cairo cell of the Secret Organization; Ibrahim al-Tayyib, head of the Cairo branch of the Secret Organization; and Abdel Kader Auda, a member of the Guidance Office and the alleged link with General Naguib. The last three named were lawyers. Ten other members of the Muslim Brotherhood, including the Supreme Guide, were sentenced to death, but their sentences were commuted to life imprisonment. The Special People's Tribunal also sentenced seventeen others to life terms. Terrorist leaders naturally received the most severe sentences, but about nine tenths of all the accused received sentences of some kind. See *Mideast Mirror*, December 11, 1954, pp. 2-5, and December 18, 1954, p. 6.

[8]   See *al-Ahram*, Vol. 80, No. 24824 (November 12, 1954), p. 1; Vol. 80, No. 24829 (November 17, 1954), pp. 1, 3; Vol. 80, No. 24835 (November 23, 1954), p. 7; and Vol. 80, No. 24838 (November 26, 1954), pp. 1, 2, 3. See also *Mideast Mirror*, November 20, 1954, pp. 10-14; November 27, 1954, pp. 6-9; and December 4, 1954, pp. 8-11.

Muslim Brothers adjudged guilty of conspiring against the lives of the leaders of the nation were also guilty of heresy.[9]

In the tortuous course of the trials the R.C.C. made use of some of the evidence to remove General Naguib permanently from any further association with the Revolutionary Government. During the trials, early in November, certain unsubstantiated charges were made against the President of Egypt, including that of implication in the Brotherhood conspiracy. Evidence was obtained of a plot to assassinate all members of the Revolutionary Council except President Naguib, and it was alleged by some Brotherhood witnesses that leaders of the Brotherhood's Secret Organization had been in contact with him. On November 14, 1954, President Naguib was deposed and placed under house arrest, and Colonel Nasser and the cabinet assumed the functions of the presidency. But talk of bringing the deposed president to trial led to intervention from the Sudan: an official delegation hurried from Khartum to Cairo and persuaded the R.C.C. to issue, on November 21, a joint Egyptian-Sudanese statement that General Naguib would not be tried.[10]

By 1955 Colonel Nasser and his colleagues in the R.C.C. had

---

[9] On October 29, 1954, the Ulama of al-Azhar sent a telegram to Colonel Nasser congratulating him upon his recent escape from the assassination attempt. See *al-Jumhuriyyah*, No. 322, October 29, 1954, p. 7. On November 18, 1954, the Council of Ulama of the University of al-Azhar issued a "call" (*nida'*) to the Muslims of Egypt and of other parts of the world to follow Islam. Muslims were reminded that Islam is a religion of unity, security, and amity, and that terrorism, assassination, and disunity on the part of Muslims is un-Islamic. With respect to the Muslim Brotherhood, the Council of Ulama recalled that in the beginning, i.e., during the first years of the movement, the Muslim Brothers conducted themselves peaceably and used acceptable techniques to attract people to Islam. Later however, a group of the Muslim Brothers deviated from the right path and conspired against other Muslims. According to the pronouncement of the Council of Ulama, these Muslim Brothers violated the commandments of God. The Ulama, in their denunciation, presumably referred only to those Brothers who were members of the secret, terrorist wing of the Brotherhood. The word for "heresy" is not actually used in the text of this statement issued by the Council of Ulama. But they ended their statement with a categoric repudiation of Muslim Brothers guilty of "deviation" (the word *inhiraf* is used in this connection); they declared that deviation from the Koran and the adoption of policies of terrorism and destruction were against God and His Prophet and the religion of Islam. See *al-Ahram*, Vol. 80, No. 24830, (November 18, 1954), pp. 1, 4, and *Mideast Mirror*, November 20, 1954, p. 6.

[10] *Mideast Mirror*, November 27, 1954, p. 2.

become the undisputed masters of Egypt. The organization of the Muslim Brotherhood had been broken up, without any likelihood of resurrection in the foreseeable future.[11] As of now, no attempt has been made by the dispersed members of the Brotherhood to rally their forces. They have been in no position to organize themselves anew against the Government of the Revolution. Presumably the Muslim Brotherhood has gone underground, as on several occasions in the past. But it will be given no opportunity to become again a powerful movement, above ground, unless the Egyptian people repudiate the Revolution and its achievements in the projected period of constitutional government. At the moment of writing, such a contingency seems even less likely, in 1963, than in 1955.

There is, however, at least one intriguing future possibility. Some distinguished individual, a man of the intellectual calibre of Shaykh Ahmad Hasan al-Baquri, might eventually found a new association or organization to draw together many old members of the Muslim Brotherhood, in order to absorb them into the Revolutionary stream.

---

[11]   The Muslim Brotherhood was not officially dissolved by the Government of the Revolution until after the trials of the Muslim Brothers were terminated. The actual dissolution of this organization was ordered by the "People's Court" on December 5, 1954. See *al-Ahram*, Vol. 80, No. 24847 (December 5, 1954), p. 1. See the anonymous pamphlet, *The Moslem Brothers*, published in English after the order for the dissolution of the Brotherhood. This pamphlet gives a succinct history of the Muslim Brotherhood, the eventual abandonment by the Brothers of their original movement for the "spiritual reformation" of Islam, their "deviations" from "true" Islamic practices, and their conspiracies against fellow Muslims. A list of their alleged or proven political assassinations is included in the pamphlet. The list is headed by the name of Prime Minister Ahmed Maher, "first victim of the Moslem Brotherhood" (in 1945), and includes the names of other notable Egyptian officials (pp. 9, 10, 21, 36). It is also asserted in the pamphlet that the Imam Yahya of Yemen, together with his Prime Minister and three of his sons, was assassinated (February, 1948) as the result of a plot "planned at the Moslem Brotherhood's headquarters in Cairo" (p. 14). The list ends with a brief account of the "attempted murder" of Prime Minister Gamal Abdel Nasser (p. 46). The pamphlet concludes: "The Moslem Brothers had to their credit, rather discredit, a long lost of massacres and cruelties stretching over ten years. They committed crimes, which in the view of Islam, were tantamount to the annihilation of human Society. The Revolution could not have been expected to remain idle while the safety of the country was at stake, nor could it leave the country's fate in the hands of a gang of murderers. The evils of the Moslem Brotherhood had to be eradicated once and for all. . . . The Moslem Brothers had killed by the sword, and 'he who kills by the sword shall perish by the sword'."

Shaykh al-Baquri is mentioned in this connection only because he has been closely identified with both movements. He is known to be one of the men who sought, in the early days of the new regime, to draft the constructive potential of the Brotherhood for service into the ranks of the Revolutionary movement. He it was who, reputedly, was the personal choice of the founder, Hasan al-Banna, as his successor in the office of Supreme Guide of the Muslim Brotherhood. He it was also who was invited by the R.C.C. to join the first civilian cabinet of the Government of the Revolution. Shaykh al-Baquri was the only Muslim Brother who resigned from the Brotherhood in order to take office under the new regime. He became and remained (until 1958) Minister of Waqfs (religious endowments) under the premiership and the presidency of both General Naguib and Colonel Nasser. But he retained a large popular following among the Muslim Brothers even after his defection from the Brotherhood. A devout Muslim such as Shaykh al-Baquri – one, moreover, who has had experience in the Brotherhood organization – might be tempted to try to reassemble the Muslim Brothers, now scattered underground and nameless throughout the country, and reconcile them to the Revolution. Shaykh al-Baquri seems at one time to have hoped, even after he became an ardent supporter of the Revolution, that some form of synthesis could be achieved between the reform elements of the Brotherhood and the new reform government, believing that Egypt needed the collaboration of both groups. Shaykh al-Baquri was eventually relieved of his post as Minister of Waqfs, under a cloud, and he is still in disfavor with the Government of the Revolution. But the possibility remains that some devout Muslim, some influential former member of the Muslim Brotherhood, might still feel that, for the sake of greater solidarity in Egypt, it would be wiser not to exclude indefinitely such an influential Muslim group from Egyptian public life. If the erstwhile Muslim Brothers would renounce their xenophobia and their terrorist activities, and if their energies could be harnessed to the Revolutionary Government, many of these Brethren would be capable of doing valiant work in the new Egypt.

VIII

THE END OF THE STRUGGLE?

It is difficult for an outsider to pass judgment upon the actions of the Muslim Brotherhood and the objectives of its leaders.

In the first thorough study of the Muslim Brotherhood that has been published to date, a full-length book in Arabic, Dr. Ishaq Musa al-Husayni, a Palestinian now resident in Lebanon, calls the *Ikhwan al-Muslimun* "the greatest modern Islamic movement." [1] This noted author commends highly the efficient, comprehensive organization of the Muslim Brotherhood. He points out that Hasan al-Banna, who had studied communism, fascism, nazism, and other Western politico-social systems and condemned them, patterned his Muslim association on a mixture of Eastern and Western systems, and that the resultant strength of the Brotherhood organization was a principal factor in assuring power and success to his movement.[2]

Dr. al-Husayni and other competent observers have ascribed the influence of the Brotherhood movement to other factors as well. Hasan al-Banna, though he was no socialist in the Western sense, was successful in presenting to Muslims the principles of Western socialism under the guise of religion. And his concept of Islam was all-embracing – it reached into every phase of life. He formulated a progressive program for reform, at a time when the political parties of Egypt lacked any clear platforms or long-range planning for reform. His program for the Brotherhood included the social, educa-

[1]   *Al-Ikhwan al-Muslimun; kubra al-harakat al-Islamiyyah al-hadithah* [The Muslim Brotherhood; The Greatest Modern Islamic Movement] (Beirut, 1952, 1955).
[2]   For this and succeeding conclusions ascribed to Dr. al-Husayni see chap. viii of the English edition of his book, *The Moslem Brethren: The Greatest of Modern Islamic Movements* (Beirut, 1956), pp. 87-110.

tional, economic, industrial, agricultural, political, and military aspects of life, as well as the spiritual.

The flexibility and modernity of al-Banna's social and economic program, however, were in marked contrast to the inflexibility of his religious-revivalist objectives. The narrow and literal interpretation of the Koran, upon which he always insisted, prevented his realizing that a truly progressive society can only march forward and achieve progress with the aid of a flexible legal system.

It has been thought by many that Hasan al-Banna organized and led a "class movement" against privilege, against capitalism, and against the ruling groups. This is too easy a judgment. There is an element of truth in the thought, but only, as it were, by accident. Hasan al-Banna's condemnation of the failures and inadequacies of a government based on privilege and composed of a wealthy and irresponsible ruling class lent color to this view of his movement. His publicly declared political objective, to substitute an Islamic government for the secularized government of the day, likewise contributed to this misconception. Adding to the same impression were the evidences of his growing ambition to seize power and mold the Brotherhood into a strong political force. But the religious essence of his movement is lost sight of in any such estimate of the place of the Muslim Brotherhood in Egyptian life.

Hasan al-Banna's ideal of the regeneration of Muslim society, by means of the revival of a wholly Muslim way of life for all Believers, was a total concept that reached beyond the confines of any one class of society. All the Muslims of Egypt, more than ninety per cent of the population of the whole country, were the target of his campaign for spiritual uplift and social welfare. The countless benefits provided through al-Banna's elaborate mechanism for his welfare program did at first seem to have been established largely in the interest of the lower classes: to aid the underprivileged and the undernourished. But here again, the principle involved was that of spreading wide the umbrella of Muslim brotherhood and mutual assistance – one of the Koranic precepts most cherished by Muslims – over as many members of the Islamic community as possible.

The later strength and importance of the Muslim Brotherhood derived from the fact that its appeal and its propaganda were directed to all Muslims in every class of society: it succeeded in recruiting

Muslim youths from all walks of life. The universality of its program was what eventually made the Muslim Brotherhood so strong a competitor of the Government of the Revolution in 1952. Undeniably the teachings of Hasan al-Banna appealed in the first instance to all the oppressed Muslim elements in Egyptian society – all those who were oppressed and neglected in the days of the monarchy. So it happened inevitably that the vast majority of his early adherents came from the poorest classes. They first heeded his teachings and responded to his leadership; they were the most in need of spiritual and bodily food. And they naturally benefited most from the Brotherhood's program of religious uplift and social welfare. The ideal of social solidarity, and the sense of belonging to a group and participating in group activities, filled a hitherto unsatisfied need for security and gave Muslim Brothers an assured place in the social life of the day which extended beyond the family and the mosque.

Dr. al-Husayni and others are critical of the principles and policies of the Muslim Brotherhood on other counts. The anti-Westernism of the Brethren, which became increasingly fanatical as the movement developed politically, contributed to their being branded as reactionaries. Their anti-Westernism, moreover, was not discriminating. They failed to differentiate between the negative aspects of Western imperialism and the constructive elements in Western civilization. They concentrated upon the evils, real and alleged, in Western social customs, and they condemned Western civilization as materialistic and essentially nonreligious.

With respect to their own religion, the Muslim Brothers made no serious attempt to achieve unity within Islam and among its differing sects. And they signally failed either to diagnose or to solve the spiritual crisis confronting the Muslims of their day.

Finally, the Muslim Brothers fell short of their own original ideal of peace and the pursuit of their aims by peaceful means. Their movement was eventually vitiated by aggressive xenophobia and discredited by terrorist activities.

One of the most penetrating criticisms of the Muslim Brothers was leveled against them by Muslim observers who were originally inclined to be sympathetic to the movement. These critics had at first nourished hopes that the essentially religious association of the Muslim Brotherhood would initiate a new and healthy development in

Islamic modernism, that it would make the first forward move, in the footsteps of Shaykh Muhammad 'Abduh, toward reconciling Islamic fundamentalism with modern progress. They became disillusioned on two counts. For one, as the Muslim Brotherhood grew in membership and in influence, it gradually turned into a political movement; and as it later gained in power, it became politically irresponsible. Secondly, the Muslim Brothers' increasing preoccupation with political power and position blinded them to the impracticalities of some of the reforms which they sponsored. Less than thirty years after its founding, the Brotherhood had become a threat to the national security of Egypt and the position of orthodox liberal Muslims was being jeopardized by the politically irresponsible ambitions of Muslim Brotherhood leaders.

Even before the death of their founder in 1949, the Muslim Brothers had begun to sow the seed of their own self-destruction. The young intellectuals who were drawn to the movement – members of professional groups, university students, and others – were sucked into a maelstrom of factionalism within the organization and were also encouraged to dissipate their energies in contending with fellow Egyptians and even with fellow Muslims. The theological and intellectual arrogance of Brotherhood spokesmen alienated many potential sympathizers among educated Egyptian Muslims, and the terrorist activities which the Brotherhood organization alternately instigated or condoned filled many with apprehension and aversion.

The increasing preoccupation of Brotherhood leaders with the attainment of political power resulted in diminishing their capacity to plan for basic reforms in Islamic society. They continued to offer clamorous lip-service to an extensive reform program, but they became progressively less competent either to initiate or to carry out such a program. After the Revolution, moreover, when the R.C.C. made it clear to all Egyptians that the Government of the Revolution was prepared to inaugurate a basic reform program, and especially after the Revolutionary leaders actually began to implement reforms that were so much in line with the reforms demanded by the Muslim Brothers, the latter lost overnight the moral ground for their opposition to the Egyptian government. The refusal of Brotherhood leaders to co-operate with a reform government fatally undermined their position. This was true of all the members of the Brotherhood Guidance Office – the Supreme Guide and the Secretary-General as well as ʿAshmawi and his faction. On the shoulders of the Supreme Guide, however, falls the ultimate responsibility for failing to grasp the full implications of the new political situation that developed in Egypt after July 26, 1952. Hasan Ismaʿil al-Hudaybi, through that failure, lost a unique opportunity to establish the Muslim Brotherhood solidly in the life of the new Egypt.

From the point of view of the intellectuals of Egypt, the Muslim Brothers had an organic weakness, over and above their lack of political acumen, which they themselves were unable to diagnose. The educational philosophy of the founder of the Brotherhood, an ideal that committed him and his disciples to the narrow confines of rigid Islamic fundamentalism, had excluded the Muslim Brothers from full participation in the ever expanding opportunities of secular education. The hallmark of Muslim intellectuals, a rising and influential elite group in Egypt, is linguistic bi-culturalism, to borrow a happy phrase coined by Professor Wilfred Cantwell Smith.[3] The Muslim intellectual of contemporary Egypt has been thoroughly exposed to the ideas and the achievements of at least one, frequently more than one, culture other than his own. He has been thus exposed owing to his proficiency in foreign languages – usually English or French, or both, and frequently also Italian. He is capable of *thinking* in one or more of these languages – not merely of reading, writing, and talking them – in addition to his native Arabic. Egyptians such as Dr. Taha Hussein, to mention only one among many, are on intimate terms with the thought and the literature of France and England, they are completely at home in the intellectual worlds of the West and of Arab Islam, and they write and publish in English, French, and Arabic with almost equal facility.

The Muslim Brothers, on the other hand, owing to their educational emphasis on Arabic and on Islamic history, and to their exclusive religious concentration on fundamentalist Islam, had disqualified themselves from belonging to this elite Muslim group. And in circumscribing their own intellectual horizons they fell short of the ideal of Muslim scholars, an ideal first inculcated in Islamic society during the golden age of Arab Islam, when the new Faith was emi-

[3]   In Sydney N. Fisher (ed.), *Social Forces in the Middle East* (Ithaca, N. Y., 1955), p. 201.

nently receptive to thought as alien as that of Aristotle. The Muslim Brothers were not equipped to hold their own among Muslim intellectuals, and therefore they could not hope to attain to a position of intellectual leadership in their own country. Their obsessive desire to reinstate fundamentalist theology, to uphold the letter of the Sacred Law of Islam, and to establish an exclusive Islamic state in Egypt caused them to renounce for themselves, and to seek to deny to others, the broader intellectual birthright of Egyptian Muslims.

The theological dilemma of the Muslim Brothers, in the final analysis, lay in the necessity they felt for remolding the whole of Egyptian society in their own image. So passionate was their conviction that Islam alone could provide the only pattern for right living, and so fierce and exclusive was their reliance on the Koran and the letter of the Sacred Law, that there was no room in their thinking for any shadow of compromise with other manners or other customs. In their belief, Islam presents to mankind a unified and comprehensive, unique, and perfect system of life, and the introduction of foreign elements on a large scale into Muslim society would be ruinous. But – and here was their dilemma – modern Egyptian life had long been permeated with foreign elements. In education, administration, science and the arts, foreign influences had been cumulatively penetrating; and the modern Egyptian Muslim had long lived and moved and had his being within a composite framework of Islamic and Western-inspired laws. It was recognition of the strength of these influences in Egypt that originally inspired Hasan al-Banna, in the early 1930's, to put his fingers into the dike in an effort to stop the inrushing flood of Western cultural invasion. But the dike had sprung too many holes by mid-20th century, and the Muslim Brothers were suffering from an acute sense of urgency.[4] They believed that Muslim life must be purged, now and immediately, before it became further contaminated by foreign matter. But was not the battle of the Brotherhood lost before ever it was begun?

Still another group, the Muslim progressive liberals, stood in contradistinction to the Muslim reactionaries who sought to "renew" Islam without benefit of the fresh waters of Europe. These liberals, in the spirit of the golden age, welcomed all constructive thought and

[4] For developments in the world of Islam since 1945 see Kenneth Cragg, *The Call of the Minaret* (New York, 1956), chap. i.

modern achievement, whatever their source, and believed with equal conviction that there was sufficient inherent strength and flexibility in the Muslim system and ethic to adapt and to use foreign influences to its own betterment. And Muslim liberals took over the helm of government with the Revolution. General Muhammad Naguib, first spokesman of the Muslim group in power after July, 1952, explained the situation clearly as it appeared to the R.C.C. Commenting on "our unanimous desire to make Egypt a secular republic," he said:

... what most of the Moslem Brothers wanted was to go back to the days of the Sultan Saláh ed Din [Saladin of the Crusades] when Egypt was a theocratic state. The rest of us, while sympathizing with the desire to apply the teachings of Mohammed to modern life, were convinced that to do so blindly would spell disaster. The rebirth of Egypt, in our opinion, depended on the continued modernization of its social, political, and economic institutions.

Egypt is the melting pot of the Middle East. Such prosperity as it has enjoyed in modern times has been largely due to its ability to attract and absorb foreigners and assimilate their ideas. There is nothing in the Koran that calls for theocratic government; on the contrary, the Prophet was in favor of parliamentary rule . . . . It is thus not only permissible but desirable for a cosmopolitan country like Egypt to be governed by means of a secular republic in which the rights of minorities shall be respected so long as the minorities, in turn, respect the Islamic way of life.

This does not mean that my colleagues and I have chosen to turn our backs on the Islamic faith. On the contrary, we hope to strengthen the faith by applying its teachings judiciously rather than blindly, as some groups in Egypt would have us do . . . . The injunctions of the Koran have as much meaning in application today as they ever did, provided they are interpreted with due regard for the great changes that have occurred in human society since the Prophet preached his message.[5]

The recurrent challenge of the Muslim Brotherhood, as of other fundamentalist Islamic groups, is in essence this: Can the government of a Muslim country be secularized without jeopardizing the basic religious structure of its Islamic civilization? Can the spirit of the Sacred Law be maintained without enforcing the letter of that Law? The point at issue is neither irrelevant nor inconsequential to the True Believer. Herein lies the strength of the Muslim Brothers in Egypt, the valid premise for their religious fundamentalism. It is necessary

[5] Mohammed Neguib, *Egypt's Destiny* (London, 1955), pp. 150-151, and also pp. 32, 177; in the American edition, pp. 134-135, and also pp. 32, 158.

to acknowledge that no fruitful compromise can be assured, as between these two essentially divergent points of view. A religious group which takes its stand on a crystallized and sacrosanct law cannot logically tolerate any breach in its ramparts. That attitude puts the burden of the proof on those – in this particular instance on the shoulders of the leaders of the Egyptian Revolution – who stoutly insist that a secularized government can maintain intact a Muslim society.

One morally crucial question can be properly raised with respect to the Muslim Brothers. How long can a religious group hope to defend its faith by terrorism and assassination? How long can it justify war, not against the foreign infidel, but against its own Muslim government and against Muslim fellow countrymen? [6] Can the spiritual values of a faith be thus defended?

The leaders of the Revolution have had another basic criticism of the Muslim Brothers. Their greatest fault, in the eyes of certain members of the R.C.C., was to emphasize and exaggerate the cultural and other differences between the Muslim majority and the Christian and Jewish minorities of Egypt. All three communities had contributed historically to the development of Egypt; the talents of all three communities were needed to build the new Egypt. Insistence upon the unity of Egypt, the equality of all Egyptians, and social justice for all was the new regime's message of hope.[7] It was obvious that the predilection of the Brotherhood for emphasizing the religious and cultural differences between these three communities, especially when coupled with their repeated demands for a wholly Islamic state, could only promote disunity in the country. Old frictions would thus be perpetuated, rather than eliminated, and justifiable doubts would be raised in the minds of Christian and Jewish Egyptians concerning their future status in Egypt and their relations with fellow citizens of the Muslim faith.

---

[6] Compare the proclamation of the Council of Ulama of al-Azhar (November 18, 1954) after the Government of the Revolution took drastic action against the Muslim Brothers. For a summary of this significant proclamation see chap. vii, note 9.

[7] The Egyptian Constitution of January 16, 1956, Preamble, *passim*; Part II, Articles 4, 5, 17, 22; and Part III, Articles 31, 34, 35, 38, 43. – For an illuminating discussion of the attitude of the R.C.C. toward the minorities see Neguib, *op. cit.*, English ed., pp. 194-196; American ed., pp. 173-174.

The Muslim Brothers were faced with another dilemma, a practical rather than a theological one. Much has been said in the preceding pages about the socio-economic reform program of the Brotherhood and its genuinely progressive character. The reforms the Muslim Brothers sponsored in this field could be reconciled with their religious fundamentalism because there was nothing in their modernized welfare program that militated against either the spirit or the letter of the Islamic Law. Their practical dilemma was quite other. They had not found it possible to implement the desired reforms, in this modern scientific age, without using the tools provided by Western technology. Inevitably they relied upon Western printing for their propaganda, and upon Western engineering, bookkeeping methods, and all the like paraphernalia of modern scientific and industrial enterprise. Hasan al-Banna himself used a microphone and loudspeaker to broadcast his speeches, and his dress was normally European. He and all the Muslim Brothers had long lived by laws that were Western in origin as well as Islamic. And yet, he and his Brotherhood repudiated Westernism and education of the Western type, and fulminated against the subversion of Muslim social customs by Western influences. They found that Western technological importations could not easily be separated from Western social infiltration.

The contradictions inherent in their attitude created tensions which drove the Muslim Brothers relentlessly into xenophobia. They reacted intemperately against the alleged imperialism of the West, and they resorted to violence and employed terrorist tactics against Westerners and also against fellow Muslims who showed interest in or sympathy for the West.

There was still another reason for the anti-Westernism of the Muslim Brothers. Because they were religious fundamentalists and reactionaries, they had a nostalgic yearning for one special aspect of the golden age of Islam, namely, the military strength of the Islamic empire which had given power and universal authority to Muslim theological leaders. At the same time, owing to this undue concentration on the power aspects of Islam's golden age, the Muslim Brothers failed to comprehend the intellectual dimensions of that era. They did not realize that the receptivity of the earliest Muslim elite to alien thought and learning was one of the golden aspects of the early period of Islamic development, a source of strength to the body politic. It seems probable that this failure of understanding was wrought by a psychological factor. In the early days the Muslims were aggressors; they were actively expanding the frontiers of Islam, swept forward on the tidal wave of their newly established Faith. They absorbed the multitudinous foreign populations which they engulfed, and they voluntarily absorbed alien cultures. Because the Muslims were powerful and self-confident, they could do so without fear. By the 20th century, however, the area of Islamic dominance had greatly contracted. Muslim Arabs were politically weak and on the defensive. Western foreigners in their turn had become the aggressors in the lands of the eastern Mediterranean and apparently sought to undermine Arab-Islamic society. It was because the Muslim Brothers recognized the weakness of Muslims vis-à-vis the West that they first became fearful of, and then antagonistic to, Westerners.

It is impossible to predict whether an organization that has already survived several periods of existence underground might, or might not, be capable of resurrection. As of now, the Muslim Brotherhood has had its official existence terminated. How can one estimate the survival potential of a movement such as this, with all its traditional undertones, its emotional overtones, and its hard core of reactionary objectives? The future role of a fundamentalist movement like the Muslim Brotherhood is not predictable. It would certainly seem that the secular, tolerant spirit of the times in Egypt would militate against a revival in the near future. But equally certain is the fact that when the Muslim Brotherhood was founded, not quite thirty years ago, it filled a popular need and evoked a wide response among the masses. Equally true is the fact that this movement fought its way to the top in Egyptian politics and eventually enlisted the support of many of Egypt's young intellectuals. Were a Muslim Brother of character and determination to arise, prepared to reassemble the now scattered membership of the Brotherhood and to lead them against a future government in Egypt, he might succeed in resurrecting the movement of Hasan al-Banna. Who can say? There are too many imponderables, too many unknown factors to be reckoned with. Much would depend upon the nature of political life in Egypt after the inauguration of fully representative government. And much would depend upon the general climate of Muslim opinion in Egypt when that time comes.

Indications are not lacking that certain of the Brotherhood principles have undergone some modification over the years – for example, the willingness of some of the Muslim Brothers to declare themselves in favor of a republican form of government for Egypt, and the attitude of some of the Brethren toward the status and the political rights of women. But none of the Muslim Brothers has ever renounced publicly the organization's basic objective of an Islamic state, a state based exclusively on the Sacred Law of Islam.

One relevant fact is worth mentioning in any consideration of the possible future resurrection of the Muslim Brotherhood. Some influential Muslim Brethren succeeded in escaping from Egypt when their organization was suppressed late in 1954, notably Saʿid Ramadan, son-in-law of the late founder of the movement, and ʿAbd al-Hakim ʿAbidin, Secretary-General of the Brotherhood. They and others are doing their best to hold the exiles together and to keep the Brotherhood alive outside Egypt, particularly in Syria and in Jordan. They attend secret meetings and all public conferences of the Muslim Brotherhood in these and other neighboring countries. The Muslim Brothers of Jordan form a large and militant group. Reportedly, there are several thousand of them, and they helped organize the riots of December, 1955, and January, 1956 – with the support of other subversive Jordanian groups (including the Communists). It is possible that through their activity in exile the Egyptian Brethren may hope eventually to recapture Egypt for the Muslim Brotherhood.[8]

[8]   The Muslim Brotherhood, of course, could not hope to accomplish this feat so long as Nasser controls Egypt. But they can build their strength outside Egypt and bide their time until the death of President Nasser. Like the Communists, though for different reasons, the Muslim Brothers deplored the union between Syria and Egypt in February, 1958. The work of the Brotherhood in Syria was, naturally, circumscribed thereafter. Since the secession of Syria from the United Arab Republic (September, 1961), however, it is quite possible that activities have been intensified. It is even likely that the dissolution of the Syro-Egyptian unitary government was encouraged by members of the Muslim Brotherhood organization in Syria. And since the signing of the latest U.A.R. pact in the spring of 1963, and the proposed federation of Syria and Iraq with Egypt, the Muslim Brotherhood of Syria has reportedly been one of the several Syrian groups which have opposed reunification. Certain news reports from the Arab Middle East (e.g., *Atlas: The World Press in Translation,*

Thus far, the Muslim Brothers have failed to enlist the allegiance of the majority of educated Muslim Egyptians. At the same time, no Egyptian Muslim has succeeded in establishing a contemporary movement to carry forward the reforms and to implement the vision of Shaykh Muhammad 'Abduh. What devout orthodox Egyptian Muslims need today is a champion – a theologian and a reformer to rehabilitate this first Islamic reform movement. They are in need of the capable and practical leadership of a second Muhammad 'Abduh – a devout Muslim possessed of the intellectual and human qualities of this earlier leader, a man who, like him, would have a sufficiently profound knowledge of Islamic theology and law to bridge the gap between Muslim fundamentalists and Muslim progressive liberals. To succeed in his reforming mission, such a leader would need to command the respect of Muslim intellectuals and to hold the confidence of Muslim liberals, without alienating the sensitive religious consciences of Muslim fundamentalists. Such a man might achieve a synthesis between the modernists and the fundamentalists of Egypt. He might even be able to salvage the dynamic essence of Hasan al-Banna's Brotherhood movement, canalize its constructive potential, and conciliate the Muslim reactionaries – a group that has shown itself confused and fearful in the face of cumulative modernist pressures.

May, 1963, p. 292, col. 2) have claimed that the Muslim Brothers of Syria have taken a stand for Syrian separatism. It is logical that all Muslim Brotherhood organizations would fear their incorporation in any federation presided over by President Abdel Nasser of Egypt, the man who had suppressed the Muslim Brotherhood of Egypt at the end of 1954.

SELECTED BIBLIOGRAPHY

A useful bibliography for the Muslim Brotherhood of Egypt must include many works on the society in which the Muslim Brothers lived and worked and propagated their doctrines. They bridged the old era and the new, they faced and tried to solve the problems that faced all Egyptian Muslims under the monarchy and under the Revolution. For this reason a number of general works are included in this bibliography: some standard histories of modern Egypt and Anglo-Egyptian relations; a few standard works on Islam and on Islam and modernism in Egypt; monographs that shed light on the special problems of Egypt and on the social, economic, and political conditions of Egyptian life; special studies and articles on nationalism and Egyptian nationalist leaders from 1881 to, and including, the present Government of the Revolution. A special group of representative publications, by Hasan al-Banna and the press of the Muslim Brotherhood, is included in the Arabic section of this bibliography.

I. REFERENCE WORKS

A. *General*

Four general reference works are indispensable for the student of modern Egypt:

Encyclopaedia of Islam: A Dictionary of the Geography, Ethnography, and Biography of the Muhammadan Peoples. 4 vols. Leyden: Brill, London: Luzac, 1913-1936. (Now in the process of revision.)

Oriente Moderno. (*Monthly publication of the Istituto per l'Oriente,* Rome.) Between the years 1921-1939 this important journal gave a detailed coverage of Egyptian affairs based on the Arabic press of Egypt – i.e., it did not rely exclusively upon *al-Ahram*; it cited or quoted from the principal Arabic newspapers.

Survey of International Affairs, 1920-1939, 1945. London: Oxford University Press, H. Milford, 1925-1952.
This is especially important for events between 1920 and 1939.

Who's Who in Egypt and the Near East: The Leading Biographical Dictionary in the Near East. Cairo: Paul Barbey Press, 1952 and 1955.
This is helpful to identify many contemporary Egyptian leaders and men of affairs.

B. *Useful Bibliographies*

Coult, Lyman H. (with Durzi, K.). *An Annotated Research Bibliography of Studies in Arabic, English, and French, of the Fellah of the Egyptian Nile, 1798-1955.* Miami, Florida: University of Miami Press, 1958.

Ettinghausen, Richard (ed.). *A Selected and Annotated Bibliography of Books and Periodicals in Western Languages Dealing With the Near and Middle East, With Special Emphasis on Medieval and Modern Times.* Washington, D.C.: Middle East Institute, 1954.

Maunier, René. *Bibliographie économique, juridique et sociale de l'Egypte moderne (1798-1916) (Travaux spéciaux de la société sultanieh d'économie politique, de statistique et de legislation,* No. 1). Cairo, 1918.

II. GOVERNMENT DOCUMENTS AND PAMPHLETS

Egypt, Embassy, U.S. *The Labor Movement in Egypt.* Washington, D.C., 1955.
——. *Rural Social Welfare Centres in Egypt.* Washington, D.C., 1954. First printed by the Egyptian Ministry of Social Affairs in 1951.
——. *The Story of Education in Egypt.* Washington, D.C.: Washington Embassy Publication, 1955.
——. *Today's Egypt, the Agrarian Reform.* Washington, D.C.: Washington Embassy Publication, 1954.

Egypt, Government of. *Constitution of the Republic of Egypt,* [January 16] *1956.* [Cairo, n.d.] Authorized texts in Arabic, English, and French.

——. *Draft of the Charter, May 21, 1962.* "Draft of the National Charter presented by President Gamal Abdel Nasser at the Inaugural Session of the National Congress of Popular Powers on the evening of 21st May, 1962." Information Department, United Arab Republic. Al-Shaab Printing House.

——. *Journal Officiel du Gouvernement Egyptien.* Arabic ed., *al-Waqā'iᶜ al-Misriyyah, jarīdah rasmiyyah.*

——, Press Department, Higher Committee of Agrarian Reform. *Land Reform Law, Full Text.* Cairo, 1954. "Decree-Law No. 178 of 1952 on Land Reform" (including additions and "modifications" to 1954).

Egypt, Higher Committee of Agrarian Reform. *Agrarian Reform in Egypt.* Release No. 10. Cairo: Press Office, 1954.

Egypt, Ministère d'Economie Nationale, Département de la Statistique Générale. *Annuaire statistique de poche, 1949-1950.* Cairo, 1951.

——. *Annuaire statistique de poche, 1953.* Cairo, 1954.

Egypt, Ministry of National Economy, Department of Statistics. *Al-Ihsa' al-Sanawi* [Statistical Year Book (1949-1950)]. Cairo, 1951.

Egypt, Ministry of Social Affairs. *Rural Social Welfare Centres in Egypt.* Cairo, 1951.

——. *Social Welfare in Egypt.* Cairo, 1950.

Egypt (United Arab Republic), Information Department. *Pocket Book, 1962.* Cairo: Al-Shaab Printing House.

France, Government of. Ministère des Affaires Etrangères, Commission de publication des documents relatifs aux origines de la guerre de 1914. *Documents diplomatiques français (1871-1914),* 1ʳᵉ série (1871-1900), Tome IV. Paris, 1932.

Great Britain, Parliament. *Accounts and Papers: State Papers.*

Great Britain, Department of Overseas Trade. *Overseas Economic Surveys: Egypt.* London, 1947 and 1952.

——. *Report on Economic and Commercial Conditions in Egypt.* London, 1937.

Great Britain, Foreign Office. *British and Foreign State Papers.* (Hertslet ed.) Vols. 73 (1881-1882) and 74 (1882-1883). London, 1890.

Great Britain, Special Mission to Egypt. *Report of the Special Mission to Egypt.* (Egypt No. 1, 1921; C. 1131.) London, 1921.

Great Britain, Government of, Middle East Supply Centre. *The Agricultural Development of the Middle East,* by B. A. Keen. London, 1946.

——. Middle East Supply Centre. *Rural Education and Welfare in the Middle East,* by H. B. Allen. London, 1946.

Great Britain, British Information Services. *The Anglo-Egyptian Sudan.* London, 1951.

——. *The Background of Anglo-Egyptian Relations.* London, 1951.

——. *The British Middle East Office.* London, 1951.

——. *British Policy in the Middle East.* London, 1951.

III. BOOKS AND PAMPHLETS IN WESTERN LANGUAGES

Abdel Nasser, Gamal. *The Philosophy of the Revolution.* Cairo: Dar al-Maaref, n.d.

———. *Egypt's Liberation; The Philosophy of the Revolution.* Washington: Public Affairs Press, 1955.

———. *The Philosophy of the Revolution.* Buffalo, N. Y.: Smith, Keynes and Marshall – Economica Books, 1959.

———. *Speeches and Press Interviews, 1958-1960.* Cairo: Information Department (U.A.R.), 1960.

Abou Alam, Abdel Raouf. *The Labor Movement in Egypt.* Washington: Egypt, Washington Embassy Publication, 1955.

Adam, Juliette (Juliette Lamber). *L'Angleterre en Egypte.* Paris: Imprimerie du Centre, 1922.

Adams, Charles C. *Islam and Modernism in Egypt.* London: Oxford University Press, 1933.

Ahmed, Jamal Mohammed. *The Intellectual Origins of Egyptian Nationalism* (= *Middle Eastern Monographs,* III, Royal Institute of International Affairs). London and New York: Oxford University Press, 1960.

Alexander, J., *The Truth About Egypt.* London: Cassell, 1911.

Amer, Ibrahim (ed.). *Encyclopedia of Egyptian Affairs.* Cairo, 1953.

Amin, Osman. *Muhammad 'Abduh.* Translated by Charles Wendell. Washington, D.C.: American Council of Learned Societies, 1953.

Ammar, 'Abbas M. *The Unity of the Nile Valley, Its Geographical Bases and Its Manifestations in History.* Cairo: Government Press, 1947.

Ammar, Hamed. *Growing Up in an Egyptian Village.* London: Routledge & Kegan Paul, 1954.

Anderson, J. N. D. *Islamic Law in the Modern World.* New York: New York University Press, 1959.

Antonius, George. *The Arab Awakening: The Story of the Arab National Movement.* New York: Lippincott, 1939.

Atiyah, Edward. *The Arabs: The Origins, Present Conditions, and Prospects of the Arab World.* Harmondsworth, Middlesex: Penguin Books Ltd., 1955 and 1958.

Ayrout, Henry Habib. *The Fellaheen.* Translated by Hilary Wayment. Cairo: Schindler, 1945.

———. *Fellahs d'Egypte.* Cairo: Editions du Sphynx, 1952.

———. *The Egyptian Peasant,* Translated by John Alden Williams. Boston: Beacon Press, 1963.

Barawy, Rashed el-. *The Military Coup in Egypt.* Cairo: Renaissance Bookshop, 1952.

Beaman, Ardern Hulme. *The Dethronement of the Khedive.* London: Allen and Unwin, 1929.

Berger, Morroe. *The Arab World Today.* New York: Doubleday and Co., 1962.

———. *Bureaucracy and Society in Modern Egypt: A Study of the Higher Civil Service.* Princeton, N.J.: Princeton University Press, 1957.

———. *Military Elite and Social Change: Egypt Since Napoleon.* Princeton, N.J.: Princeton University Center of International Studies, 1960.

Berque, Jacques. *Histoire d'un Village Egyptien au XXème Siècle.* Paris and The Hague; Mouton, 1957.

Blackman, Winifred S. *The Fellahin of Upper Egypt.* London: Harrap, 1927.

Blunt, Wilfrid Scawen. *My Diaries, Being a Personal Narrative of Events 1888-1914.* 2 vols. New York: Knopf, 1921.

——. *Secret History of the English Occupation of Egypt, Being a Personal Narrative of Events.* New York: Knopf, 1922.

Boehm, Y. *The Organization of the Moslem Brotherhood in Egypt.* Tel-Aviv, 1952. (In Hebrew. Cited by Walter Z. Laqueur on p. 342 of his book, *Communism and Nationalism in the Middle East.* The author of this study has not had an opportunity to consult Boehm's work.)

Boktor, Amir. *School and Society in the Valley of the Nile.* Cairo: Elias' Modern Press, 1936.

Bonné, Alfred. *State and Economics in the Middle East: A Society in Transition.* London: K. Paul, Trench, Trubner, 1948.

Bowman, Humphrey Ernest. *Middle-East Window.* London: Longmans, Green, 1942.

Brinton, Jasper Yeates. *The Mixed Courts of Egypt.* New Haven, Conn.: Yale University Press, 1930.

Broadley, Alexander Meyrick. *How We Defended Arabi and His Friends.* 2d ed. London: Chapman and Hall, 1884.

Bullard, Sir Reader W. *Britain and the Middle East, from the Earliest Times to 1950.* London and New York: Hutchinson's University Library, 1951.

Chirol, Sir Valentine. *The Egyptian Problem.* London: Macmillan, 1921.

Cleland, Wendell. *The Population Problem in Egypt.* Lancaster, Pa.: Science Press, 1936.

Clerbet, Marcel. *Le Caire,* 2 vols. Cairo: Schindler, 1934.

Colombe, Marcel. *L'Evolution de l'Egypte, 1924-1950.* Paris: G. P. Maisonneuve, 1951.

Colvin, Sir Auckland. *The Making of Modern Egypt.* London: Seeley, 1906.

Craig, James I. *Egypt in the Post War Economy.* Cairo, 1945.

Cromer, The Earl of (Evelyn Baring). *Modern Egypt.* 2 vols. London: Macmillan, 1908.

Crouchley, A. E. *The Economic Development of Modern Egypt.* London: Longmans, Green, 1938.

Davis, Helen M. *Constitutions, Electoral Laws, Treaties of States in the Near and Middle East.* Durham, N. C.: Duke University Press, 1947 and 1953.

Dodge, Bayard. *Al-Azhar: A Millennium of Muslim Learning.* Washington, D.C.: Middle East Institute, 1961.

——. *Muslim Education in Medieval Times.* Washington, D.C.: Middle East Institute, 1962.

Driault, Edouard. *La question d'Orient depuis ses origines jusqu'à nos jours.* Preface by Gabriel Monod. 7th ed. Paris: F. Alcan, 1917.

Duff-Gordon, Lucie (Austin), Lady. *Last Letters from Egypt.* 2d ed. London: Macmillan, 1876.

Egypt and the United Nations: Report of a Study Group Set Up by the Egyptian Society of International Law. New York: Manhattan Publishing Co. and the Carnegie Endowment for International Peace, 1957.

Le Groupe d'Etudes de l'Islam. *L'Egypte indépendante,* Centre de Politique Etrangère, Publication No. 7. Paris: Paul Hartman, 1938.

Elgood, P. G. *Egypt and the Army.* London: Oxford University Press, 1924.

Fernau, Friedrich Wilhelm. *Flackernder Halbmond: Hintergrund der islamischen Unruhe.* Erlenbach-Zurich: E. Reutsch, 1953. (English ed., *Moslems on the March: People and Politics in the World of Islam.* Translated by E. W. Dickes. New York: Knopf, 1954.)

Fisher, Sydney N. (ed.). *Evolution in the Middle East: Reform, Revolt and Change.* Washington, D.C.: Middle East Institute, 1953. (A series of addresses presented at the Seventh Annual Conference on Middle East Affairs, sponsored by the Middle East Institute, March 6-7, 1953.)

——. *Social Forces in the Middle East.* Ithaca, N.Y.: Cornell University Press, 1955. (Papers presented at a conference sponsored by the Committee on the Near and Middle East of the Social Science Research Council.)

Franck, Dorothea Seelye (ed.). *Islam in the Modern World.* Washington, D.C.: Middle East Institute, 1951. (A series of addresses presented at the Fifth Annual Conference on Middle East Affairs, sponsored by the Middle East Institute.)

Freycinet, Charles de. *La question d'Egypte.* 2d ed. Paris: Calmann-Levy, 1905.

Galatoli, Anthony Michelangelo. *Egypt in Midpassage.* Cairo: Urwand and Sons Press, 1950.

Galt, Russell. *The Effects of Centralization on Education in Modern Egypt.* Cairo: Department of Education, American University at Cairo, 1936.

Garzouzi, Eva. *Old Ills and New Remedies in Egypt.* Cairo: Dar al-Maaref, 1958.

Gaudefroy-Demombynes, Maurice. *Les institutions musulmanes.* Paris: Flammarion, 1946. (English ed., *Muslim Institutions.* Translated by J. P. Macgregor. London: Allen & Unwin, 1950.)

Ghali, Mirrit Boutros. *The Policy of Tomorrow.* Cairo, 1938 and 1951, Washington, D.C.: American Council of Learned Societies, 1953.

Ghazzali, Muhammad al-. *Our Beginning in Wisdom.* Translated by Isma'il R. el Faruqi. Washington, D.C.: American Council of Learned Societies, 1953.

Gibb, H. A. R. *Modern Trends in Islam.* Chicago: University of Chicago Press, 1947.

——. *Mohammedanism: An Historical Survey.* London and New York: Oxford University Press, 1950.

—— (ed.). *Whither Islam? A Survey of Modern Movements in the Moslem World.* London: Gollancz, 1932.

Gibb, H. A. R., and Bowen, Harold. *Islamic Society and the West: A Study of the Impact of Western Civilization on Moslem Culture in the Near East.* London and New York: Oxford University Press, 1950.

Grunebaum, Gustave E. von. (ed.). *Unity and Variety in Muslim Civilization.* Chicago: University of Chicago Press, 1955. (Notably the contribution of Dr. Werner Caskel.)

Guillaume, Alfred. *Islam.* London: Pelican Books, 1954.

Hakim, Tewfik el-. *Maze of Justice.* Translated by A. S. Eban. London: Harvill Press, 1947.

Harbison, Frederick A., and Ibrahim, Ibrahim Abdelkader. *Human Resources for Egyptian Enterprise.* New York: McGraw-Hill. 1958.

Hartmann, Martin. *The Arabic Press of Egypt.* London: Luzac, 1899.

Hesseltine, William B., and Wolf, Hexel C., *The Blue and the Gray on the Nile.* Chicago: University of Chicago Press, 1961. (Contains annotated list of Americans who served in Egypt in the 1870's.)

Heyworth-Dunne, Gamal-Eddine (James Heyworth-Dunne). *Egypt: The Co-operative Movement.* Cairo: Renaissance Book Shop, 1952.

Heyworth-Dunne, James. *An Introduction to the History of Education in Modern Egypt.* London: Luzac, 1939.

——. *Religious and Political Trends in Modern Egypt.* Washington, D.C.: Published by the author, 1950.

——. *Select Bibliography on Modern Egypt.* Cairo, 1952.

Hitti, Philip K. *History of the Arabs.* 3rd ed., rev. London: Macmillan, 1946.

Hoskins, Halford L. *The Middle East, Problem Area in World Politics.* New York: Macmillan, 1954.

Hourani, Albert H. *Minorities in the Arab World.* London and New York: Oxford University Press, 1947.

Hurewitz, J. C. *Diplomacy in the Near and Middle East: A Documentary Record.* 2 vols. Princeton, N.J.: D. Van Nostrand, 1956.

Hurst, H. E. *The Nile: A General Account of the River and the Utilization of Its Waters.* London, 1952.

Husaini, Ishak Musa (Ishaq Musa al-Husayni). *The Moslem Brethren; The Greatest of Modern Islamic Movements.* Translated by John F. Brown and John Racy. Beirut: Khayat's College Book Cooperative, 1956.

Hussein, Ahmed. *Rural Social Welfare Centres in Egypt.* Cairo: Ministry of Social Affairs, 1951.

Hussein, Taha (Taha Husain). *An Egyptian Childhood.* Translated by E. H. Paxton. London: Routledge, 1932.

——. *The Future of Culture in Egypt.* Translated by Sidney Glazer. Washington, D.C.: American Council of Learned Societies, 1954.

——. *The Stream of Days: A Student at the Azhar.* Translated by Hilary Wayment. 2d ed. London and New York: Longmans, Green, 1948.

Ionides, Michael. *Divide and Lose: The Arab Revolt, 1955-1958.* London: Geoffrey Bles, 1960.

Issawi, Charles Philip. *Egypt: An Economic and Social Analysis.* London and New York: Oxford University Press, 1947.

——. *Egypt at Mid-Century: An Economic Survey.* London and New York: Oxford University Press, 1954.

Kabbani, Isma'il el-. *A Hundred Years of Education in Egypt.* Cairo: Government Press, 1948.

Kedourie, Elie. *England and the Middle East; The Destruction of the Ottoman Empire, 1914-1921.* London: Bowes & Bowes, 1956.

Khalid, Khalid Muhammad. *From Here We Start.* Translated by Isma'il R. el Faruqi. Washington, D.C.; American Council of Learned Societies, 1953.

Kirk, George. *The Middle East in the War.* London and New York: Oxford University Press, 1952 and 1953.

Klingmüller, Ernst. *Geschichte der Wafd-Partei im Rahmen der gesamtpolitischen Lage Aegyptens.* Berlin: Druck Triltsh und Huther, 1937.

Kohn, Hans. *Nationalism and Imperialism in the Hither East.* London, 1932.

——. *Western Civilization in the Near East.* New York, 1936.

Kotb, Sayed. *Social Justice in Islam.* Translated by John B. Hardie. Washington, D.C.: American Council of Learned Societies, 1953.

Lacouture, Jean, and Lacouture, Simonne. *L'Egypte en mouvement.* Paris: Editions du Seuil, 1956.

Lammens, Henri. *L'Islam; croyances et institutions.* 3d ed., rev. Beirut: Imprimerie Catholique, 1943.

Landau, Jacob M. *Parliaments and Parties in Egypt.* New York: Praeger, 1954.

Landes, David S. *Bankers and Pashas: International Finance and Economic Imperialism in Egypt.* London: Heinemann, 1958. [Harvard University Press, 1958].

Langer, William L. *European Alliances and Alignments, 1871-1890.* New York: Knopf, 1931.

Laqueur, Walter Z. *Communism and Nationalism in the Middle East.* New York: Praeger, 1956.

Little, Tom. *Egypt.* New York: Praeger, 1958.

Lloyd, George Ambrose, Lord. *Egypt Since Cromer.* 2 vols. London: Macmillan, 1933-1934.

Longgood, William F. *Suez Story: Key to the Middle East.* New York: Greenberg, 1957.

Low, Sidney. *Egypt in Transition.* New York: Macmillan, 1914.

Macdonald, Duncan Black. *Development of Muslim Theology, Jurisprudence and Constitutional Theory.* New York: Scribner, 1926.

Marlowe, John. *Anglo-Egyptian Relations, 1800-1953.* London: Cresset Press, 1954.

Marriott, J. A. R. *The Eastern Question: An Historical Study in European Diplomacy.* London, 1940.

Matthews, R. D., and Akrawi, Matta. *Education in Arab Countries of the Near East.* Washington, D.C.: American Council on Education, 1949.

Middle Eastern Affairs. ("St. Antony's Papers," No. 4.) London: Chatto and Windus, 1958.

Middle Eastern Affairs. ("St. Antony's Papers," No. 11.) London: Chatto and Windus, 1961.

Milner, Alfred [Lord]. *England in Egypt.* 2d ed. London: E. Arnold, 1894. 4th ed., 1907.

Mosharrafa, M. M. *Cultural Survey of Modern Egypt.* 2 vols. London: Longmans, Green, 1947.

Naguib, Mohammed. *Egypt's Destiny: A Personal Statement.* Garden City, N.Y.: Doubleday, 1955.

Nasser, — See Abdel Nasser, Gamal.

Neguib, Mohammed (Mohammed Naguib). *Egypt's Destiny.* London: V. Gollancz, 1955. (The English Edition has identical Text but different pagination.)

Newby, P. H. *The Picnic at Sakkara.* New York: Knopf, 1955.

Radwan, Abu Al-Fatouh Ahmad. *Old and New Forces in Egyptian Education: Proposals for the Reconstruction of the Program of Egyptian Education in the Light of Recent Cultural Trends.* New York: Bureau of Publication, Teachers College, Columbia University, 1951.

Rifaat Bey, Mohammed Ali. *The Awakening of Modern Egypt.* New York: Longmans, Green, 1947.

Rivlin, Helen Anne B. *The Agricultural Policy of Muḥammad ʿAlī in Egypt.* ("Harvard Middle Eastern Studies," No. 4.) Cambridge, Mass.: Harvard University Press, 1961.

Royal Institute of International Affairs. *Great Britain and Egypt, 1914-1936.* London and New York, 1936. (Information Papers.)

——. *Great Britain and Egypt, 1914-1951.* London and New York, 1952. (Information Papers.)

——. *The Middle East: A Political and Economic Survey.* London and New York: Oxford University Press, 1950, 1954, and 1958.

Russell, Sir Thomas W. *Egyptian Service, 1902-1946.* London: J. Murray, 1949.

Sabry, Muhammad. *La question d'Egypte depuis Bonaparte jusqu'à la révolution de 1919.* Paris: Association Egyptienne, 1920.

——. *La Genèse de l'esprit national égyptien (1863-1882).* [Paris (?),] 1924.

——. *La révolution égyptienne d'après des documents authentiques et des photographies prises au cours de la révolution.* Preface by M. A. Aulard. Paris: J. Urin, 1919.

Sadat, [Colonel] Anwar El. *Revolt on the Nile.* London: Allan Wingate, 1957.

Safran, Nadav. *Egypt in Search of Political Community: An Analysis of the Intellectual and Political Evolution of Egypt, 1804-1952.* Cambridge, Mass.: Harvard University Press, 1961.

Sanhoury, A. *Le Califat, son évolution vers une société des nations orientales.* Paris: Librarie Orientaliste Paul Geuthner, 1926.

Sayegh, Fayez A. *Arab Unity: Hope and Fulfillment.* New York: Devin-Adair Co., 1958.

Schonfield, Hugh J. *The Suez Canal in World Affairs.* London: Constellation Books, 1952.

Sékaly, Achille. *Le Congrès du Khalifat (Le Caire, 13-19 mai 1926) et Le Congrès du Monde Musulman (La Mekke, 7 juin-5 juillet 1926).* Paris: Editions Ernest Leroux, 1926.

Shafik, Doria Ragai. *La Femme et le Droit Religieux de l'Egypte Contemporaine.* Paris: Paul Geuthner, 1940.

Sidarrous, Sesostris. *Des Patriarcats dans l'Empire Ottoman.* Paris, 1907.

Sparrow, Gerald. *The Sphinx Awakes.* London: R. R. Hale, 1956.

Spencer, William. *Political Evolution in the Middle East.* New York: Lippincott, 1962.

Storrs, Sir Ronald. *Orientations.* London: I. Nicholson and Watson, 1937. (Published in the United States as *The Memoirs of Sir Ronald Storrs.* New York: G. P. Putnam, 1937.)

Toynbee, Arnold J. *The Islamic World Since the Peace Settlement.* (Vol. I of the *Survey of International Affairs,* of the Royal Institute of International Affairs.) London: Oxford University Press, 1927.

Tritton, Arthur Stanley. *Islam: Belief and Practice.* London and New York: Hutchinson's University Library, 1951.

UNESCO. *Compulsory Education in the Arab States.* ("Studies on Compulsory Education," No. 16.) Paris: United Nations Educational, Scientific and Cultural Organization, 1956.

Vatikiotis, P. J. *The Egyptian Army in Politics – Pattern for New Nations?* Bloomington: Indiana University Press, 1961.

Ward, Sir A. W., and Gooch, G. P. (eds.). *The Cambridge History of British Foreign Policy, 1783-1919.* Vol. III (1866-1919). Cambridge: University Press, 1923.

Warriner, Doreen. *Land and Poverty in the Middle East.* London and New York: Royal Institute of International Affairs, 1948.

——. *Land Reform and Development in the Middle East: A Study of Egypt, Syria, and Iraq.* London: Royal Institute of International Affairs, 1957 and 1962.

——. *Land Reform and Economic Development.* Cairo: National Bank of Egypt, 1955.
Wheelock, Keith. *Nasser's New Egypt: A Critical Analysis.* New York: Praeger, 1960.
Willcocks, W. *Egyptian Irrigation.* London, 1889.
Wilson, Sir Arnold Talbot. *The Suez Canal: Its Past, Present and Future.* London and New York: Oxford University Press, 1939.
Wint, Guy, and Calvocoressi, Peter. *Middle East Crisis.* Harmondsworth, Middlesex: Penguin Books, 1957.
Wynn, Wilton. *Nasser of Egypt: The Search for Dignity.* Cambridge, Mass.: Arlington Books, 1959.
Young, [Sir] George. *Egypt.* London: E. Young, 1927. 2d ed., 1930.
Young, T. Cuyler (ed.). *Near Eastern Culture and Society: A Symposium on the Meeting of East and West.* Princeton, N.J.: Princeton University Press, 1951. (Notably the contributions of Professors Gibb, Kurani, and Zurayk.)
Youssef Bey, Amine. *Independent Egypt.* London: J. Murray, 1940.

IV. BOOKS AND PAMPHLETS IN ARABIC

ʿAbd al-Rāziq, ʿAlī. *al-Islām wa uṣūl al-ḥukm; baḥth fī al-khilāfah wa al-ḥukūmah fī al-Islām* [Islam and the principles of government; a study of the caliphate and the government in Islam]. 2d and 3d ed. Cairo: Maṭbaʿat Miṣr, 1925.
Aḥmad, Muḥammad Ḥasan. *al-Ikhwān al-Muslimūn fī al-mīzān* [The Muslim Brotherhood in the balance]. [N.p., Maṭbaʿat al-Ikhā, 1946?]
ʿArafah, Muḥammad Aḥmad. *Naqd maṭāʿin fī al-Qurʾān al-karīm* [Refutation of attacks on the Koran]. Ed. and commented on by Rashīd Riḍā. 1st ed. Cairo: Maṭbaʿat al-Manār, 1351 A. H. [1932].
ʿAṭiyyat Allāh, Aḥmad. *Qāmūs al-thawrah al-Miṣriyyah* [Dictionary of the Egyptian revolution]. [Cairo]: Maktabat al-Anglo-al-Miṣriyyah, [1954].
al-Bannā, Ḥasan. *Bayna al-ams wa al-yawm* [Between yesterday and to-day]. [Cairo]: Maṭbaʿat al-Ḥurriyyah, [195–].
——. *Daʿwatunā fī ṭawr jadīd* [Our teachings in a new era]. Cairo: Dār al-Kitāb al-ʿArabī, 1954.
——. *Hal naḥnu qawm ʿamaliyyūn?* [Are we a people of action?]. [1st ed.] [N.p.]: al-Ikhān al-Muslimūn, [1946].
——. *Ilā ayy shay' nadʿū al-nās* [The beliefs which we preach to people]. [Amman: al-Maṭbaʿah al-Waṭaniyyah, 1949].
——. *Kayfa nafham al-Islām* [Our understanding of Islam]. Damascus: Maṭbaʿat al-Ittiḥād al-Sharqī, [1949?].
——. *Mudhakkirāt* [Memoirs]. Cairo, [1949?].
——. *Mushkilātunā fī ḍaw' al-niẓām al-Islāmī* [Our problems in the light of Muslim institutions]. [Cairo: al-Maṭbaʿah al-ʿĀlamiyyah, 1948?]
——. *Naḥwa al-nūr* [Toward the light]. [Cairo: al-Ikhwān al-Muslimūn, 1950.] [Cairo, 1936.] [Amman, 1950.]
——. *Ṣafwat aḥādīth al-Jumuʿah; majmūʿat maqālāt tawjīhiyyah Islāmiyyah* [Selected Friday talks, a collection of articles on Muslim guiding principles]. [Cairo]: Muḥammad Khayr al-ʿIrqsūsi, [194–]. (These lectures were origi-

nally published in *al-Ikhwān al-Muslimūn* newspaper in 1946.)

Ḥusayn, Ṭāhā. *Fī al-shiʿr al-Jāhilī* [On pre-Islamic poetry]. 1st ed. Cairo: Maṭbaʿat Dār al-Kutub al-Miṣriyyah, 1926.

al-Ḥusaynī, Isḥāq Mūsā. *al-Ikhwān al-Muslimūn; kubrā al-ḥarakāt al-Islāmiyyah al-ḥadīthah* [The Muslim Brotherhood; the greatest modern Islamic movement]. 1st ed. Beirut: Dār Bayrūt, 1952. 2d ed. Beirut: Dār Bayrūt, 1955. (The second edition includes, on pp. 277-308, a bibliography based principally on the publications of the Muslim Brotherhood.)

al-Ikhwān al-Muslimūn. *Daʿwatunā* [Our teachings]. [Amman: al-Maṭbaʿah al-Waṭaniyyah], 1949. Cairo, 1943 or 1944.

——. *Qism al-Usar. Niẓām al-usar, nash'atuh wa ahdāfuh* [The group, or cell, system: its development and aims]. [Egypt], 1372 A.H. [1952].

Khālid, Khālid Muḥammad. *Min hunā nabda'* [From here we start]. 4th ed. [Cairo]: Dār al-Nīl, 1950.

Quṭb, Sayyid. *al-ʿAdālah al-ijtimāʿiyyah fī al-Islām* [Social justice in Islam]. 2d ed. Cairo: Lajnat al-Nashr li al-Jāmiʿiyyīn, [195–].

al-Rāfiʿī, ʿAbd al-Raḥmān. *ʿAsr Ismāʿīl* [The era of Ismail]. Cairo: Maṭbaʿat al-Nahḍah, 1932.

——. *Thawrat sanat 1919* [The revolution of the year 1919]. 1st ed. Cairo: Maktabat al-Nahḍah al-Miṣriyyah, 1946.

al-Rāfiʿī, Muṣṭafā Ṣādiq. *Taḥt rāyat al-Qurʾān . . .* [Under the banner of the Koran]. 1st ed. Cairo: al-Maktabah al-Ahliyyah, 1926.

V. ARTICLES IN WESTERN LANGUAGES

Abdel Nasser, Gamal. "The Egyptian Revolution," *Foreign Affairs*, XXXIII (January, 1955), 199-211.

Alami, Musa. "The Lesson of Palestine," *Middle East Journal*, III (October, 1949), 373-405.

Badeau, John S. "A Role in Search of a Hero: A Brief Study of the Egyptian Revolution," *Middle East Journal*, IX (Autumn, 1955), 373-384.

Batal, James. "Notes on the New Egypt," *The Muslim World*, XLIV, Nos. 3-4 (July-October, 1954), 227-235.

Berger, Morroe. "Military Elite and Social Change: Egypt Since Napoleon," *Bulletin of the School of Oriental and African Studies* (London), Vol. XXIV, No. 2 (1961).

"Developments of the Quarter," *Middle East Journal*, III (April, 1949), 182-184.

Flavin, Martin. "Egypt's Liberation Province, the Beginning of a Beginning," *The Reporter* (November 3, 1955), pp. 23-29.

Gherson, Randolph. "The Anglo-Egyptian Question," *Middle East Journal*, VII (Autumn, 1953), 456-483.

Gibb, H. A. R. "Anglo-Egyptian Relations, A Revaluation," *International Affairs* (Royal Institute of International Affairs), XXVII (October, 1951), 440-450.

——. "Middle Eastern Perplexities," *International Affairs* (Royal Institute of International Affairs), XX (October, 1944), 458-472.

——. "Social Reform: Factor X. The Search for an Islamic Democracy," *Atlantic Monthly*, CXCVIII (October, 1956), 137-141.

——. "The University in the Arab-Moslem World," in *The University Outside Europe*, ed. Edward Bradby. New York: Oxford University Press, 1939.

Harris, Christina Phelps. "Egyptian Nationalism and the Revolution of 1952," *World Affairs Quarterly* (University of Southern California), XXVI (January, 1956), 358-377.

Hourani, Albert. "The Anglo-Egyptian Agreement: Some Causes and Implications," *Middle East Journal*, IX (Summer, 1955), 239-255.

Husaini, Ishak M. (Ishaq Husseini). "Islam Past and Present," *Atlantic Monthly*, CXCVIII (October, 1956), 169-172.

Hussein, Ahmed. "Social Reform in Egypt with Special Reference to Rural Areas," *The Muslim World*, XLIV, No. 1 (January, 1954), 12-19.

Hussein, Aziza. "The Role of Women in Social Reform in Egypt," *Middle East Journal*, VII (Autumn, 1953), 440-450.

Lichtenstadter, Ilse. "The 'New Woman' in Modern Egypt – Observations and Impressions," *The Muslim World*, XXXVIII, No. 3 (July, 1948), 163-171.

Mattison, Beatrice McCown. "Rural Social Centers in Egypt," *Middle East Journal*, IV (Autumn, 1951), 461-480

Metaweh, J. E. "An Egyptian Experiment in Functional Education," *Rural Sociology* (Cornell University), Vol. XVIII, No. 4 (December, 1953).

Morrison, S. A. "Arab Nationalism and Islam," *Middle East Journal*, II (April, 1948), 147-159.

Nolte, Richard H. "Year of Decision in the Middle East," *Yale Review*, XLVI (Winter, 1957), 228-244.

Peters, Donald. "Moslem Brotherhood – Terrorists or Just Zealots?" *The Reporter*, March 17, 1953, pp. 8-10.

Rosenthal, Franz. "The 'Muslim Brethren' in Egypt," *The Moslem World*, XXXVII (October, 1947), 278-291.

Winder, R. Bayly. "Islam as the State Religion – A Muslim Brotherhood View in Syria," *The Muslim World*, XLIV, Nos. 3-4 (July-October, 1954), 215-226.

Wright, E. "Egypt: Nationalism in Adolescence," *World Affairs* (London), IV (July, 1950), 335-349.

Wright, Edwin M. "Conflicting Political Forces and Emerging Patterns," *Academy of Political Science Proceedings* (Columbia University), XXIV (January, 1952), 500-512.

Wynn, C. Wilton. "The Latest Revival of Islamic Nationalism," *The Muslim World*, XXXVIII, No. 1 (January, 1948), 11-16.

VI. NEWSPAPERS AND PERIODICALS

A. *In Western Languages*

La Bourse égyptienne (daily), Cairo.
L'Egypte contemporaine (quarterly in Arabic, French, and English), Cairo. Revue de la Société Fouad 1er d'Economie Politique, de Statistique et de Législation.

The Egyptian Economic and Political Review (monthly), Cairo.
Middle Eastern Affairs (monthly), New York.
Middle East Forum (monthly), Beirut. (Publication of the Alumni Association of the American University of Beirut, Lebanon.)
Middle East Journal (quarterly), Washington, D.C. (Publication of the Middle East Institute.)
Middle East Report (twice-monthly), Washington, D.C. (Publication of the Middle East Institute.)
Mideast Mirror (weekly in Arabic and English editions), Cairo. (Publication of the Arab News Agency.)
Le Monde (daily), Paris.
Muslim World (quarterly), Hartford, Connecticut. (Publication of the Hartford Seminary Foundation. Before January, 1948, entitled the *Moslem World*.)
The New York Times (daily), New York.
Orient (quarterly), Paris. Edited by Marcel Colombe.
Oriente moderno (monthly), Rome. (Publication of the Istituto per l'Oriente.)
Revue du Caire (monthly), Paris. (Les Editions des Cahiers du Sud.)
Revue des études islamiques (monthly), Paris. (Centre National de la Recherche Scientifique.)
Revue du monde musulman (monthly), Paris (to 1926). Superseded in 1927 by *Revue des études islamiques.*
The Times (daily), London.
Die Welt des Islams (irregular), Berlin (to 1950), Leiden (from 1951). (Publication of the Deutsche Gesellschaft für Islamkunde, Berlin.)

B. *In Arabic (Published in Cairo unless other place is given)*

al-Abhath (quarterly), Beirut. (Journal of the American University of Beirut; published by Dar Al-Kitab, Beirut.)
al-Hilāl (Al-Hilal) (twice-monthly; later monthly).
al-Manār (Al-Manar) (weekly; later monthly).
al-Muqattam (Al-Mokattam) (daily, evening).
al-Ahrām (Al-Ahram) (daily).
al-Jumhūriyyah (Al-Goumhouria) (daily).
Mir'āt al-Sharq al-Awsat (Mideast Mirror) (weekly; Arabic and English editions).
al-Miṣrī (Al-Misri) (daily).

ADDENDA

Anonymous. *The Moslem Brothers.* n.p., n.d. 48 pages, with photographs illustrating "the atrocities of the Moslem Brotherhood." From internal evidence, this pamphlet was published in Egypt after the public trials of Muslim Brothers and the official dissolution of the Muslim Brotherhood by the Government of the Revolution, as ordered by the "People's Court" on December 5, 1954. This pamphlet purportedly reflects the views of the Government of the Revolution.

Cragg, Kenneth. *The Call of the Minaret.* New York: Oxford University Press, 1956.

Hazard, Harry W. (comp.). *Atlas of Islamic History.* 3d ed., rev. Princeton, N.J.: Princeton University Press, 1954.

Monroe, Elizabeth. *Britain's Moment in the Middle East, 1914-1956.* London: Chatto & Windus, 1963.

Stevens, Georgiana G. *Egypt, Yesterday and Today.* New York: Holt, Rinehart and Winston, 1963.

Zurayk, Constantine K. *The Meaning of the Disaster.* Translated by R. Bayly Winder. Beirut: Khayat's College Book Cooperative, 1956.

Kaplinsky, Zvi. "The Muslim Brotherhood," *Middle Eastern Affairs* (New York), V, No. 12 (December, 1954), 377-385. N.B.: Earlier that year *Middle Eastern Affairs* had published a "Document," translated from *al-Ahram*, January 15, 1954: a "Statement of the Council of the Revolution Command" (on the Muslim Brotherhood). *Middle Eastern Affairs*, V, No. 3 (March, 1954), 94-100.

INDEX

Note: Where "Pasha" is given, Governor of Egypt is indicated; all other "Pashas" have been omitted.

Farghaly, Muhammad, 222 and n
Farid, Muhammad: 128; leads 2d National Party, 75, 77; attempts to gain support for party, 78-79
Farouk, King: 142, 178n, 195, 196; implicated in assassination of al-Banna, 185
Fashoda: Marchand mission to, 60-61 and n, 68
Fatwa (judicial opinion): of ʿAbduh, 125, 129
Federations of Students: membership in Brotherhood, 159
Fertile Crescent, the: McMahon's 1915 pledge of qualified independence for Arabs of, 88; permeated by Brotherhood, 160, 180
Fidaiyan-i Islam (Iranian Islamic organization): contrasted with Brotherhood, 216n
Figaro, Le, 70
Firman (of Sultan-Caliph): 44; of autonomy for Ismail (1873), 27n, 37, 40; of investiture for Tawfiq (1879), 40, 43
Foreigners in Egypt: 19, 41, 125, 128; landholdings of, 20; European mission schools, 29; Ismail encourages influx of, 33-35; population (1836-1882), 34 and n; in Mixed Courts, 35-36, 65; privileged position of, 34-35, 37, 52; panic of, during Arabi Rebellion, 52; Arabi's attitude toward, 52n; their reaction to Dinshaway incident, 74; European interests a vital issue in treaty negotiations, 94-95; European casualties in riots of 1921, 95; aid Muhammad Ali in modernization program, 115; in Suez Canal Zone, 148-149; al-Banna's view on their enterprises vs. national interest, 172n; major enterprises nationalized, 209n. See also Capitulations
France: 68, 72, 84, 87, 95 and n, 105; Napoleonic occupation of Egypt, 18, 19; influence of French language, culture, and technical aid, 21, 64-65, 112, 113-114; Franco-Turkish commercial agreement

(1838) operative in Egypt, 33-34; influence of French Revolution, 40; withdraws from joint action with British in 1882 crisis, 50 and n, 53; renounces special interests in Egypt (1904), 59; Anglo-French rivalry in Egypt, 59, 65; French-Abyssinian threat to Nile thwarted, 60-61; influence of French legislation, 36, 65, 125n, 131; management of Suez Canal Company by, 148-149. *See also* Dual (Financial) Control; Joint Note
Free Officers, the: 195n, 198 and n, 217, 219; reject alliance with Brotherhood, 180n; restricted Brotherhood membership in, 195; their coup d'état inaugurates Revolution, 195-196; nationalist goals of, 196. *See also* Revolution of 1952
Freycinet, Charles de, 50n
Fuad I, Ahmad (Sultan; 1st King of Egypt): 95, 97, 123, 178n; triangular struggle with Wafdists and British, 98; his powers under Constitution of 1923, 98-99; inaugurates royal dictatorship, 102
Fuad II, Ahmad (heir to Egyptian throne), 195n

Gambetta, Léon: fears expanding Pan-Islamic movement, 45. *See also* Joint Note
Gambetta Note. *See* Joint Note
Geneva, 71
Germany: 50n, 84, 182; limited cultural influence of, 65
Gezira, the Sudan, 101
Ghali, Boutros (Coptic Prime Minister): 63, 74, 90; unpopular with extreme nationalists, 79; assassinated, 79
Ghali, Mirrit Boutros: as reform leader, 203
Ghezireh (Gezira) Island, 28, 87
Gibb, H. A. R., Sir Hamilton, 112
Gladstone, William Ewart: 43 and n, 46, 49; quoted on 1st National Party, 46n
Gordon, General Charles ("Chinese"):

188n, 215, 222, 229; al-Banna's political ambitions cause split in, 179 and n; and Free Officer group, 180n, 195; becomes largest and most cohesive Islamic association, 180-181; al-Banna-Nahhas bargain a moral victory for, 182-183; Wafdist seceders in, 183; al-Banna as charismatic leader and martyr, 183, 215; dominant member of united Islamic groups, 183-184; ardently participates in Arab-Israeli war, 184; becomes acute security problem, 184; assassinates Amin Zaki, 184; dissolved by Nuqrashi, 184-185; assassinates Nuqrashi, 185, 198; al-Banna assassinated, 185; numerical strength when dissolved, 185; quiescent period of reorganization, 185; legally reinstated, 185; resumes hostility toward government, 186-187; Associations Law's control over, 186-187, 212; militant Secret Organ, 188 and n, 222 and n; pyramidal structure of, 188-190; Founders' Committee, 189; Regional Committees, 190; Secretariat, 190, 214; military role of unofficial "Phalanx" (*Katibat*), 190-192; role in "Black Saturday" incident, 192; relations with and attitude toward Communists, 192-194; limited army membership in, 195; struggle with R.C.C., 195n, 197-200, 209-211, 213-219 *passim*; competes with Revolutionary Government in reform program, 199, 203, 229-230; reforms advocated by, 200-202, 216n, 217, 234; proposals for new constitution, 202-203; concern for priority rights of Egyptian Muslims, 207; insists on "return" to wholly Islamic government, 210, 231, 233, 236; hamstrung by Parties Law, 212-213; as non-political association, 212-213, 220; and Liberation Rally, 214, 215; emphasis on dedication to Islam, 215, 215n-216n; aims and "peaceful" policy publicized by

emissary to U.S., 215n-216n; contrasted with *Fidaiyan-i Islam*, 216n; Revolutionary Government's charges cited against, 217-218; public trials of Muslim Brothers, 221-222, 222n; completely quashed by Revolutionary Government, 221-224, 224n; denounced by Ulama of al-Azhar, 222-223, 233n; unlikely possibility of its resurrection, 224-225, 235-237; denounced in anonymous pamphlet, 224n-225n; al-Husayni evaluates "greatest modern Islamic movement," 226-228; universality of its program, 227-228; fails to achieve unity within Islam, 228; criticized by former sympathizers, 228-229; rigid educational philosophy censured by Egyptian intellectuals, 230-231; belief in Islam as total way of life, 231; Naguib quoted on reactionary views of, 232; validity of its Islamic fundamentalism appraised, 232-233; attitude toward minority communities vs. Islamic state criticized by R.C.C. members, 233; stresses military, rather than intellectual, strength, 234-235; activity in exile, 236 and n. *See also* al-Banna, Hasan; al-Hudaybi

Muslim Brotherhood publications:
—*al-Da'wah*, 175
Da'watuna: literal meaning of, 174 and n; summary of, 174-175
al-Ikhwan al-Muslimun: 155n, 156; history of, 175; attacks British, 176
al-Muslimun, 175, 176n, 215n
Nahwa al-Nur: al-Banna's statement on objectives of Brotherhood, 169-174

Muslim Press Company and Daily Newspaper, 157

Muslim world. *See* Islamic society

Muslims: world population of, 12; revolt against French in Tunis and Algeria, 45; need religious leader for reform of static society, 115; al-Banna's knowledge of early heterodox sects, 152; the *da'is* as